A difficult legal problem is a disaster for most people. Lawyers are expensive and not always trustworthy. Court procedures and language are difficult to understand and often frightening. The person with the legal problem (the client) is commonly denied the right to participate in his or her own dispute, except to pay and pay and pay.

In the midst of this unhappy picture there are several rays of light. One is Small Claims Court—a place where decisions are made cheaply, quickly and with the participation of the disputing parties. In this book Ralph Warner shows you how to use Small Claims Court to your best advantage. With the information given here and your own creativity and determination, there is much that you can do to liberate yourself from the oppression of lawyers, judges and our traditional court system.

"Warner's book takes you by the hand through all the potential pitfalls of trying your own case. But, before you file against someone who has done you in, Warner says you should make an honest attempt at settling the dispute. He has devoted a whole section of the book on how to wangle a settlement..."

—Peter Weaver
Los Angeles Times

"This is a superb book! Flawless! No small business should be without it..."

—Michael Phillips
The Next Whole Earth Catalogue

"Everybody's Guide to Small Claims Court *gives step-by-step advice on how to prepare your case, how to file it, and perhaps most importantly, how to collect if you win. It outlines several ways to determine if it's worth suing and also presents various methods of collecting the money if you do win.*"

—Steve Fox
Associated Press

EVERYBODY'S
GUIDE TO

SMALL
CLAIMS
COURT

by Attorney Ralph Warner

Editorial Assistance: Robin Leonard

Illustrated by Linda Allison

NOLO PRESS ■ 950 PARKER STREET, BERKELEY CA 94710

IMPORTANT

Nolo Press is committed to keeping its books up-to-date. Each new printing, whether or not it is called a new edition, has been revised to reflect the latest law changes. This book was printed and updated on the last date indicated below. Before you rely on information in it, you might wish to call Nolo Press, (415) 549-1976 to check whether a later printing or edition has been issued.

PRINTING HISTORY

New "Printing" means there have been some minor changes, but usually not enough so that people will need to trade in or discard an earlier printing of the same edition.

New "Edition" means one or more major, or a number of minor, law changes since the previous edition.

FIRST EDITION	April 1978
SECOND EDITION	February 1979
Second Printing	July 1979
THIRD EDITION	March 1981
FOURTH EDITION	March 1982
FIFTH EDITION	September 1983
Second Printing	June 1984
Third Printing	January 1985
SIXTH EDITION	February 1986
SEVENTH EDITION	May 1987
Second Printing	March 1988

Legal Editing	David Brown
	Robin Leonard
	Mary Randolph
	Steve Elias
Illustrations	Linda Allison
Production	Jackie Clark
	Stephanie Harolde
Graphics	Keija Kimura
	Amy Ihara

Library of Congress Catalog No. 81-80355
ISBN 0-87337-044-9

Update Service
● Introductory Offer ●

Our books are as current as we can make them, but sometimes the laws do change between editions. You can read about law changes which may affect this book in the NOLO NEWS, a 24-page newspaper which we publish quarterly.

In addition to the Update Service, each issue contains comprehensive articles about the growing self-help law movement as well as areas of law that are sure to affect you (regular subscription rate is $7.00).

To receive the next 4 issues of the NOLO NEWS, please send us $2.00:

Name _____

Address_____

_____

Send to: NOLO PRESS, 950 Parker St., Berkeley CA 94710

sc ca 3/88

Recycle Your Out-of-Date Books & Get 25%off your next purchase!

Using an old edition can be dangerous if information in it is wrong. Unfortunately, laws and legal procedures change often. To help you keep up to date we extend this offer. If you cut out and deliver to us the title portion of the cover of any old Nolo book we'll give you a 25% discount off the retail price of any new Nolo book. For example, if you have a copy of TENANT'S RIGHTS, 4th edition and want to trade it for the latest CALIFORNIA MARRIAGE AND DIVORCE LAW, send us the TENANT'S RIGHTS cover and a check for the current price of MARRIAGE & DIVORCE, less a 25% discount. Information on current prices and editions is listed in the NOLO NEWS (see above box). Generally speaking, any book more than two years old is of questionable value. Books more than four or five years old are a menace.

OUT OF DATE = DANGEROUS

This offer is to individuals only.

THANK YOU

Nolo Press is as much family as business. Without the help of many Nolo family members, there would be no books such as this one. For work on this edition, I am particularly grateful to Stephanie Harolde, Keija Kimura, Alison Towle, Linda Allison and Carol Pladsen.

A number of talented friends read the original manuscript of this book and made helpful suggestions for improvement. With enough help, even a tarnished penny can be made to shine. Thanks to Dan Armistead, Leslie Ihara Armistead, David Brown, Peter Honigsberg, Ellen Roddy, Jeanne Stott, Roderic Duncan, Linda Dyson, Delores Huajardo, Jody Ann Becker, Jeff Rubin, and Robert Olson of Educational Seminars.

In addition, Steve Elias made literally hundreds of suggestions for change and improvement at the time I completely revised this book for its Seventh Edition. Thanks to Steve's inspired (and dogged) work, this is now a much improved book.

CONTENTS

Chapter 9: Where Can You Sue?

Chapter 10: Plaintiff's and Defendant's Filing Fees, Court Papers and Court Dates

Chapter 11: Serving Your Papers

Chapter 17: Motor Vehicle Purchase Cases

Chapter 18: Cases Where Money Is Owed

Chapter 19: Vehicle Accident Cases

Chapter 20: Landlord-Tenant Cases

Chapter 21: Small Business, Small Claims

Introduction

Here is a practical book on how to use Small Claims Court. It is a tool which will help you answer such questions as:

"How does Small Claims Court work?"

"Do I have a case worth pursuing or defending?"

"How do I prepare my case to maximum advantage?"

"What witnesses and other evidence should I present?"

"What do I say in court?"

"Can I appeal if I lose?"

"How do I collect my judgment?"

Proper presentation of your Small Claims action can often mean the difference between receiving a check and writing one. This isn't to say that I can tell you how to take a hopeless case and turn it into a blue ribbon winner. It does mean that with the information you will learn here and your own creativity and common sense, you will be able to develop your position in the best possible way. It does mean that I can show you how a case with a slight limp can be improved and set on four good legs.

Just as important as knowing when and how to bring your Small Claims Court action is knowing when not to. You don't want to waste time and energy dragging a hopeless case to court. Here I will teach you to understand the difference between winners and losers, and hopefully to keep the losers at home.

The goal of this book is to give both people bringing a case and those defending one all the step-by-step information necessary to make the best possible use of Small Claims Court. From deciding whether you have a case, through gathering evidence, arranging for witnesses, planning your courtroom presentation, and collecting your money, you will find everything you need here.

Certain arbitration decisions have had to be made as to order and depth of coverage. For example, the question of whether an oral contract is valid is discussed in Chapter 2, but not again in Chapter 16 on automobile repairs, where you may need it. So please take the time to read, or at least skim, the entire book before you focus on the chapters that interest you most. You may find something on page 106 that will change what you learned on page 32. A good way to get an overview of the entire Small Claims process is by carefully reading the

Table of Contents. It would be worthwhile to read it through several times before starting the text itself.

Chapter 23 is the last part of this book designed to help you win your case and collect your money. Chapter 24 is devoted to a different cause--how our court system must be changed to deliver more justice and less frustration. In many ways this material is intensely personal in that it reflects my own experience with our formal, lawyer-dominated legal delivery system. It springs from my own painful realization that neither law, nor justice, nor the resolution of disputes is what our courts are presently about. We have instead allowed them to become the private fiefdom of lawyers, judges and other professionals, and it is their selfish interests rather than the common good that are being served too much of the time.

I have included this material because I believe that it will be of interest to all of you who have become involved in the resolution of your own disputes in Small Claims Court. You have had the courage to take responsibility for solving your own problems. Given the opportunity, you can do a great deal more. It is past time that you are allowed to participate in your own legal system. It is past time that you are made welcome in your own courthouses. It is past time that all of us realize that a society whose legal system is run by and for lawyers can't long survive.

Now a few words about two potentially sensitive subjects. First, when grappling with the ever tricky personal pronoun, I have decided to simply take turns rather than using the cumbersome "he or she" and "his or her" every time both men and women could be involved.

Second, I want to say a few words about the many referrals to other Nolo Press self-help law books you will find sprinkled throughout this one. At first glance it may appear that I am trying to sell you another book on every third page. In my own defense, however, I would like to make three points. First, Nolo Press is by far the largest and most comprehensive publisher of self-help law materials in the United States. As a result, there are many legal areas where Nolo publishes the only materials aimed at non lawyers. Second, I simply don't have the space in this already chunky book to repeat all the information in Nolo's fifty or so other volumes. Third, as Nolo's books are available at most libraries (public or law) in the United States, it shouldn't be hard to read any other Nolo volumes pertinent to your problem at no cost.

CHAPTER 1

In the Beginning

A. First Things

The purpose of Small Claims Court is to hear disputes involving small amounts of money, without long delays and formal rules of evidence. Disputes are presented by the people involved and lawyers are normally prohibited.[1] The maximum amount of money that can be sued for in California is $1,500. In legal jargon, this is often called the "jurisdictional amount."[2]

There are three great advantages of Small Claims Court:

• First, you get to prepare and present your own case without having to pay a lawyer more than your claim is worth.

---

[1] In California, a lawyer may sue in his own case and as the representative of a corporation under some circumstances (see Chapter 8).

[2] The laws listing how much you can sue for, as well as the procedures in Small Claims Court, are listed in the California "Code of Civil Procedure" (CCP), in Secs. 116 through 117.20.

• Second, bringing a dispute to Small Claims Court is simple. The gobbledygook of complicated legal forms and language prevalent in other courts are kept to a minimum. To start your case, you need only fill out a few lines on a simple form (i.e., "Honest Al's Used Chariots owes me $500 because the 1979 Chevette they sold me in supposedly 'excellent condition' died less than a mile from the car lot"). When you get to court, you can talk to the judge without a whole lot of "res ipsa loquiturs" and "pendente lites." If you have documents, or witnesses, you may present them for what they are worth with no requirement that you comply with the thousand year's accumulation of rusty, musty procedures, habits and so-called rules of evidence of which the legal profession is so proud.

• Third, and perhaps most important, Small Claims Court doesn't take long. Most disputes are heard in court within a month or two from the time the complaint is filed. The hearing itself seldom takes more than 15 minutes. The judge announces her decision either right there in the courtroom, or mails it out within a few days.

But before you decide that Small Claims Court sounds like just the place to bring your case, you will want to answer a basic question. Are the results you are likely to achieve in proportion to, or greater than, the effort you will have to expend? This must be answered by looking at each dispute individually. It is all too easy to get so involved in a particular dispute that you lose sight of the fact that the time, trouble and expense of bringing it to court are way out of balance with any likely return.

In order to profitably think about whether your case is worth the effort, you will want to understand the details of how Small Claims Court works—who can sue, where, for how much, etc. You will also want to learn a little law—are you entitled to relief, how much, and how do you compute the exact amount? Finally and most importantly comes the detail that so many people overlook to their later dismay. Assuming that you prepare and present your case brilliantly, and get a judgment for everything you request, can you collect? This seems a silly thing to overlook, doesn't it? Sad to say, however, it is often done. Plaintiffs commonly go through the entire Small Claims procedure with no chance of collecting a dime because they have sued a person who has neither money nor any reasonable prospect of getting any.

The purpose of the first dozen chapters of this book is to help you decide whether or not you have a case worth pursuing. These are not the sections where grand strategies are brilliantly unrolled to baffle and confound the opposition—that comes later. Here we are more concerned with such mundane tasks as locating the person you want to sue, suing in the right court, filling out the necessary forms and getting them properly served. Perhaps it will disappoint those of you with a dramatic turn of mind, but most cases are won or lost before anyone enters the courtroom.

Throughout this book we reproduce sample forms. Most California Small Claims forms are uniform for the entire state, although a few local forms may vary slightly from one judicial district to the next. Blank copies of all these forms are available at your local Small Claims clerk's office.

B. Checklist of Things to Think Out Before Initiating or Defending Your Case

Here is a preliminary checklist of things you will want to think about at this initial stage. As you read further, we will go into each of these areas in more detail. But let me remind yo again, if you haven't already gotten a copy of your local Small

Claims Court rules, do it now. It's silly to come to bat with two out in the ninth and the bases loaded and not know if you are supposed to run to first or third. Oh, and one more thing. When you read the rules you will see that a free Small Claims Court advisor is available to you. I discuss what this means in more detail in Chapter 13, Sec. C. For now, it's enough to know that if you become confused when preparing a Small Claims case, help is available.

CHECKLIST OF QUESTIONS NEEDING ANSWERS BEFORE YOU FILE IN SMALL CLAIMS COURT

1. Does the other person owe you the money, or, put another way, "Is there liability"? (See Chapter 2)

2. How many dollars is your claim for? If it is for more than the Small Claims maximum, do you wish to waive the excess and still use Small Claims Court? (See Chapter 4)

3. Is your suit brought within the proper time period (Statute of Limitations)? (See Chapter 5)

4. Which Small Claims Court should you bring your suit in? (See Chapter 9)

5. Whom do you sue? As you will see in many cases, especially those involving businesses and automobiles, this can be a little more technical and tricky than you might have guessed. (See Chapter 8)

6. Have you made a reasonable effort to contact the other party to offer a compromise? (See Chapter 6)

7. And again, the most important question—assuming that you can win, is there a reasonable chance that you can collect? (See Chapters 3 and 23)

CHECKLIST OF QUESTIONS NEEDING ANSWERS BEFORE DEFENDING A CASE

1. Do you have a good legal defense against the claim of the plaintiff? (See Chapters 2 and 12)

2. Has the plaintiff sued for a reasonable or an excessive amount? (See Chapter 4)

3. Has the plaintiff brought his suit within the proper time limit (Statute of Limitation)? (See Chapter 5)

4. Has the plaintiff followed reasonably correct procedures in bringing suit and serving you with the court papers? (See Chapters 11 and 12)

5. Have you made a reasonable effort to contact the plaintiff in order to arrive at a compromise settlement? (See Chapters 6 and 12)

Defendant's Note: In addition to your right to defend a case, you also have the right to file your own claim (Chapters 10 and 12). You will want to do this if you believe that you suffered damage arising from the same incident or transaction that forms the basis of the plaintiff's suit against you, and that the plaintiff is responsible for your loss. Defendants' claims commonly develop out of a situation in which both parties are negligent (say in a car accident) and the question to be decided is who was more at fault.

C. Legal Jargon Defined

Mercifully, there is not a great deal of technical language in use in Small Claim Courts. But there are a few terms that may be new to you and which you will have to become familiar with. Don't try to learn all of these terms now. Refer back to these definitions when you need them.

Abstract of Judgment: A document which you get from the Small Claims Court clerk's office which indicates that you have a money judgment against another person. Filing it with the County Recorder places a lien on real property owned by the judgment debtor.

Appeal: In the Small Claims context, a request that the Superior Court rehear the case from scratch and reverse the decision of the Small Claims Court. A Small Claims appeal can only be brought by a defendant. It is heard in the appellate division of the Superior Court, and the parties may (but do not have to) be represented by attorneys.

California Civil Code (CC) and California Code of Civil Procedure (CCP): Books which contain some of California's substantive and procedural laws. They are available at all public libraries and law libraries (which are located at the county courthouse and are open to the public.) They can also be purchased from Nolo Press (see order information at the back of this book).

Calendar: List of cases to be heard by a Small Claims Court on a particular day. A case taken off calendar is removed from the list. This usually occurs because the defendant has not been served or because the parties jointly request that it be heard on another day.

Claim of Defendant: A claim by a defendant that the plaintiff owes him money. A Claim of Defendant, also called a "Defendant's Claim," is filed as part of the same Small Claims action that the plaintiff has started.

Claim of Exemption: A procedure by which a "judgment debtor" can claim that, under federal and/or California law, certain of his money or other property is exempt from being grabbed to satisfy a debt.

Continuance: A court order that a hearing be postponed to a later date.

Default Judgment: A court decision given to the plaintiff (the person filing suit) when the defendant fails to show up (defaults).

Defendant: The person being sued.

Dismissed Case: A dismissal usually occurs when a case is dropped by the plaintiff. If the defendant has not filed a claim, the plaintiff can do this by filing a written request. If the defendant has filed a claim, they must agree in writing before a dismissal will be allowed. If a plaintiff does not show up in court on the appointed day, the judge may dismiss the case.

Equity: The value of a particular piece of property that you actually own. For example, if a car has a fair market value of $2,000 and you owe a bank $1,000 on it, your equity is $1,000.

Exempt Property: Under California law, certain personal and real property is exempt from being used to pay ("satisfy") court judgments if the debtor follows certain procedures. See Chapter 23.

Garnish: To attach (legally take) money—usually wages, or commissions, or a bank account—for payment of a debt.

Hearing: The court trial.

Homestead Declaration: A piece of paper that any home-owner can file with the County Recorder's office which protects the equity in her home from attachment and sale to satisfy most debts. The equity protected is $45,000 for a family, $60,000 for persons who are over 65, blind, or disabled, and $30,000 for a single person. A homeowner is entitled to substantial protection even if a homestead is not filed. See *Homestead Your House* by Warner & Ihara (Nolo Press).

Judgment: The decision rendered by the court.

Judgment Creditor: A person to whom money is owed under a court decision.

Judgment Debtor: A person who owes money under a court decision.

Judgment Debtor's Statement of Assets: A form which accom-panies a notice of entry of judgment which must be completed by a defendant unless the judgment is appealed or paid. See Chapter 23.

Jurisdiction: A Small Claims Court has jurisdiction to hear cases involving money damages up to $1,500. (This is often called the "jurisdictional amount.") Small Claims Court also has jurisdiction over certain types of unlawful detainer (evic-tion) actions (see Chapter 19) and may award several other types of remedies, including recission, restitution, reparation and specific performance, as discussed in Chapter 4.

Levy: A legal method to seize property or money for unpaid debts under court order. For example, a sheriff could levy on (sell) your automobile if you refused to pay a judgment.

Lien: A legal right to an interest in the real estate of another for payment of a debt. To get a lien, you first must get a court judgment and then take proper steps to have the court enter an "Abstract of Judgment." You can then take the Abstract to the County Recorder's office in a county where the judgment debtor has real estate to establish the lien.

Motion to Vacate a Judgment: The motion the defendant must file to reopen a proceeding because he or she did did not appear in court to defend a case on the proper date and the judge has entered a Default Judgment. See Chapter 10.

Order of Examination: A court procedure allowing a judgment creditor to question a judgment debtor about the extent and location of his or her assets.

Plaintiff: The person who starts a lawsuit.

Process Server: Person who delivers court papers to a party or witness. See Chapter 14.

Recorder (Office of the County Recorder): The person employed by the county to make and record documents. The County Recorder's office is usually located in the main county courthouse.

Satisfaction of Judgment: A written statement filed by the judgment creditor when the judgment is paid. See Chapter 22.

Statute of Limitations: The time period in which you must file your lawsuit. It is normally figured from the date the act or omission giving rise to the lawsuit occurs, and varies depending on the type of suit. See Chapter 5.

Stay of Enforcement: When a Small Claims Court judgment is appealed to the Superior Court by a defendant, enforcement (collection) of the judgment is stayed (stopped) until the time for appeal has expired.

Stipulation: An agreement to compromise a case which is entered into by the parties and then presented to the judge.

Submission: When a judge wants to delay decision on a case until a later time, she "takes it under submission." Some judges announce their decision as to who won and who lost right in the courtroom. More often, they take the case under submission and mail out a decision later.

Subpoena: Court order requiring a witness to appear in court. It must be served on the person subpoenaed to be valid. See Chapter 14.

Subpoena Duces Tecum: A court order requiring that certain documents be produced in court.

Substituted Service: A method by which court papers may be served on a defendant who is difficult to serve by other means. See Chapter 11.

Trial De Novo: The rehearing of a Small Claims case from scratch by a Superior Court judge when an appeal has been taken by a defendant. In this situation, the previous decision by the Small Claims judge has no effect and the appeal takes the form of a new trial (trial de novo).

Unlawful Detainer: Legalese for eviction. Unlawful detainers may be brought in Small Claims Court for month-to-month tenancies based on non-payment of rent. See Chapter 20.

Venue: This basically refers to the proper location (court) to bring a suit, and is discussed in detail in Chapter 9. If a suit is brought in the wrong place, it can be transferred to the right court or dismissed, in which case the plaintiff must refile in the right court.

Wage Garnishment: After a judgment has been issued (and the defendant's time to appeal has elapsed), the Small Claims Court clerk will issue a writ of execution upon request. This may be turned over to a sheriff, marshal or constable with orders to collect (garnishee) a portion of the judgment debtor's wages directly from his employer.

Writ Of Execution: An order by a court to the sheriff, marshal or constable to collect a specific amount of money due.

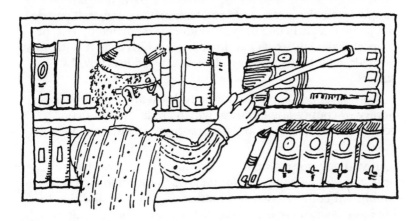

D. Legal Research

As part of using Small Claims Court, you may want more information on one or another California law. I refer to many of the most relevant ones in this book, but there are, of course, a great many more than I can possibly list here. If you imagine a child standing on a beach with a pailful of sand, with the sand in the pail representing the laws discussed in this book and the sand on the beach representing the total body of California law, you will have some idea of how many more laws you can sift through if you have the energy.

California laws are roughly divided by subject matter into sets of books called codes. Thus, there is the Civil Code, the Probate Code, the Penal Code, the Vehicle Code, and many more. The majority of California laws, including those having to do with consumer protection (e.g., credit cards, landlord/tenant, auto lemon laws, etc.) are found in the Civil Code (abbreviated CC). Other codes that you may want to refer to as part of preparing a Small Claims case are the Code of Civil Procedure (CCP), which includes the laws having to do with the operation of Small Claims Court., the Business and Professions Code (Bus. & Prof. Code), which includes rules regarding the collection of professional fees, contractor's license regulations, etc., the Vehicle Code, which contains the rules of the road, and the Commercial Code (Com. Code), which contains information about warranties. To locate a particular law, simply locate the correct code and look up the number. If you do not know if a particular area of conduct is regulated by law, or suspect that a law exists but don't know which code it is in or its number, refer to the master code index which lists laws by subject.

You can get access to California codes at any large public library or county law libraries, which are located in main county courthouses (and in some branch courthouses) and are open to the public.

If you do your research at a law library, you will have an opportunity to look up California laws in the annotated codes (published both by West and Mathew Bender). In addition to the basic laws, these codes also list relevant court decisions (called "cases") interpreting each law. If you find a case that seems to fit your situation, you may want to read it, and if it still seems relevant, point it out to the judge as part of your Small Claims presentation. If you are confused about how to find and understand a particular case, ask the law librarian or see *Legal Research: How to Find and Understand the Law*, by Stephen Elias (Nolo Press), an invaluable guide to doing your own legal research.

CHAPTER 2

Do You Have a Case?

Before you even start thinking about going to court—any court—you must answer a basic question: Do you have a good case? Before you can collect for a loss you have suffered, you must show that the other party is legally responsible for it. Put into legal slang, this means that you must show that there is "liability." Obvious, you say. Perhaps it is to you, but apparently not to lots of others.

Here is what often seems to happen. People focus on their own loss—the amount of money that they are out as a result of whatever incident occurred. They think that, because they have been damaged they must have a right of recovery against someone. But the fact that a loss has occurred isn't enough to make a winning case. You must state facts that indicate to the judge that the person you are suing should legally be held accountable.

If you have suffered monetary damage as a result of the conduct of someone else, and you feel that person was in the wrong, by all means, pursue your case to court. But as you do, understand that the judge will be trying to see if what happened to you ("your loss") can be made to fit the requirements of one or another legal theory that justifies your recovery. The rest of this chapter constitutes a discussion of the theories most commonly used to do this. The point of my presenting these to you is not to give you a mini law school course, although at times I fear it may seem like one, but to give you an opportunity to think about how to best present the story of what happened to you in a way that will make it easy for the judge to rule in your favor.

Let's now look at the relevant legal theories, one by one, to see if you can make your loss fit at least one of them:

1. A valid contract (written, oral or implied) has been broken by the person you are suing and that, as a result, you have suffered a monetary loss (see Section A below for more);

2. The intentional behavior of the person you are suing has caused you to suffer a monetary loss (see Section B below for more);

3. The negligent behavior of the person you are suing has caused you to suffer a monetary loss (see Section B below for more);

4. The negligent or intentional behavior of the person you are suing has caused you a personal injury or severe mental distress (see Section C below for more);

5. You were injured by a defective product and qualify for recovery under the "doctrine of strict liability (see Section D below for more);

6. A written or implied warranty extended to you by a merchant has been breached and as a result, you have suffered a monetary loss (e.g., a new car suffers mechanical problems shortly after purchase). (See Section E below for more on this.)

7. A right created by statute has been violated and as a result of this violation, you have suffered a monetary loss. This would be the case if a consumer protection law was violated and the violation resulted in your being out some money (see Section F below for more).

Now, before we consider each of these legal theories individually, here is an example of why it's so important to establish not only that you have suffered a loss, but that someone is legally liable to make it good. One night someone entered the garage in the plaintiff's apartment complex, smashed a window in her car and stole a fancy AM-FM radio and tape deck worth $528. Upon discovery of the theft, the plaintiff (let's call her Sue) immediately got several witnesses to the fact that her car had been broken into. She took pictures and then called the police. After the police investigation was complete, Sue obtained a copy of their investigation report. She also got several estimates as to the cost of repairing the damage to the car window, the lowest of which was $157. Sue added the cost of the window to the value of the tape deck and filed suit in Small Claims Court against the building owner for $685.

Sue overlooked only one thing. Unfortunately for her, it was an important one. Under the circumstances the building owner wasn't liable. He had never promised (orally or in writing) to keep the garage locked, had never done so, had never led Sue to believe that he would do so, and indeed could point to requests from other tenants that the garage be kept open. All the tenants were reasonably on notice that it was easy to gain access to the garage either from inside or outside the building. Put simply, the building owner was neither in violation of a contract, nor guilty of any negligent behavior in failing to lock the garage. The situation facing Sue was no different than it would have been if her car had been damaged on the street.

Now let's take this same situation, but change a few facts. Instead of a situation where the door was always open and no one ever expected it to be closed, let's now assume that the lease contract signed by the landlord and tenant stated that the tenant would be assigned a parking place in a "secured garage." Let's also assume that the garage had always been locked until the lock broke seven days before the theft occurred. Finally, let's assume that Sue and other tenants had asked the owner to fix the lock the day after it broke, but that he hadn't "gotten around to it."

In this situation, Sue should win. The landlord made certain promises to the tenant (to keep the garage locked) and then failed to keep them in a situation where he had ample opportunity to do so. The failure presumably allowed the robber access to the car.

Note: In both fact situations above, the total amount of damage $685.50, was the same. But in the first, there was no right of recovery (the defendant wasn't liable), and in the second, the apartment owner's failure to keep the door locked violated the defendant's lease contract. In addition, the failure of the apartment owner to fix the lock within a reasonable time constituted negligence.

A. How to Approach a Breach of Contract Case

In broad outline, a contract is any agreement between parties where one person agrees to do something for the other in exchange for something in return. The agreement may be written, oral, or implied from the circumstances (i.e., I deliver milk to your house and you pay for it).[1]

Note: See Section E below for breach of warranty information.

Example 1: "I promise to give you $750 on the first of January." This is not a contract because you have promised to do nothing for me in return. I have only indicated that I will give you a gift in the future. This sort of promise is not enforceable.

Example 2: "I promise to pay you $750 on January 1 in exchange for your promise to shine my door knob every morning before 7 o'clock." This is a valid contract. If I refuse to pay you, you can go to court and get a judgment for the $750.

Example 3: I ask you if you want your house painted. You say "yes." I paint the house. You refuse to pay, claiming that since you never agreed on a price, there was no contract. You are wrong. A court will use the doctrine of "quantum meruit" (as much as is deserved for labor) to rule that when one person does work for another that the second person consents to (implied consent is often enough), a contract exists. In other words, the law will require that a person getting the benefit of work, where there is a reasonable expectation that such work should be paid for, is contractulally obligated to pay for it.

Perhaps the largest number of cases coming before Small Claims Court involve the breach of a contract. Often the contract that has not been honored involves a failure to pay money. Hardly a day goes by when someone isn't sued for failing to pay the phone company, the milkman, the local hospital, or even book fines to the public library. But sometimes a breach of contract suit stems, not from failure to pay a bill, but because one party has performed his duties under the contract badly, or not at all, and the other person has been damaged as a result. Such

---

[1] Generally speaking, contracts that can't be performed within a year must be in writing. However, the great majority of consumer-type contracts can be performed in a year and therefore oral contracts are normally enforceable. Also, a person who lacks mental capacity cannot make an enforceable contract and contracts made by people not yet 18 can be cancelled (disaffirmed) under some circumstances. See CC Secs 34 and 35.

might be the case if an apartment owner accepted a deposit and agreed to rent an apartment to a tenant and then rented it to someone else.[2]

Damages resulting from a breach of contract are normally not difficult to prove. You must show that the contract existed (if it is written, the document should be presented to the court, and if it's oral or implied from the circumstances, the facts necessary to establish it should be stated). You must then testify as to the circumstances of the other person's breach of the contract and the amount of damages you have suffered. In many situations this involves no more than stating that a legitimate bill for X dollars has not been paid.

Example: "Joe Williams owes me $200 because he failed to pay for car repairs that he asked me to perform. I did all the repairs properly. Here is a work order signed by Joe authorizing me to do the work."

The fact that many contract cases are easy to win doesn't mean that all are. I have seen a good number of plaintiffs lose what to them seemed to be open and shut cases. Why? Simply because they failed to show the defendant owed them any money. Put another way: they failed to show either that a contract existed (see *Example* 2 below) or that it was breached if it did exist (see *Example 1* below). In other situations the plaintiff is able to show that a contract existed, but not that the defendant breached it (*Example 1* below).

---

[2] Leases and rental agreements, whether written or oral, are contracts. They are discussed in detail in the *California Tenants' Handbook* and *The Landlord's Law Book (Vol.1): Rights and Responsibilities,* Nolo Press (see back of this book for more information).

Example 1: Let's look at the facts of a situation that I witnessed recently in Small Claims Court in Oakland, California. Plaintiff sued defendant for $650, the cost of replacing a pigskin suede jacket that was ruined (it shrunk dramatically) by the defendant's cleaning establishment. Plaintiff had taken the jacket to defendant for cleaning and given him a $50 fee. Defendant, by accepting the jacket and the fee, clearly implied that he would properly clean the jacket. A contract existed.

Plaintiff was very sure of his loss. He stood in the courtroom, a great bear of a man, looking as if he had just escaped from a professional football team and slowly put the jacket on. As he wiggled into the coat, the whole courtroom, including the judge who almost choked trying to keep a straight face, burst out laughing. The sleeves barely came to the man's elbows and the coat itself didn't reach his waist. With a little luck the jacket would have fit a good-sized jockey.

As I sat watching, I thought that the case was over and that the plaintiff had won easily. Certainly by putting on the jacket he had made his point more effectively than he could have with ten minutes of testimony. I was wrong. The plaintiff had overlooked two things, one obvious, and one not so obvious. By the time the defendant finished his presentation, the plaintiff's case had shrunk almost as much as the jacket.

The obvious thing that plaintiff overlooked in asking for the $650 replacement value of the jacket was that the jacket was eight months old and had been worn a good bit. Valuation is a common problem in clothing cases and we discuss it in detail in Chapter 4. Let's just say here that the jacket was worth no more than $400 in its used condition and that, in any case where your property is damaged or destroyed, the amount of your recovery will be limited to the fair market value of the goods at the time the damage occurs—not their replacement value.

Now let's look at defendant's other defense. He testified that, when he saw the jacket after cleaning, he had been amazed. His cleaning shop specialized in leather goods and the cleaning process used should have resulted in no such shrinking problem. What's more, he testified that he had examined a number of other leather goods in the same cleaning batch and found no shrinking problem with any of them. To find out what happened, he sent the jacket to an "independent testing laboratory." Their report, which he presented to the court, stated that the problem was not in the cleaning, but in the jacket. It was poorly made in that the leather had been severely overstretched prior to assembly. When it had been placed in the cleaning fluid, it had shrunk as a result of this poor original workmanship.

What happened? The judge was convinced by the testing lab report and felt that defendant had breached no contract as far as the cleaning was concerned.[3] However, he also felt that the defendant, as a leather cleaning specialist, had some responsibility to notify plaintiff that the jacket should not have been cleaned in the first place. Therefore, the judge held mostly for the defendant, but did award the plaintiff $100 in damages.

---

[3] Plaintiff could bring suit against the person who made the jacket for defective workmanship. It could be argued that, by using inferior material, they had breached an implied warranty (contract) that the goods sold were reasonably fit for the purpose they were designed to fulfill. Warranty actions must, however, be filed promptly (see Sec. E below).

Example 2: A few weeks later I saw another contract case where the plaintiff had suffered an obvious loss, but failed to show that defendant was responsible for making it good. This time it was a plaintiff landlord suing the parent of a tenant for damages that the tenant had caused to her apartment. The parent was sued because he had co-signed his daughter's lease contract. The plaintiff easily convinced the judge that the damage had, in fact, occurred and the judge seemed disposed toward giving judgment for the $580 requested until the parent presented his defense. He showed that the lease between his daughter and the landlord had been rewritten three times after he originally co-signed the agreement without his again adding his signature and that the changes, which included the replacement of several of his daughter's original roommates with others, were significant. He claimed that, because he had not co-signed any of the subsequent lease contracts, he wasn't liable. The judge agreed. The judge was probably relying on the noteworthy case of *Wexler v. McLucas*, 48 CA 3 Supp 9 (1975). Leases, rental agreements and the rights and responsibilities of co-signers are discussed in more detail in the *California Tenants' Handbook*, Moskovitz and Warner, Nolo Press.

Note: We will go further into individual fact situations that commonly arise in the area of contracts in Chapters 16-21. You will want to read these before you decide whether or not you have a good case. Also, if your breach of contract situation involves fraud or undue influence committed by the other party, or you received little or nothing for your money through the direct fault of the seller, you may have a right to have the contract ended (rescinded) and be returned to your position before you entered into it (i.e., get your money or goods back). I discuss the remedy known as "recission" in Chapter 4, Sec. E, "Equitable Relief."

B. How To Approach a Case Where Your Property Has Been Damaged By the Negligent or Intentional Acts Of Someone Else

After cases involving breach of contract, the most common disputes that come to Small Claims Court involve damage to one person's property caused by the negligent actions of another. Less often, the plaintiff claims that he suffered loss because the defendant intended to damage his belongings.

A technical definition of what constitutes negligence could easily fill the next few pages. Indeed, whole law texts have been written on the subject. I remember thinking in law school that the more scholarly professors wrote about the subject of negligence, the more mixed up they got. Like good taste or bad wine, negligence seems to be easy to recognize, but hard to define.

Despite the problems involved, let me try and give you a one-sentence definition: If, as a result of another person's conduct, your property is injured and that person didn't act with reasonable care in the circumstances, you have a case based on his negligence.[4] It's as simple—or complex—as that. If you want to get into the gory details of the subject, go to your nearest law library and get any recent legal text on "Torts." "Torts" are wrongful acts or injuries.

Example: Jake knows the brakes on his ancient Saab are in serious need of repair, but does nothing about it. One night when the car is parked on a hill, the brakes fail and the car rolls across the street and destroys Keija's persimmon tree. Keija sues Jake for $125, which is the reasonable value of the tree. Jake would lose because he did not act with reasonable care in the circumstances.

Another obvious situation involving negligence would be a car or bus that swerves into your driving lane and sideswipes your fender. The driver of the offending vehicle has a duty to operate it in such a way as to not harm you. By swerving into your lane, it is extremely likely that he has failed to do so. A situation where negligence could be difficult to show might involve your neighbor's tree that falls on a car parked in your driveway. Here you have to be ready to prove that for some reason (age, disease, an obviously bad root system, etc.) the tree was in a weakened condition, and the neighbor was negligent in failing to do something about it. If the tree had looked to be in good health, you would have a tough time proving that your neighbor was negligent in not cutting it down or propping it up.

There is no fool-proof way to determine in advance if someone is or is not negligent. It's often a close question—a matter of judgment. If you are in doubt, bring your case and let the judge decide. After all, he or she gets paid (by you, the taxpayer) to do it.

Here are a couple of questions which may help you make a decision as to whether you have a good case based on someone else's negligence.

---

[4] Sometimes negligence can occur when a person who has a duty or responsibility to act fails to do so. For example, a car mechanic who fails to check your brakes after you tell him they have been working poorly and he promises to do so would be negligent.

• Did the person whose act (or failure to act) injured you behave in a reasonable way? Or to put it another way, would you have behaved differently if you were in his or her shoes?

• How much did your conduct contribute to causing the injury?

If you believe that the person who caused you to suffer a monetary loss behaved in an unreasonable way (ran a red light when drunk) and that you were acting sensibly (driving at 30 m.p.h. in the proper lane), you probably have a good case. Even if you were partly to blame, you can still recover from the other party for his share of fault. For instance, if a judge finds that one person (drunk and speeding) was 80% at fault, and that the other (too inattentive under the circumstance) was 20% at fault, the comparatively innocent party can recover 80% of his or her loss.

C. How To Approach a Personal Injury (And Mental Distress) Case

The considerations here are much the same as outlined in Section B just above. You must show not only that you were injured but that someone's intentional or negligent behavior caused your injury, unless your case qualifies as one where the law applies the doctrine of strict liability (see Section D below). Most personal injury cases involve amounts of money which are clearly over the Small Claims maximum and should therefore be pursued in Municipal (up to $25,000) or Superior Court, but occasionally a minor personal injury case will be appropriate for Small Claims.

Example 1: Keija takes Harry, her Pekinese puppy, for a walk without a leash. Soto walks by and Harry takes an instant dislike to his purple and orange socks and shows it with a quick nip on Soto's right ankle. As Soto was on a public side-walk where he had a right to be, we can safely assume that Keija was negligent in allowing Harry to bite him. Why? Because, as a society, we have decided that you can't let you dog run about biting people in public places, even if they do have horrible taste in socks. If you do, you are negligent and are going to have to pay for it.

Example 2: Now, let's change our example and assume that, instead of biting Soto, Harry went after a burglar who was trying to sneak into Keija's garage window. Let's also assume that after the dust cleared and the cops hauled the burglar away it was discovered that he had suffered the same injury as Soto. Although the burglar's blood was just as red as Soto's, he can recover nothing. Why? Because Keija is entitled to protect herself and her property and as a society we have decided that keeping a dog is a reasonable way to do it.

Example 3: Now let's change the example again. This time Harry bites Walter, Keija's next door neighbor, who had climbed over the back yard fence to get some apples from Keija's tree. Keija didn't know that the neighbor was in the habit of trespassing. The neighbor, however, knew that Harry was kept in the yard and was a watch dog. Here again, there would be no liability. Keija had taken reasonable precautions to secure Harry in her own yard. She owed no duty of care to her apple-poaching neighbor in this situation.

Example 4: I know you're getting sick of hearing about nasty little Harry, but bear with him a moment longer. Let's assume now that Harry bites a travelling carrot-peeler salesman who knocks at the front door. Can the salesperson recover? Probably. Even though Keija didn't invite him and never let a carrot in the house, the salesperson had the right to assume that it was safe to go up the walk to the front door. But suppose Keija had a fence around the front yard with a latched gate and two large signs, one saying "Beware of the Dog," with a picture of Harry hanging onto someone's leg, and another saying "No Tres-passing, No Soliciting"? This would probably be enough to satisfy Keija's duty of care to the rest of the world and if the carrot-peeler salesman entered the gate anyway, he would do so at his own risk.

Suggestion: Before you sue someone for a personal injury (or for property damage), think not only about your loss, but whether the other party acted reasonably under the circumstances. In other words, were they negligent? If they were not, you have no right to recover, no matter what your injury, unless your situation qualifies under Section D, below. If in doubt, go ahead and sue, but be prepared to deal with the liability question, as well as simply showing the extent of your injury. In later chapters I will give you some practical advice as to how to prove your case.

Mental Distress Note: As discussed further in Chapter 4, you do not have to suffer a physical injury to successfully recover in court as a result of someone else's negligent or intentionally obnoxious behavior. Invasion of privacy and the intentional infliction of mental distress are but two of the types of lawsuits that can be based on non-physical injuries. For example, if your landlord enters your apartment without permission several times and you request that she cease doing so, but she persists, causing you to become genuinely upset and anxious, you have a good case. Obviously, not every instance of obnoxious behavior that makes you mad qualifies as being serious enough to bring a successful lawsuit. Generally, to recover, the other person's actions must:

• Be truly obnoxious;

• Violate a state law or local ordinance (i.e., noise);

• Continue after you have asked the person to stop (it's best to do this in writing and to do it more than once).

In addition, you must be able to convince a judge that you have genuinely suffered mental distress as a result of the other person's conduct.

D. How to Approach a Case When You Are Injured By a Defective Product (Doctrine of Strict Liability)

There is a legal concept called "strict liability." When this doctrine applies, there is no need to prove negligence. It's enough that an injury occurred as a result of something going wrong with the defendant's product or activity. This concept was traditionally applied to such things as nuclear reactors, munitions storage, people who keep wild and inherently dangerous animals (a cheetah in the city) and other extremely hazardous activities. More recently it has been extended to other legal areas, including a landlord's responsibility for injury-causing defects in rented property. A landlord is held to a strict duty of care toward tenants when a defective condition which existed at the time the tenant moved in caused the injury (e.g., a tenant slips in the shower and is injured when she cuts herself on a non-shatter resistant glass door). This is true even though the landlord didn't know about the condition that caused the defect.

The most important area where the strict liability doctrine is applied is where a manufactured product such as an appliance or automobile breaks for no apparent reason and causes injury or property damage. The people injured are entitled to recover damages from the manufacturer, landlord or other strictly liable defendant without having to prove negligence. Of course, most product liability cases will end up in Superior Court, but now and then a defect in a product or rental property will cause an injury small enough that the damage caused falls within the Small Claims Court maximum ($1,500).

As noted above, personal injury cases, whether involving the concept of strict liability or not, are normally brought in Municipal or Superior Court because of the amounts of money involved. To do this, you will very likely need the help of a lawyer.

E. How to Approach a Breach of Warranty Case

First you need to understand that warranty law is almost impossibly confusing, even to lawyers. A principal reason for this is that three separate and distinct warranty laws can apply to the retail sale of goods.[5] The sad result is that, short of presenting you with a major treatise, it's impossible to thoroughly explain warranty law. The best I can do in the short space I have here is to give you several general rules of thumb.

Note: I discuss warranties as they apply to new and used car transactions, as well as the California Lemon Law, in Chapter 17.

1. If a new or used product comes with a written warranty, you have the right to rely on it.

---

[5] Song-Beverly Consumer Warranty Act (CC Secs.1747-1748.5); California Commercial Code (Com. Code Secs. 2313, 2315); Magnuson-Moss Consumer Warranty Act, 15 USC 2302.

2. If a seller makes written or oral statements describing a product's features (e.g., "these tires will last at least 25,000 miles") or what it will do, and you rely on these statements as part of your decision to purchase the product, these statements constitute an express warranty that you have a right to rely on. This is true even though the written warranty states there are no other warranties.

3. In most situations an implied warranty of general fitness for the intended use or "merchantability" is also present (e.g., that a lawnmower will cut grass, a tire will hold air, a calculator will subtract, etc.). This warranty exists in addition to the written and express warranties discussed just above and applies even though there is a statement (often called a "warranty disclaimer") saying no warranties exist beyond the written warranty, or that no warranty exists at all, or that all implied warranties are specifically disclaimed. Implied warranties apply to new products of all kinds, except clothing and consumables [CC Sec. 179(a)]. Under the Song-Beverly Act, they last for the same time period as the written warranty, but in no case longer than one year or shorter than 60 days. Under the California Commercial Code and Magnuson-Moss Act, implied warranties may last for a longer time under some circumstances. Implied warranties apply to used products only in transactions in which a written warranty is given, and then only last for as long as the written warranty, but no shorter than 30 days or longer than 90 days.

4. If a warranty is breached (e.g., a TV set with a six-month warranty on parts and labor breaks the day after purchase), you should notify the seller and manufacturer in writing, keeping a copy of your letter. Give them a reasonable chance to make necessary repairs or replace the defective product. Thirty days to accomplish this is usually considered to be reasonable. If they don't, it's time to think about filing in Small Claims Court.

5. In considering whether and how to pursue a breach of warranty case, realize that Small Claims Court judges usually consider this type of dispute based on a broad view of fairness. In other words, if you purchase goods that are clearly defective, or do not accomplish the task they were represented by

the seller to handle (either in an advertisement or a personal statement to you), and you have made and documented a good faith effort to have the seller or manufacturer either fix or replace the goods or refund your money, file in Small Claims Court and let the judge worry about the details of warranty law.

Let's now examine a couple of examples of breach of warranty situations:

Example 1: Alan purchases a computer and some expensive accounting software from ABC Computer. He explains his bookkeeping needs to the salesperson in detail and is assured that the computer and software will do the job. The computer contains a written warranty against defects in parts and labor for 90 days. The warranty statement says that all implied warranties are disclaimed. The software contains no written warranty statement. It is apparent to Alan after a couple of days work that the software simply is not sophisticated enough to meet the bookkeeping needs he had explained to the salesperson and that the salesperson didn't know what he was talking about when he said it was "perfect for the job."

Two days later the computer breaks. Alan calls ABC and asks for the computer to be fixed or replaced and for his money back on the software. As to the computer, Alan should have no problem—it broke within the written warranty period. The software raises a different problem. In asking for his money back Alan can claim a breach of an express warranty (the salesperson's statement that it would meet his needs), and the implied warranty of general fitness or merchantability (it simply doesn't meet the reasonable standard of accounting packages). This latter claim would be hard to prove, however, if the software is adequate to accomplish more routine accounting tasks, just not sophisticated enough for Alan's special needs. If the seller won't make good and Alan thinks about whether he can win in court, he should give considerable thought to how he can prove that he relied on the salesperson's statements that the software would meet his specific bookkeeping needs as part of his decision to purchase it. If he had given the salesperson written specifications as to his accounting needs and had a copy, or if he had a witness to the salesperson's grandiose promises, he would be in good shape. Otherwise, it might come down to his word against the salesperson's.

F. How to Approach a Case When Your Rights Under California Law Have Been Breached

There are thousands of California laws which purport to protect consumers. Everything from the construction of home swimming pools, to regulation of retail sales, to the moving of household goods, to the types of contracts that you can be offered by a health studio are covered. I list a number of these laws in the Appendix to this book. If you think any of these, or the many others discussed in the book, may apply to your situation, you can look up the law involved yourself (see Chapter 1, Sec. D).

Many California laws provide specific consumer remedies. For example, Bus. & Prof. Code Sec. 17500, which prohibits false or deceptive advertising, provides that private parties may recover the money they spent for goods or services advertised in this fashion. The point is simple: if you believe that the person you have a claim against has violated a California law and that this violation is directly related to the monetary damage you have suffered, call the judge's attention to the law in question as part of your oral presentation in Small Claims Court.

Example: Steve E. purchased a set of cookware from a very persuasive door-to-door salesperson. That afternoon he checked at a discount store and found a very similar cookware set for half the price. Realizing that he had been talked into a bad deal, Steve wondered if he had any rights to cancel the door-to-door purchase. On the way home he stopped at a local library and looked up door-to-door sales in the index to the West California Codes. He found nothing. Being a persistent sort, Steve next looked up the word home. Sure enough, he found an entry for "Home Solicitation Contracts," and under that a subheading for "Cancellations." He was referred to Section 1689.7 of the Civil Code. Looking up this section, Steve read, "...the buyer has the right to cancel a home solicitation contract or offer until midnight of the third business day after the day on which the buyer signs an agreement or offer to purchase...." Steve immediately wrote a letter cancelling his contract and asking the sales company to refund his money and pick up the cookware. When it refused, Steve filed an action in Small Claims Court, pointed the statute out to the judge, and walked away with a judgment for the amount of the purchase.

In addition to the specific consumer protection rights embedded in literally thousands of California laws, there are several general legal rules you should know about. One of the most important of these deals with fraud (CC Sec. 1572). Generally speaking, if fraud is present as part of a transaction (contract, sale, etc.), the deal can be cancelled. Fraud can take the form of intentional misrepresentation; negligent misrepresentation (a positive assertion without adequate information that it is true); fraudulent concealment (suppression of that which is true); a false promise (a promise with no intention to perform);

or any other act designed to deceive. If you think you have been defrauded, make sure the judge knows about your claim. The judge has the power to "rescind" the sale or other contract that forms the basis of the fraudulent conduct and order that your money be refunded, along with any damages you have suffered as a result of the fraud.

G. Stating Your Claim On Your Court Papers

Before you get too far into theories of law, let me bring you back to earth. While it is helpful to have a good grasp of what's involved in proving a contract or other type of negligence case (the judge, after all, is a lawyer), it is more important that you stay grounded on the facts of your grievance. One of the joys of Small Claims Court is that you don't plead theories of law—you state facts. So, even if you are not sure that what happened to you fully matches one of the legal theories discussed here, bring your case anyway if you have suffered real monetary damage and you believe the person you are suing caused that damage.

Let's jump ahead and take a look at the form you will fill out when you file your case. Turn to Chapter 10 and find the form entitled "Plaintiff's Statement." Look at Line 5. As you can see, there is little space for theory. Indeed, there is barely room to set down the facts of your dispute. You should state your case like this:

"I took my coat to John's Dry Cleaners and it was returned in a damaged (shrunk) condition."

"Defendant's dog bit me on the corner of Rose and Peach Streets in West Covina, California."

"The car repairs that Joe's Garage did on my car were done wrong, resulting in my engine burning."

"Defendant refused to return the cleaning deposit for my apartment even though I left it clean."

Note: When you state your case on the court papers, your only goal is to notify the other party and the court as to the broad outline of your dispute. You don't want to try to argue the facts of your case or the law that you believe applies to it. Your chance to do this will come later in court.

Important: Now is a good time to start organizing your materials in one place. Get a couple of manila envelopes or file folders, label them carefully, and find a safe place for storage. One folder or envelope should be used to store all documentary evidence such as receipts, letters, photographs, etc. The other is for your court papers, filing fee receipts, etc. It's no secret that more than one case has been won or lost because of good (or bad) record keeping.

CHAPTER 3

Can You Recover
If You Win?

This is the shortest chapter in the book and the most important. In it, I ask all of you who are thinking of filing a Small Claims suit to focus on a very simple question—can you collect if you win? Collecting from many individuals or businesses isn't a problem as they are solvent and will routinely pay any judgments entered against them. But all too often, the main problem you face in Small Claims Court is not winning your case, but collecting your money when you do win.

I am co-author with Stephen Elias of the book published by Nolo Press entitled *Billpayers' Rights*. It contains information for people who are over their heads in legal debts and don't know how they are going to keep the roof over their heads and clothes on their kids' backs. The message of the book is that, surprisingly, there are many ways for a debtor to protect himself. A creditor, it turns out, can't legally take the food from the debtor's table, or the T.V. from his living room, or even (in many cases) the car from his driveway.[1]

What do these facts mean to you? Simply that many Californians who are not completely without money are nevertheless "judgment proof." You can sue them and get judgments against them until red cows dance on the yellow moon, but you can't collect a dime. Unfortunately, just this sort of frustrating thing happens every day—people go to lots of trouble to win cases only to realize that the judgment is uncollectable. This, of course, compounds the misery. Not only has the person suing lost the money from the original debt or injury, but also the time, trouble and expense of the Small Claims suit. As my grandmother used to say, "no one ever got to live in the big house on the hill by throwing a good quarter after a bad dime."

Whenever a dispute develops, it is all too easy to get caught up in thinking and arguing about who was wrong—so easy that perspective is lost and the problems of collection are forgotten. I emphasize this because I have so often observed people bringing cases to court in which there was never a hope of collecting. How can I tell ahead of time? I can't always, but in many situations, it's not hard. One thing I look for is whether or not the defendant is working. If a person fails to voluntarily pay a judgment, the easiest way to collect it is to garnish his or her wages. Thus, if the person sued is working, there is an excellent chance of collecting if payment is not made voluntarily. But you can't garnish a welfare, social security, unemployment, pension or disability check. So, if the person sued gets his income from one of these sources, red flags should be flying.

---

[1]A debtor's motor vehicles are protected if the amount of equity in the vehicle(s) totals no more than $1,200, unless he uses the vehicle as a tool of his trade, in which case the car is exempt from attachment as long as the equity is $2,500 or less. CCP 704.010, 704.060.

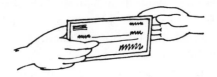

But what about other assets? Can't a judgment be collected from sources other than wages? Yes, it can—bank accounts, motor vehicles and real estate are other common collection sources. But remember, as stated above, many types of property are exempt from attachment. Did you know that you can't effectively get at the judgment debtor's equity in a family house unless it exceeds $45,000 ($60,000 if the owner is over 65, blind, or disabled, $30,000 if the debtor is single and not yet 65), or that a whole list of other possessions, including furniture, a motor vehicle(s) with $1,200 in equity, the tools of a person's trade valued up to $2,500, and at least 75% of wages are exempt?[2] So before you go down and file your papers, ask yourself these questions:

1. Does the person you wish to sue voluntarily pay debts—or are you dealing with a person who will make it as difficult as possible to collect if you win?

2. Does he have a job or is he likely to get one? Judgments can be collected for ten years (this period can usually be renewed) and accrue interest as long as they are not paid.

3. If this person doesn't have a job, does she have some other means of support or assets that convince you that you can collect?

4. If you have your doubts about voluntary payment and the person you are suing doesn't have a job, can you identify some

---

[2]In California property that is exempt from being taken to satisfy debts is listed in the Code of Civil Procedure Section 704.010. Also, see *Billpayers' Rights*, Warner and Elias, Nolo Press. This book contains forms and instructions necessary for a debtor to take advantage of his rights.

non-exempt assets that you can attach, such as a bank account, or real property other than the place where the person lives?

5. If a business is involved, is it solvent and does it have a good reputation for paying debts?

6. Is the person or business you wish to sue living or doing business in California? Normally, it is not possible to get a judgment against out-of-staters in a California Small Claims Court unless they are present in California or actively do business here.

Note: If a person or a business declares a straight bankruptcy under Chapter 7 and lists you as a creditor, your right to recover is cut off. If you are owed money on a secured debt (there was a security agreement as in the case of a car or major appliance), you are entitled to recover your security. If the judgment was obtained because you or your property was injured by the malicious behavior of the person declaring bankruptcy (e.g., they hit you when drunk), your right to collect is not cut off.

In Chapter 23, we deal in detail with the mechanics of collecting after you get your judgment. If you think that collection may pose a problem, you should read this chapter now. But remember what my canny old grandmother said about bad dimes and good quarters and don't waste your time chasing people who have no money.

CHAPTER 4

How Much Can
You Sue For?

The maximum amount you can sue for in Small Claims Court is $1,500. With a few exceptions, Small Claims Court does not hear cases unless they are for money damages. Thus, you can't use Small Claims Court to get a divorce, stop (enjoin) the city from cutting down your favorite oak tree, change your name, or do any of the thousands of other things that require some solution other than the payment of money. However, Small Claims Court may be used for certain types of evictions (see Chapter 20) and in rare situations, equitable relief (see Section D of this chapter), which can include such things as ending (rescinding) a contract arrived at fraudulently or ordering that a prevailing party be awarded an object of property instead of money damages when this is the only way to resolve the dispute fairly (specific performance).

A. Cutting Down a Claim That's Over the Limit to Fit Into Small Claims

It is legal to reduce an excessive claim so that it will fit into Small Claims Court. Thus, you could take a $2,100 debt and bring it into Small Claims Court, claiming only $1,500. But if you do this, you forever waive the $600 difference between $1,500 and $2,100. In legal parlance, this is called "waiving the excess." Why might you want to do this? Because the alternative to Small Claims Court involves filing your suit in a formal court with dozens of complicated rules and the considerable expense involved in having a lawyer fill out the papers, etc. A lawyer would probably charge considerably more than $600 to represent you. It is possible to represent yourself in Municipal or Superior Court, but doing so requires a good bit of homework and the guts to walk into an unfamiliar and sometimes hostile arena. Law libraries exist in most major courthouses and are open to the public. Law librarians are usually very helpful in assisting you to find materials. However, neither the librarians nor the court clerks will help you decipher the numerous confusing procedural rules that you must follow in the "formal" courts.

I don't mean to discourage you. Lots of people have successfully handled their cases in our formal courts, but you should be aware before you start that your path may be lonely and frustrating. If you wish to take your case to Municipal or Superior Court yourself, you might start by looking at a series of books entitled *California Forms*. This encyclopedia-like series shows you how to prepare most of the papers that you may ever need to file. For help in finding your way around the law library, and interpreting what you find there, I recommend you obtain a copy of *Legal Research: How to Find and Understand the Law*, Elias (Nolo Press).

B. Splitting Small Claims Court Cases

It is not legal to split an over-the-limit claim into two or more pieces to fit each into Small Claims Court. Taking the $2,100 figure we used above, this means you couldn't sue the same person separately for $1,100 and $1,000.[1] As with most rules, however, a little creative thought will take you a long way. While you can't split a case that's too big to get it into Small Claims Court, you can bring multiple suits against the same person as long as they are based on different claims. This is where the creativity comes in. There is often a large grey area in which it is genuinely difficult to differentiate between one divided claim and several independent ones. If you can reasonably argue that a $2,100 case actually involves two or more separate contracts, or injuries to your person or property, you may as well try dividing it. The worst that will happen is that a judge will disagree and tell you to make a choice between taking the entire claim to Municipal Court, or waiving

---

[1] Defendant's claims that are over the $1,500 limit are discussed in Chapters 10 and 12.

any claim for money in excess of $1,500 and staying in Small Claims.

Example 1: Recently I watched a man in the private telephone business come into Small Claims Court with three separate lawsuits against the same defendant for a combined total of $2,000. One, he said, was for failure to pay for phone installation, another was for failure to pay for phone maintenance and the third was for failure to pay for moving several phones to a different location. The man claimed that each suit was based on the breach of a separate contract. The judge, after asking a few questions, told the man that he was on the borderline between one divided (no good) and several separate (okay) claims, but decided to give him the benefit of the doubt and allowed him to present each case. The man won all three and got two judgments for $700 and a third for $600.

Example 2: Another morning a woman alleged that she had lent a business acquaintance $1,000 twice and was therefore bringing two separate suits, each for $1,000. The defendant said that this wasn't true. She claimed that she had borrowed $2,000 to be repaid in two installments. A different judge, after listening to each person briefly, told the plaintiff that only one claim was involved and that, if she didn't want to waive all money over $1,500, she should go to Municipal Court.[2]

Suggestion: If you wish to sue someone on two related claims, which you believe can be viewed as being separate, you may be better off to file your actions a few days apart. This will result in their being heard on different days, and in most metropolitan areas, by different judges. Unless the defendant shows up and argues that you have split one claim, you will likely get your judgments without difficulty. There is, however, one possible drawback to this approach. If you bring your claims to court on the same day and the judge rules that they are one claim, he will give you a choice as to whether to waive the excess over $1,500 or go to Municipal Court. However, if you go to court on

------

[2] In the landlord-tenant area there is a ruling that a landlord must sue for all unpaid rent for a rental unit in one action and can't bring separate Small Claims suits based on each month's unpaid rent. *Leske v. Municipal Court,* 138 CA 3d 188.

different days and the question of split claims is raised on the second or third day, you may have a problem. If the judge decides that your action in splitting the claims was improper, he has no choice but to throw the second and third claims out of court with no opportunity to refile in Municipal Court. This is because you have already sued and won and you are not entitled to sue the same person twice for the same claim.

C. How to Compute the Exact Amount of Your Claim

Sometimes it's easy to understand exactly what dollar amount to sue for, but it's often tricky. Before we get to the tricky part, let's go over the basic rule. When in doubt, always bring your suit a little on the high side. Why? Because the court has the power to award you less than you request, but can't give you more, even if the judge feels that you are entitled to it. But don't go overboard—if you sue for $1,500 on a $500 claim, you are likely to spur your opponent to furious opposition, ruin any chance for an out-of-court compromise, and lose the respect of the judge.

1. Computing the Exact Amount—Contract Cases

To arrive at the exact figure to sue on in contract cases, compute the difference between the amount you were supposed to receive under the contract and what you actually received. For example, if Jeannie Goodday agrees to pay Homer Brightspot $1,200 to paint her house to look like a rainbow, but then only gives him $800, Homer has a claim for $400 plus the cost of filing suit and serving Jeannie with the papers (costs are discussed in more detail in Chapter 15). The fact that Jeannie and Homer made their agreement orally does not bar Homer from suing. Oral contracts are generally legal as long as they can be carried out in a year. Of course, people tend to remember oral contracts differently and this can lead to serious proof problems once you get to court. It is always wise to reduce agreements to writing, even if only to a note or letter agreement dated and signed by both parties.[3]

Where the contract involves lending money in exchange for interest, don't forget to include the interest due in the amount you sue for.[4] I have seen several disappointed people sue for the exact amount of the debt (say $500) and not include interest (say $50), thinking that they could have the judge add the interest when they got to court. This can't be done—the judge doesn't have the power to make an award larger than the amount you request.[5] Of course, you can't sue for interest if the interest amount would make your claim larger than the Small Claims maximum.

Unfortunately, not all claims based on breach of contract are easy to reduce to a money amount. This is often due to a legal doctrine known as "mitigation of damages." Don't let the fancy term throw you. Like so much of our law the concept behind the "mumbo jumbo" is simple. "Mitigation of damages" means simply that the person bringing suit for breach of contract must himself take all reasonable steps to limit the amount of damages he suffers. Let's take an example from the landlord-tenant field. Tillie the tenant moves out three months before the end

---

[3] Many useful consumer-oriented agreements, including one for home repair and maintenance situations, can be found in *Make Your Own Contract*, Elias (Nolo Press).

[4] As a general rule, you can only recover interest when it is called for in a written or oral contract. If you loaned a friend $100, but never mentioned interest, you can sue only for the return of the $100.

[5] If you find yourself in court and realize you have asked for too little, you should request that the judge allow you to amend your claim. Some judges will do this and offer the defendant a continuance to deal with defending against the higher amount if they wish it.

of her lease (remember a lease is a contract). Her monthly rent is $350. Can Lothar the landlord recover the full $1,050 ($350 x 3 months) from Tillie in Small Claims Court? Probably not. Why? Because Lothar has control of the empty apartment and must take reasonable steps to attempt to find a new tenant. If Lothar can rerent the apartment to someone else for $350 or more per month, he has suffered no damage. Put another way, if Lothar rerents the apartment, he has fulfilled his responsibility to "mitigate damages." In a typical situation it might take Lothar several weeks (unless he had plenty of advance notice, or Tillie herself found a new tenant) to find a suitable new tenant. If it took three weeks and $25 worth of newspaper ads, Lothar could recover approximately $300 from Tillie.

The "mitigation of damages" concept isn't only applicable to landlord-tenant situations, but applies to every contract case where the person damaged can take reasonable steps to protect himself. In the earlier example, if Jeannie Goodday had agreed to pay Homer Brightspot $100 per day for seven days to paint her house and then had cancelled after the first day, Homer could sue her for the remaining $600, but, if he did, he would surely be asked whether he had earned any other money during the six days. If he had, it would be subtracted from the $600. But what if Homer refused other work and slept in his hammock all week? If Jeannie could show that he had turned down other jobs, or had refused to make reasonable efforts to seek available work, this too would be used to reduce Homer's recovery.

Suggestion: Sue only for the amount of money you are out. Don't try to collect money in court that you have already recovered from someone else.

2. Computing the Exact Amount— Property Damage Cases

When your property has been damaged by the negligent or intentional act of someone else, you have a right to recover for your loss.[6] This amount is often, but not always, the amount of money that it would take to fix the damaged item.

Example: John Quickstop bashes into Melissa Caretaker's new Dodge, smashing in the left rear. How much can Melissa recover? The amount that it would cost to fix, or, if necessary, replace the damaged part of her car. Melissa should get several estimates from responsible body and fender shops and sue for the amount of the lowest, one if John won't pay voluntarily (see Chapter 19).

There is, however, a big exception to the rule that a person who has had property damaged can recover the cost of fixing the damaged item. This occurs when the cost to fix the item exceeds its actual cash market value. You are not entitled to a new or better object—only to have your loss made good. Had Melissa Caretaker been driving a 1961 Dodge, the cost to fix the fender might well have exceeded the value of the car. If this were the case, she would be entitled to the value of the car, not the value of the fender repair.

Think of it this way. In any situation where the value of the repair exceeds the value of the object, you are limited to the fair market value of the object (the amount you could have sold it for) a minute before the damage occurred. From this figure, you have to subtract the value, if any, of the object after the injury. Of course, in deciding how much to claim, you should give yourself the benefit of the doubt as to how much a piece of property is worth, but don't be ridiculous. A $300 motor scooter might conceivably be worth $450 to $500, but it's not worth $750.

---

[6] If you haven't done so, read Chapter 2. It is important to remember that you not only have to establish the amount of your loss, but that the person you are suing is legally responsible ("liable") to pay your damages.

Example: Let's return to Melissa. If her 1961 Dodge was worth $700 and the fender would cost $800 to replace, she would be limited to a $700 recovery, less what the car could be sold for in its damaged state. If this was $50 for scrap, she would be entitled to $650. However, if Melissa had just gotten a new engine and transmission and her car was worth $1,200, she would legally be entitled to recover and sue for the entire $800 needed to get her Dodge fixed.

Note: Many people insist on believing that they can recover the cost of getting a replacement object when theirs has been totalled. As you should now understand, this isn't necessarily true. If Melissa's $700 car was totalled and she claimed that she simply couldn't get another decent car for less than $900, she would still be limited to recovering $700. To get $900, she would have to show that her car had a sale value of that much just before the accident. This rule can cause you a real hardship when an older object that is in great shape is destroyed. The fair market value may be low, while the cost of replacement high.

Knowing what something is worth and proving it are quite different. A car that you are sure is worth $800 may look like it's only worth $500 to someone else. In court, you will want to be prepared to show that your piece of property is worth every bit of the $800. The best way to do this is to get some estimates (opinions) from experts in the field (i.e., a car dealer if your car was ruined). This is best done by having the expert come to court and testify, but can also be done in writing. You will also want to check newspaper and flea market ads for the prices asked for comparable goods and creatively explore any other approaches that make sense given the type of damage you have suffered. We talk more about proving your case in court in Chapters 16-21.

3. Computing the Exact Amount— Cases Involving Damage to Clothing

Clothing is property, so why am I separating it out for special treatment? For two reasons. Cases involving clothing are extremely common in Small Claims Court and judges seem to apply a logic to them that they apply to no other property damage cases. The reason for this is that clothing is personal to its owner and often has small or little value to anyone else even though it may be in good condition. If the rules that we just learned (i.e., you can recover the repair cost of a damaged item unless this would be more than its market value before the damage occurred, in which case you are limited to recovering its total value) were strictly applied to clothing, there would often be little or no recovery. This is because there is not much market for used clothing.

When suing for damage to new or almost new clothing, sue for its cost. If it is older, sue for that percentage of the value of the clothing which reflects how worn it was when the damage occurred. For example, if your two-year-old suit which cost $400 new were destroyed, sue for $200 if you feel the suit would have lasted another two years. In clothing cases, most judges want answers to these questions:

• How much did the clothing cost originally?

• How much of its useful life was consumed at the time the damage occurred?

• Does the damaged item still have some value to the owner, or has it been ruined?[7]

Example 1: Wendy took her new $250 coat to Rudolph, a tailor, to have alterations made. Rudolph cut part of the back of the coat in the wrong place and ruined it. How much should Wendy sue for? $250—as the coat was almost new. She could probably expect to recover close to this amount.

---

[7] The International Fabricare Institute publishes a very useful pamphlet called the *Fair Claims Guide for Consumer Textile Products*, which contains a number of tables designed to tell you what any object of used clothing is worth. It's available from IFI, 12251 Tech Road, Silver Spring, MD 20904 for 50¢.

Example 2: The same facts as just above, but the coat was two years old and had been well worn, although it was still in good condition. Here Wendy would be wise to sue for $200 and hope to recover between $100 and $150.

Example 3: This time we will return Wendy's coat to its almost new condition, but have Rudolph only slightly deface the back, instead of completely destroying it. I would still advise Wendy to sue for the full $250. Whether she could recover that much would depend on the judge. Most would probably award her a little less on the theory that the coat retained some value. Were I Wendy, however, I would strongly argue that I didn't buy the coat with the expectation that I could only wear it in a closet and that, as far as I was concerned, the coat was ruined.

4. Computing the Exact Amount— Personal Injury Cases

Lawyers quickly take over the great majority of cases where someone is injured. These claims are routinely inflated (a sprained back might be worth $3,000-$5,000 or more), because it is in everyone's selfish interest to do so. The insurance adjusters and insurance company lawyers are as much a part of this some-thing-for-nothing syndrome, as are the ambulance-chasing plaintiff's attorneys. If there aren't lots of claims, lots of lawsuits, lots of depositions and negotiations, it wouldn't take lots of people making lots of money to run the system. Even in states with so-called "no-fault" automobile insurance, the dispute resolution bureaucracy has managed to protect itself very well.

Some small personal injury cases do get to Small Claims Court, however. Dog bite cases are one common example and there are others. You figure the amount to sue for by adding:

- Out of pocket medical costs,
  including medical transportation   _____

- Loss of pay, or vacation time
  for missing work   _____

- Pain and suffering[8]   _____

- Damage to property[9]   _____

                            TOTAL   _____

Medical and hospital bills, including transportation to and from the doctor, are routinely recoverable as long as you have established that the person you are suing is at fault. However, if you are covered by health insurance and the insurance company has already paid your medical costs, you will find that your policy says that any money that you recover for these costs must be turned over to the company. Often, insurance companies don't make much effort to keep track of, or recover, Small Claims judgments as the amounts of money involved don't make it worthwhile. Knowing this, many judges are reluctant to grant judgments for medical bills unless the individual can show that he is personally out-of-pocket the money.

Loss of pay or vacation time is viewed in a similar way. If the cocker spaniel down the block lies in wait for you behind a

---

[8] In more serious cases you would also have to figure the monetary value of any permanent injury. These cases do not, however, get to Small Claims Court. Also, contrary to the erroneous "advice" many small claims clerks give, you can sue for pain and suffering expenses in Small Claims Court, just as you can in regular Municipal or Superior Court. The only limitation is that the amount you can sue for is $1,500. See *Leuschen v. Small Claims Court* (1923) 191 Cal. 133 and 59 Cal. Ops. Atty. Gen. 321 (1976).

[9] Often a personal injury is accompanied by injury to property. Thus, a dog bite might also ruin your pants. You add all of your damages together as part of the same suit. You can't sue separately for your pants and your behind

hedge and grabs a piece of your derriere for breakfast, and as a result you miss a day of work getting yourself patched up, you are entitled to recover the loss of any pay, commissions or vacation time. However, if you are on a job with unlimited paid sick time, so that you suffer no loss for missing work, you have nothing to recover.

The third area of recovery is for what is euphemistically known as "pain and suffering." This is a catch-all phrase that simultaneously means a great deal and nothing at all. Generations of lawyers have made a good living mumbling it. Their idea is often to take a minor injury (sprained ankle) and inflate its value as much as possible by claiming that the injured party underwent great "pain and suffering." "How much is every single minute that my poor client suffered an unbearably painful ankle worth—$1, $5, $10,000?" etc. When you read about million dollar settlements, a good chunk of the recovery routinely falls into the "pain and suffering" category. I don't mean to suggest that recovery for "pain and suffering" is always wrong—just that it is often abused.

But back to the case of the nasty cocker spaniel. If you received a painful bite, spent the morning getting your rump attended to, had to take several pain killers and then make sure that the dog was free of rabies, you would very likely feel that you were entitled to some recovery. One judge I know doesn't pay much attention to the evidence in this type of case. He simply awards $500 for a painful bite by a medium-sized dog, adds $100 for anything the size of a lion, and subtracts $100 if the dog looks like a mouse.

Suggestion: In thinking about how much you wish to sue for, be aware that lawyers often bring suit for three to four times the amount of the out-of-pocket damages (medical bills and loss of work). Therefore, if you were out of pocket $150, you might wish to ask for $500, the overage being for "pain and suffering." If you have no medical bills (there is no blood or at least x-rays), you will find it difficult to recover anything for "pain and suffering." This is why lawyers routinely encourage their clients to get as much medical attention as possible.

Example 1: Mary Tendertummy is drinking a bottle of pop when a mouse foot floats to the surface. She is greatly nauseated, loses her lunch and goes to the doctor for medication. As a result, she is out an afternoon's pay. She sues the pop company for $500. This is reasonable. She will probably recover most of this amount.

Example 2: The same thing happens to Roy Toughguy. He just throws the pop away in disgust and goes back to work. A few weeks later he hears about Mary's recovery and decides that he too could use $500. How much is he likely to recover? Probably not much more than the price of the soda—he apparently suffered little or no injury.

Note: Certain costs of suit such as filing fees, subpoenaed witness fees, costs of serving papers, etc., can be recovered, but many, such as compensation for time off from work to go to court, transportation to and from court, etc., cannot. See Chapter 15 for more information. You do not add costs to the amount of your suit. The judge does this when the case is decided.

5. Computing the Exact Amount— Emotional or Mental Distress

As noted in Chapter 2, in our increasingly crowded urban environment, there are all sorts of ways we can cause one another real pain without even making physical contact. For example, if I live in the apartment above you and wake up every morning and pound on my floor (your ceiling) for an hour, I will probably quickly reduce you to the status of a raving maniac. What can you do about it besides bashing me over the head? One remedy is for you to sue me in Small Claims Court based on the fact that my actions constitute the intentional infliction of emotional distress. But how much should you sue for? Unfortunately, there is no good rule of thumb I can give you.

It depends on how obnoxious my behavior is, how long it has gone on, how clearly you have asked me to cease it (this should be done in writing), how well you can convince the judge you have suffered and, probably at least as important, the personality of the judge. My gut reaction is that in this type of case you do better if you appear to be very reasonable. Thus, I would normally advise against suing for $1,500, or any amount over $1,000, unless the other person's behavior clearly makes him out to be first cousin to Attila the Hun.

D. Bad Checks

There are several major exceptions to the information on how to compute the amount of your claim set out in Section C, just above. These involve situations where a statute establishes the right to receive extra damages, over and above the amount of the financial injury.[10] The most common of these involves bad checks, where you receive a bad check (or a check on which the

---

[10] In the landlord-tenant area, a tenant is eligible to get $100 per day in damages in addition to the amount of her actual loss if a landlord disconnects her utilities (even if the rent or utility bill is not paid). Also, if a landlord acting in bad faith fails to return a security deposit to a tenant within 14 days of the tenant moving out, or provide a written itemization of the reasons for keeping it, the tenant is eligible for up to $200 in punitive damages plus interest at 2% per month (see Chapter 20).

writer stops payment in bad faith)[11] and the person giving it to you does not make it good within 30 days of your written demand mailed via certified mail to do so. Where a bad check is involved—whether it was for payment of a contract,

---

[11] According to CC Sec. 1719, "There shall be no cause of action under this section if a maker stops payment in order to resolve a good faith dispute with the payee. The payee is entitled to the damages only upon proving by clear and convincing evidence that there was no good faith dispute. A 'good faith dispute' is one in which the court finds that the maker of the check had a reasonable belief of his or her legal entitlement to withhold payment. Grounds to such entitlement include, but are not limited to, the following; services were not rendered, goods were not delivered, goods or services purchased are faulty, not as promised, or otherwise unsatisfactory, or there was an overcharge . . . In the case of a stop payment, the notice to the maker of the check shall be in substantially the following form:

NOTICE

To: _____(name of maker)_____
_____(name of payee)_____ is the payee of a check you wrote for $____(amount)____ . The check was not paid because you stopped payment, and the payee demands payment. You may have a good faith dispute as to whether you owe the full amount. If you do not have a good faith dispute with the payee and fail to pay the payee the full amount of the check in cash within 30 days after this notice was mailed, you could be sued or held responsible to pay at least all of the following:

(1) The amount of the check.

(2) Damages of at least $100, or, if high, three times the amount of the check, up to $500.

(3) The cost of mailing this notice.

If the court determines that you do have a good faith dispute with the payee, you will not have to pay the damages and mailing cost mentioned above. If you stopped payment because you had a good faith dispute with the payee, you should try to work out your dispute with the payee. You can contact the payee at:

_____(name of payee)_____

_____(street address)_____

_____(telephone number)_____

You may wish to contact a lawyer to discuss your legal rights and responsibilities."

personal injury or property damage claim— Civil Code Sec. 1719 states that you are entitled to recover the amount of the check plus three times the amount of the check, to the maximum of $500, with the following exceptions:

1. You can sue for $100 in damages, no matter how small the bad check. Thus, if you get a $25 bad check, you can sue for $125.

2. You can't sue for more than $500 in damages, no matter how large the check. Thus , for a $200 bad check, you can sue for $700 (the amount of the check plus the $500 maximum).

Example: If you receive a bad check (say $150), write a letter to the person who gave it to you demanding payment in cash. Keep a copy. Send the letter certified mail. Wait 30 days. If you are not paid in full in cash (you don't have to accept another check), file in Small Claims Court. You can sue for the amount of the bad check ($150) plus three times that amount ($450, for a total of $600).

One final point. The law says that if you follow these rules, you shall get triple damages. This is not an area in which the judge has discretion as to whether to award them or not.

E. Equitable Relief (Or Money Can't Always Solve the Problem)

California allows judges to grant relief in ways that do not involve the payment of money, if equity (fairness) demands it. In California (CCP Sec. 116.3), "equitable relief" is limited to one or more of four categories: "recission," "restitution," "reformation," and "specific performance." Let's translate these into English.

Recission: This is a remedy that is used when a grossly unfair or fraudulent contract is discovered, or where a contract was based on a mistake as to an important fact, or was induced by duress or undue influence, or one party simply didn't receive what was promised through the fault of the other. Thus, if a merchant sued you for failure to pay for aluminum siding that you contended had been misrepresented and was a total rip-off, you could ask that the contract be rescinded, and that any money you paid be returned to you. Civil Code 1689(b)(1)-1689(b)(6).

Restitution: This is an important remedy. It gives a judge the power to order that a particular piece of property be transferred to its original owner when fairness requires that the contracting parties be restored to their original positions. It can be used in the common situation in which one person sells another a piece of property (say a motor scooter) and the other fails to pay. Instead of simply giving the seller a money judgment which might be hard to collect, the judge has the power to order the scooter restored to its original owner. Where money has been paid under a contract that is rescinded, the judge can order it to be returned, plus damages. Thus, if a used car purchase was rescinded based on the fraud of the seller, the buyer could get a judgment for the amount paid for the car, plus money spent for repairs, alternate transportation, financing, etc.

Reformation: This remedy is somewhat unusual. It has to do with changing (reforming) a contract to meet the original intent of the parties in a situation where some term or condition agreed to by the parties has been left out or misstated and where fairness dictates that the contract be reformed. Thus, if Arthur the Author and Peter the Publisher orally agree that Peter will publish Arthur's 200-page book and then they write a contract inadvertently leaving out the number of pages, a court would very likely "reform" the contract to include this provision if Arthur showed up with a 2,000-page manuscript. Reformation is most commonly used when an oral agreement is written down incorrectly.

Specific Performance: This is an important remedy that comes into play where a contract involving an unusual or "one-of-a-kind" object has not been carried out. Say you agree to buy a unique antique jade ring for your mother's birthday that is exactly like the one she lost years before, and then the seller refuses to go through with the deal. A court could cite the doctrine of "specific performance" to order that the ring be turned over to you. "Specific performance" will only be ordered in situations where the payment of money will not make a party to a contract whole.

One very confusing aspect of California's equitable relief provision is that you are not allowed to demand (sue for) equitable relief, but the judge has the power to grant it when you ask for money damages. Obviously, however, you are not likely to get relief you don't ask for. So, if you want one of the equitable remedies set out above, your best bet is to sue for your monetary loss, but to ask for equitable relief in court as soon as possible. If your request is greeted with disbelief, refer the judge to Section 116.3 of the Code of Civil Procedure. You should also know that in another, somewhat weird, legal twist, the judge has power to grant equitable relief, no matter how much money doing so involves. Thus, if you sue a manufacturer for $1,500 as a result of damage suffered from a defective product, but can convince the judge that the product was so defective that the entire contract should be rescinded, she can order that you get all of your money back if you return the goods, even if the goods in question happen to be a $15,000 automobile.

CHAPTER 5

Is the Suit Brought Within the Proper Time Limits (Statute of Limitations)?

The legislature sets up time limits within which lawsuits must be filed. These are called Statutes of Limitations. Time limits are different for different types of cases. If you wait too long, your right to sue will be barred by these statutes. Why have a Statute of Limitations? Because it has been found that disputes are best settled relatively soon after they develop. Unlike wine, lawsuits don't improve with age. Memories fade and witnesses die or move away, and once-clear details tend to blur together. As a general rule, it is wise to sue as soon after your dispute arises as is reasonably possible. Statutes of Limitations are almost never less than one year, so if you file promptly, you should have little to worry about.

A. California Statute of Limitations Periods[1]

Here are the statute of limitation periods most likely to affect you:

Personal Injury: One year from the injury, or, if the injury is not immediately discovered, one year from the date it is discovered.

Oral Contracts: Two years from the day the contract is broken.

Written Contracts: Four years from the day the contract is broken.

Damage to Personal or Real Property: Three years from the date the damage occurs.[2]

Fraud: Three years from the date of the discovery of the fraud.

Professional Negligence Against Health Care Providers: Three years after the date of the injury or one year from its discovery.

Suits Against Public Agencies: Before you can sue a city, county or the state government, you must file an administrative claim form. The time period in which this must be done is normally 100 days. This is not precisely a Statute of Limitations, but it has the same effect. (See Chapter 8 for a more complete discussion of how to sue governments in Small Claims Court.)

---

[1] I only include the most common Statutes of Limitations periods here.You will find the rest in California CCP Secs. 312-363.

[2] The statute of limitations is ten years stemming from property damage that results from latent defects in the planning, construction or improvement of real property.

Note: Some contracts which you may assume to be oral may actually be written. People often forget that they signed papers when they first arranged for goods or services. For example, your charge accounts, telephone service, insurance policies as well as most major purchases of goods and services involve a written contract, even though you haven't signed any papers for years. And another thing—to have a written contract you need not have signed a document full of "whereas's" and "therefores." Any signed writing in which you promise to do something (e.g., pay money, provide services) in exchange for someone else's promise to provide you something in return is a contract, even if it's written on toilet paper with lipstick. When you go to a car repair shop and they make out a work order and you sign it—that's a contract. (See Chapter 2A for more about contracts and liability for their breach.)

B. Computing the Statute of Limitations

Okay, now let's assume that you have found out what the relevant limitations period is. How do you know what date to start your counting from? That's easy. Start with the day the injury to your person or property occurred, or, if a contract is involved, start with the day that the failure to perform under the terms of the contract occurred. Where a contract to pay in installments is involved, start with the day that the first payment was missed.[3]

Example: Doolittle owes Crabapple $500, payable in five monthly installments of $100. Both live in San Jose, California. They never wrote down any of the terms of their agreement. Doolittle misses his third monthly payment which was due on January 1, 1986. Crabapple should compute his Statute of Limitations period from January 2, 1986, assuming, of course, that Doolittle doesn't later catch up on his payments. Since the Statute of Limitations for oral contracts is two years, this means that Crabapple has until January 1, 1988 to file his suit. If a written contract had been involved, Crabapple could file until January 1, 1990, as the Statute of Limitations on written contracts is four years.

I am frequently asked to explain the legal implications of the following situation. After the Statute of Limitations runs out (say two years on an oral contract to pay for having a fence painted), the debtor commences voluntarily to make payments. Does the voluntary payment have the effect of creating a new two-year Statute of Limitations period, allowing the person who is owed the money to sue if the debtor again stops paying? No. Simply starting to pay on an obligation where the Statute of Limitations already bars the creditor from getting a judgment doesn't create a new period for suit.[4] All the creditor can do is to keep his toes crossed and hope that the debtor's belated streak of honesty continues. However, if the debtor signs a written agreement promising to make the payments, this does create a

---

[3] The Statute of Limitations (four years on a written contract) applies separately to each installment of a contract. Thus, if you agree to pay $5,000 in five installments commencing January 1, 1985 and continuing on January 1 of each succeeding year and never agree in writing to waive the Statute of Limitations, the creditor's lawsuit can successfully be defended (in legalese it is often said his suit is "barred") on the basis that the statute of limitations has expired on January 2, 1989. Your second payment will not be barred until January 2, 1990 and so on.

[4] See California CCP Sec. 360.

new Statute of Limitations period. In legal slang, this is called "reaffirming the debt."

Example: Back to the drama of Doolittle and Crabapple. Let's assume that in February, 1993, Doolittle experiences a burst of energy, gets a job and decides to pay off all of his old debts. He sends Crabapple $50. A week later, suffering terrible strain from getting up before noon, he quits his job and reverts to his old ways of sleeping in the sun when not reading the racing form. Is the Statute of Limitations allowing Crabapple to sue reinstated? No. As we learned above, once the limitation period of two years has run out, it can't be revived by simply making a payment. However, if Doolittle had sent Crabapple the $50 and had also included a letter saying that he would pay the remainder of the debt, Crabapple would again be able to sue and get a judgment if he failed to pay. Why? Because a written promise to pay a debt barred by the Statute of Limitations has the legal effect of reestablishing the debt.

Debtor's Note: If a creditor and debtor discuss an unpaid bill and the debtor asks the creditor to give her more time to pay, to lower payments, or make some other accommodation, the creditor, assuming he is willing to agree, will almost always require that the debtor waive the Statute of Limitations in writing. This means that if the debtor fails to pay, he must wait another four years before the creditor is prevented from successfully suing. The Statute of Limitations on a written contract is four years. Code of Civil Procedure Sec. 360.5 allows the statute to be waived for an additional four-year period by written agreement.

Suspending the Statute of Limitations: In a few situations, the Statute of Limitations is suspended for a period of time (lawyers say "tolled"). This occurs if the person sued is in prison, living out of the state, insane or a minor. If the Statute of Limitations is suspended ("tolled") by one of these events, it starts up again when the event causing the tolling ends. See CCP Secs. 351,352.

Example: Jack borrows money from Tim under a written contract. Jack fails to pay the money back on the day required. Six months later, Jack is sentenced to a year in jail. The four-year Statute of Limitations would be tolled (suspended) during this period and Tim would still have three-and-one-half years after Jack gets out of jail to collect.

C. Telling the Judge That the Statute of Limitations Has Run Out

What should a defendant do if he believes that the Statute of Limitations period has run out? Tell the judge. Sometimes a judge will figure this out without a reminder, but sometimes he won't. If you are a defendant, don't ever assume that because the clerk has filed the papers and you have been properly served, this means that the plaintiff has started his or her suit on time. The clerk never gets involved in Statute of Limitations questions. They will cheerfully file a suit brought on a breach of contract occurring in 1916.

CHAPTER 6

How to Settle Your Dispute

Litigation should be a last, not a first, resort. Suing is not as bad as shooting, but neither is it as much fun as a good back rub. Rarely does anyone have a high time in court. In addition to being time-consuming and emotionally draining, lawsuits tend to polarize disagreements into "all win-all lose" propositions where face (and pocketbook) saving compromise is difficult. Most of us are terrified of making fools of ourselves in front of strangers. When forced to defend our actions in a public forum, we tend rather regularly to adopt a self-righteous view of our own conduct, and to attribute the vilest of motives to our opponents. Many of us are willing to admit that we have been a bit of a fool in private—especially if the other person does too—but in public, we will stonewall all the way, even when it would be to our advantage to appear a little more fallible.

I have witnessed dozens of otherwise sensible people litigate the most appalling trivia including one case in which the parties effectively tied up over $2,000 of each other's property (and had a fist fight) over a fishing pole worth $15. This doesn't mean that I don't think you should take your case to court if necessary. What I am suggesting is this: before you file your case, ask yourself whether you have done everything reasonably possible (and then a little more) to try to settle with the other party.

A. Try to Talk Your Dispute Out

Trying to settle your case isn't a waste of time. Indeed, you are required to make the attempt. The law in California states that a "demand" for payment must be made prior to filing a court action. Increasingly the "demand" requirement is being interpreted to mean that the "demand" be in the form of a letter.

But first things first. Before you reach for pen and paper, try to talk to the person with whom you are having the dispute. I can't count how many times people have consulted me about supposedly insurmountable disputes in situations where they had never once tried to talk it out with the other person.[1] Apparently many of us have a strong psychological barrier to talking to people we are upset with, especially if we have already exchanged heated words. Sometimes we seem to think that a willingness to compromise shows weakness. But wasn't it

---

[1] I sat as judge pro tem in one case where a man sued another man for $500 resulting from a car accident. Instead of putting on a defense, the defendant said he was "willing to pay." Why haven't you paid before, then?" I asked. "No one asked me to," he replied.

Winston Churchill who said, "I would rather jaw, jaw, jaw than war, war, war"?

Important: An offer of compromise made either orally or in writing does not bind the person making the offer to that amount if the compromise is not accepted. Thus, you could make an original demand for $500, then offer to compromise for $350, and, if your compromise offer is turned down, still sue for $500.

If you take my advice and are able to talk things out with your opponent, write down your agreement. Oral understandings, especially between people who have small confidence in one another, are often not worth the breath used to express them. Here are two sample compromise agreements that you may be able to adopt to your uses.

SAMPLE AGREEMENT 1

Dusty Rider and Bigshot Owner agree as follows:

1. Dusty was to exercise Bigshot's horses every morning for two weeks from October 1 to October 15 at Golden Gate Fields Racetrack in Albany, California, and was to be paid $15 per horse exercised each morning;

2. Bigshot's horses got sick on September 29 and there was no need for Dusty's services;

3. Dusty gave up other employment to make herself available to ride Bigshot's horses, and she couldn't find another riding job at short notice;

4. Dusty and Bigshot agree that $600 is fair compensation for her loss of work and Dusty agrees to accept this amount as a complete settlement of all of her claims.

Date	Dusty Rider

Date	Bigshot Owner

SAMPLE AGREEMENT 2

Walter Spottedhound and Nellie Neighbor agree that Walter's "mixed breed" black dog Clem sneaked onto Nellie's patio and bit her behind the right knee. After taking into consideration Nellie's medical bills, the fact that she had to miss two hours' work while at the doctor's office, and the pain and discomfort she has suffered, it is agreed that Walter will pay Nellie $250 in full settlement of all her claims. The money will be paid in five equal monthly installments. The first installment is hereby paid this date and the next four will be paid on the first day of February, March , April and May, 19__.

It is also agreed that Walter will commence at once to construct a six-foot high cyclone fence to keep Clem out of Nellie's yard.

Date	Walter Spottedhound
Date	Nellie Neighbor

A number of fill-in-the-blank, tear-out release forms that may be used to settle the types of disputes which commonly end up in Small Claims Court are contained in *Make Your Own Contract*, Elias (Nolo Press).

B. Write a "Demand" Letter

If your efforts to talk your problems out fail (or despite my urging you refuse to try), your next step is to send your adversary a letter. As noted above, many courts require that a "demand" letter be sent. But even if there is no such requirement, it is almost essential that you send one. Why? Simple—the

"demand" letter is not only useful in trying to settle your dispute, it is also your best opportunity to lay your case before the
judge in a carefully organized way. In a sense, it allows you to
"manufacture" evidence that you will be permitted to use in
court if the case isn't settled. Either way, you can't lose, so take
the time to write a good letter.

Your letter should be reasonably short, directly to the point,
and, above all, polite (you catch more flies with honey than by
hitting them over the head with a mallet). Use a typewriter
and keep a carbon, or photocopy. Limit your remarks to a page,
or at most, a page and a half. Remember, if the case doesn't
settle, you will want to show the letter to the judge—and
what's more important, you will want the judge to read it. It's
my experience that aside from letters of the heart, no one ever
reads much more than the first page of any letter with attention.

Remember, the judge doesn't know anything about how your
problem started and developed. This means that you will want
to write the letter so that it briefly reviews the entire dispute.
It may seem a little odd, writing all the facts for your opponent
who well knows them, and it may result in a formal sounding

letter. So what? You want to state your position in a way the judge can understand.

Let's consider a case I watched in Los Angeles one morning. The facts (with a little editorial license) were simple. Jennifer moved into Peter's house in August, agreeing to pay $250 per month rent. The house had four bedrooms, each occupied by one person. The kitchen and other common areas were shared. Things went well enough until one chilly evening in October when Jennifer turned on the heat. Peter was right behind her to turn it off, explaining that heat inflamed his allergies.

As the days passed and fall deepened, heat became more and more of an issue until one cold, late November night when Jennifer returned home from her waitress job to find her room "about the same temperature as the inside of an icicle." After a short cry, she started packing and moved out the next morning. She refused to pay Peter any additional rent, claiming that she was within her rights to terminate her month-to-month tenancy without giving notice because the house was uninhabitable.[2] It took Peter one month to find a suitable tenant and to have that person move in. Therefore, he was without a tenant for one month and lost rent in the amount of $250.

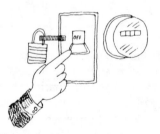

After calling Jennifer several times and asking her to make good the $250 only to have her slam down the phone in disgust, Peter wrote her the following letter:

---

[2] In California, tenants do have the right to simply leave, or in the alternative, to stay and cease paying rent, if conditions in their rented home become uninhabitable, whether the cause is no heat, water, electricity, etc. See the *California Tenants' Handbook*, Moskovitz and Warner, Nolo Press.

61 Spring St.
Los Angeles, Calif.
January 1, 19__

Jennifer Tenant
111 Sacramento St.
Palos Verdes, California

Dear Jennifer:

You are a real idiot. Actually, you're worse than that: you're malicious—walking out on me before Christmas and leaving me with no tenant when you know that I needed the money to pay my child support. You know that I promised to get you an electric room heater. Don't think I don't know that the real reason you moved out was to live with your boyfriend.

Please send me the $250 I lost because you didn't give me a month's notice like the law says you are supposed to. If you don't, I will sue you.

In aggravation,
Peter Landperson

To which Jennifer replied:

111 Sacramento St.
Palos Verdes, Calif.
January 4, 19__

Peter Landperson
61 Spring St.
Los Angeles, California

Dear Mr. Landperson:

You nearly froze me to death, you cheap bastard. I am surprised it only took a month to rent that iceberg of a room—you must have found a rich polar bear (ha ha). People like you should be locked up.

I hope you choke on an ice cube.

Jennifer Tenant

As you have no doubt guessed, both Peter and Jennifer made similar mistakes. Instead of being business-like, each deliberately set out to annoy the other, reducing any possible chance of compromise. In addition, they each assumed that they were writing only to the other, forgetting that the judge would be privy to their sentiments. Thus, both lost a valuable chance to present the judge with a coherent summary of the facts as they saw them. As evidence in a subsequent court proceeding, both letters were worthless.

(Now let's interrupt these proceedings and give Peter and Jennifer another chance to write sensible letters.)

61 Spring St.
Los Angeles, Calif.
January 1, 19__

Jennifer Tenant
111 Sacramento St.
Palos Verdes, California

Dear Jennifer:

As you will recall, you moved into my house at 61 Spring St., Los Angeles, California, on August 1, 1988, agreeing to pay me $250 per month rent on the first of each month. On November 29, you suddenly moved out, having given me no advance notice whatsoever.

I realize that you were unhappy about the fact that the house was a little on the cool side, but I don't believe that this was a serious problem, as the temperature was at all times over 60 degrees and I had agreed to get you an electric heater for your room by December.

I was unable to get a tenant to replace you (although I tried every way I could and asked you for help) until January 1, 1989. This means that I am short $250 rent for the room you occupied. If necessary, I will take this dispute to court because, as you know, I am on a very tight budget. I hope that this isn't necessary and that we can arrive at a sensible compromise. I have tried to call you with no success. Perhaps you can give me a call in the next week to talk this over.

Sincerely,
Peter Landperson

To which our now enlightened Jennifer promptly replied:

---

111 Sacramento St.
Palos Verdes, Calif.
January 4, 19__

Peter Landperson
61 Spring St.
Los Angeles, California

Dear Peter:

I just received your letter concerning the rent at 61 Spring St. and am sorry to say that I don't agree either with the facts as you have presented them, or with your demand for back rent.

When I moved in August 1, 1988, you never told me that you had an allergy and that there would be a problem keeping the house at a normal temperature. I would not have moved in had you informed me of this.

From early October, when we had the first cool evenings, all through November (almost two months), I asked that you provide heat. You didn't. Finally, it became unbearable to return from work in the middle of the night to a cold house, which was often below 60 degrees. It is true that I moved out suddenly, but I felt that I was within my rights under California law, which states that a tenant need not pay rent for an uninhabitable space (see the *California Tenant's Handbook*, Moskovitz and Warner).

Since you mentioned the non-existent electric heater in your letter, let me respond to that. You first promised to get the heater over a month before I moved out and never did. Also, as I pointed out to you on several occasions, the heater was not a complete solution to the problem, as it would have heated only my room and not the kitchen, living room, dining area, etc. You repeatedly told me that it would be impossible to heat these areas.

Peter, I sincerely regret the fact that you feel wronged, but I believe that I have been very fair with you. I am sure that you would have been able to rerent the room promptly if the house had been warm. I regret that I don't believe that any compromise is possible and that you will just have to go to court if that's what you wish to do.

Sincerely,

Jennifer Tenant

As you can see, while the second two letters are less fun to read, they are far more informative. Both Peter and Jennifer have clearly set forth their positions. In this instance, the goal of reaching an acceptable compromise was not met, but both have prepared a good outline of their positions for the judge. In court, both Peter and Jennifer will testify, present witnesses, etc. in addition to their letters. However, court proceedings are often rushed and confused and it's nice to have a written statement for the judge to fall back on. Be sure to bring a carbon or photocopy of your demand letter to court when your case is to be heard. Be sure, too, that the judge is given the copy as part of your case. The judge won't be able to guess that you have it; you will have to let him or her know and hand it to the clerk. (For more about how to conduct yourself in court, see Chapters 13-15).

Important: If you compromise your case after you have filed it in court, but before the court hearing, be sure to do so in writing. Also let the court know that you won't be appearing. Some courts will ask that the plaintiff sign a "Request for Dismissal" form. Never do this unless your compromise agreement has already been reduced to writing. Also, it is not wise to have a case dismissed unless you have been paid in full. If the compromise settlement involves installment payments, it would be wise to go to court and present your agreement to the judge. She can then enter a judgment in the same terms as the compromise. If this is done and then the judgment is not paid, it can be collected using the techniques discussed in Chapter 23.

C. Settlement at Court

Sometimes cases are settled while you are waiting for your case to be heard. It is perfectly proper to ask the other person if he or she wishes to step into the hall for a moment to talk the matter over. If you can agree on a compromise, wait until the case is called and tell the judge the amount you have agreed upon and whether the amount is to be paid all at once, or over time. The judge can either order the case dismissed if one person pays the other on the spot, or can enter a judgment for the amount that you have compromised upon, if payment is to be made later.

D. Mediation As An Alternative

Here at Nolo Press we are enthusiastic about the recent trend away from the adversary approach to dispute resolution and toward efforts to help people solve their own disputes by talking them out with the help of a trained mediator. The idea is to get the parties to arrive at an agreement— usually a reasonable compromise—that seems fair to all. The best way to do this is to include mediation as part of the formal Small Claims Court procedure. In other words, parties who were open to voluntary mediation would be encouraged to try it, instead of presenting their case to a judge as part of an adversary proceeding.

Unfortunately, at least as far as Small Claims Court is concerned, California lags behind in giving people the opportunity to mediate their disputes. Unlike New York City, for example, where everyone is offered an arbitration-mediation alternative to a court trial, mediation is currently available only in a few areas of California as isolated experiments. This is too bad, because where mediation is attempted, it is successful as much as 80% of the time.

CHAPTER 7

Who Can Sue?

In most situations, asking who can sue in Small Claims Court is an easy question. You can as long as you are eighteen years of age, have not been declared mentally incompetent in a judicial proceeding and are suing on your own claim.[1] Sometimes, however, listing yourself as the party bringing suit isn't quite so easy.

Here are the rules:

1. If you are suing for yourself alone, simply list your full name where it says "Plaintiff" on the "Plaintiff's Statement" and sign the "declaration under penalty of perjury" on the "Claim of Plaintiff" form (see sample forms in Chapter 10).

---

[1] Minors emancipated under Sections 60-70 of the California Civil Code can also sue and be sued. This includes minors on active duty with the military, married minors and minors emancipated by court order. A prisoner can sue by either waiving a personal appearance and submitting a written declaration to the court or by having another person (other than a lawyer) appear on his/her behalf. CCP 117.4.

2. If more than one person is bringing suit, list all the names on the "Plaintiff's Statement." Only one person need sign the "declaration under penalty of perjury" stating that all the information given is true and correct (see Chapter 10).

3. If you are filing a claim on behalf of an individually-owned business, the owner of the business must do the suing. She should list her name and the business name as plaintiffs on the "Plaintiff's Statement," e.g., "Jane Poe doing business as ABC Printing." The "declaration under penalty of perjury" should be signed in the business owner's name (see Chapter 10). Also, if the business uses a fictitious name (e.g., Tasty Donut Shop) as opposed to the owner's name, a form stating that the fictitious business name has been properly registered must normally be completed.

4. If you are filing a claim on behalf of a partnership, list the partnership name as plaintiff. Only one of the partners need sign the "declaration under penalty of perjury" (see Chapter 10). If the partnership uses a fictitious name, list it and the partners' real names, e.g., ABC Printing, a partnership, and Jane Poe and Phil Roe individually.

5. If you are filing a claim on behalf of a corporation, whether profit or non-profit, list the corporation as plaintiff. The "declaration under penalty of perjury" must be signed by either:

a. an officer of the corporation, or

b. a person authorized to file claims on behalf of the corporation by the Board of Directors of the corporation who is not employed for the sole purpose of representing the corporation in Small Claims Court. In this instance, the person must state under penalty of perjury that she is properly authorized to represent the corporation.

6. If you are filing on behalf of an unincorporated association, do so by listing the name of the association and the name of the officer by whom it is being represented (e.g., ABC Society, by Philip Dog, President).

7. When a claim arises out of damage to a motor vehicle, the registered owner(s) of the vehicle must file in Small Claims Court. This means that, if you are driving someone else's car

and get hit by a third party, you can't sue for damage done to the car. The registered owner must do the suing.

8. If you are suing on behalf of a public entity such as a public library, city tax assessor's office or county hospital, you must show the court clerk proper authorization to sue.

Other Pre-Suit Requirements: In certain situations, to qualify to sue in Small Claims Court, other legal requirements must be met. For example, contractors must be licensed, and car repair dealers, structural pest control operators, and TV repair people must be registered with the relevant state agency as a condition of using Small Claims Court.[2] And, as noted, anyone doing business under a fictitious name must file and maintain a fictitious business name statement. If you are being sued by anyone who you feel may not meet these requirements, make sure you tell the judge of your concern.

---

[2] In addition, car repair dealers must give their customers a written estimate of costs to be eligible to bring suit. Bus. & Prof. Code Sec. 9884-9(a).

A. Participation by Attorneys

Attorneys cannot normally appear in Small Claims Court. There are several exceptions to this rule. The major one allows attorneys to appear to sue or defend their own claims. Attorneys are also allowed to use Small Claims Court to sue or defend on behalf of a partnership when all other partners are also attorneys, and on behalf of a professional corporation of which the attorney is an officer or director and all other officers and directors are attorneys (CCP 117.4).

Getting the advice of a lawyer before going to Small Claims Court is perfectly legal, however. Indeed, many of the free Small Claims advisors available in most counties to help Small Claims litigants are lawyers (see Chapter 13, Sec. C).

B. Suits By Minors

If you are a minor (have not yet reached your eighteenth birthday), your parent or legal guardian must sue for you, unless you are emancipated under Sections 60-70 of the California Civil Code. To do this, a form must be filled out and signed by the judge appointing the parent or legal guardian as your "Guardian Ad Litem." This simply means guardian for the purposes of the lawsuit. Ask the court clerk for a "Petition for Appointment of Guardian Ad Litem" form. It must be signed by both minor and guardian. When you have filled it out, take it to the Small Claims Court clerk and arrange to have the judge add his signature at the bottom, under "ORDER."

C. Class Actions

In Small Claims Court there is no such thing as a true class action lawsuit where a number of people in a similar situation join together in one lawsuit. However, a number of community groups have discovered that if a large number of people with a particular grievance (pollution, noise, etc.) sue the same defendant at the same time, something remarkably like a class action suit is created. This technique was pioneered by a stubborn group of homeowners near the San Francisco Airport who several times won over 100 Small Claims Court judgments on the same day. They hired expert witnesses, did research, ran training workshops and paid for legal advice when needed as part of a coordinated effort while all arguing their own cases. The City of San Francisco maintained that they were in effect involved in a class action law suit and such suits are not permitted in Small Claims Court. A California Court of Appeals disagreed, saying that, "Numerous 'mass' actions against the City alleging that noise from the City airport constituted continuing nuisance were neither too 'complex' nor had such 'broad social policy import' that they were outside the jurisdiction of Small Claims Court . . . "[3]

[3] *City and County of San Francisco v. Small Claims Div.*, San Mateo Co. (1983) 190 Cal.Rptr. 340.

D. Special Rules for Prisoners and Military Personnel Transferred Out of State

A prisoner can sue in Small Claims Court by filing his papers by mail and then by either waiving personal appearance and submitting testimony in the form of written declarations *or* by having another person (other than a lawyer) appear on his behalf in court (CCP 117.4).

Similarly, a member of the U.S. military on active duty who is assigned to a duty station outside of California after her claim has occurred (except when the out-of-state assignment is for less than six months) can file in Small Claims Court by mail. Evidence can then be submitted in the form of a written declaration or by having another person (not a lawyer and not someone who has presented more than four other similar claims in the past 12 months) appear in Small Claims Court on her behalf (CCP 117.40). This code section was adopted primarily to deal with the problem of members of the military who move out of state not being refunded security deposits on rental housing.

E. Business Owners Do Not Have To Go to Court

It used to be that the owners of small unincorporated businesses were discouraged from using Small Claims Court. This was because there was a legal requirement that stated that the owner of the business both had to file the papers and show up in court himself. For example, a dentist who wished to sue on an overdue bill would have to be in court personally. But California is now more understanding of business time pressures. If a business (incorporated or unincorporated) wishes to sue on an unpaid bill, it can send an employee to court to testify about the debt as it is reflected in the written records of the business. For instance, a landlord suing for unpaid rent can send his or her property manager to court to establish the fact that the rent was unpaid (but see caution about bringing eviction cases in Small Claims Court in Chapter 20). For a business owner to invoke this time-saving procedure, the employee sent to court must be actually familiar with the company's books and able to testify about how this specific debt was entered in them. In addition (under Section 117.4 of the Code of Civil Procedure and Section 1271 of the Evidence Code) the business record evidencing the debt must have been made:

• In the normal course of business (i.e., contained in the business's regular records);

• At or near the same time as the debt arose; and

• Under conditions that indicate its reliability as evidence.

This method of obtaining relief from the Small Claims Court is only recommended when the issue is cut and dried. If there is likely to be any dispute about how the debt arose or the amount at issue, the presence of the business owner and the testimony of someone who knows about the facts of the dispute will be necessary. For example, if a T.V. repair business brings suit to collect an unpaid bill and sends a bookkeeper who knows nothing about what goes on in the repair shop to court, the suit will probably be lost if the defendant shows up and says the T.V. was not fixed properly. In this situation, some judges may postpone (continue) the case for a few days to allow the business owner to show up and present testimony about the quality of the repair, but don't count on it.

Note: California forbids the use of Small Claims Court by collection agencies ("Assignees") suing on someone else's claim (CCP 117.5).

CHAPTER 8

Who Can Be Sued?

You can sue just about anybody (person, partnership, corporation, government, etc.) in Small Claims Court. Indeed, it is more
often the "where can I sue" problem (see Chapter 9), not the
"who can I sue" problem that causes difficulties. For example,
you can sue the First National Bank of Bangor, Maine, but you
will find it very difficult to have the case heard in Sacramento, California, unless you can show that the bank does business
there, or entered into or agreed to carry out a contract with you
there. This doesn't mean that you have a problem with suing
the bank—you don't. The problem is only with bringing suit in
Sacramento. If you go to Maine, where the bank is located, you
can bring your suit with no problem.

Here are some hints that may prove helpful when it comes
to filling out your papers. You will want to check the forms set
out in Chapter 10B as you go along.

A. Suing One Person

If you are suing an individual, simply name him or her, using the most complete name that you have for that person. If the person calls himself J. R. Smith and you don't know what the J. stands for, simply sue him as J. R. Smith.

B. Suing Two or More People

If you are suing more than one person on a claim arising from the same incident or contract, you must list and serve each to properly bring them before the court. This is also required with a husband and wife.

Example: J. R. and June Smith, who are married, borrow $1,200 from you to start an avocado pit polishing business. Unfortunately, in the middle of the polishing, the seeds begin to sprout. J. R. and June get discouraged and refuse to repay you. If you wish to sue them and get a judgment, you should list them as J. R. Smith and June Smith—not Mr. and Mrs. Smith. But now suppose that J. R. borrowed $1,200 for the avocado pit business in January, June borrowed $1,000 to fix her motorcycle a month later and neither loan was repaid. In this situation, you would sue each in separate Small Claims actions.

C. Suing An Individually-Owned Business

Here you list the name of the owner and the name of the business (i.e., J. R. Smith—doing business as [d.b.a.] Smith's

Texaco). Don't assume that the name of the business is in fact the same as the name of the owner. Often it is not. Jim's Garage may be owned by Pablo Garcia Motors, Inc. (see Section E below). If you get a judgment against Jim's Garage and there is no Jim, you will find that it's worthless, unless you take steps to have the judgment changed to reflect the correct name. This can take time and trouble so be sure you know who the owner of the business is before you sue.

Note: If you sue the owner of a business using a fictitious name, but don't get the name right, CCP Sec. 117.19 allows you to substitute the correct name either at the court hearing or after judgment. Ask the Small Claims Court clerk for more information.

California requires that all people doing business in a name other than their own file a Fictitious Business Name Statement with the county clerk in the county or counties in which the business operates. This is public information and you can get it from the county clerk. Another way to figure out who owns a business is to check with the Business Tax and License Office in the city where the business is located. If the business is not in an incorporated area, try the county. The tax and license office will have a list of the owners of all businesses paying taxes in the city. They should be able to tell you, for example, that the Garden of Exotic Delights is owned by Rufus Clod. Once you find this out, you sue Rufus Clod, d.b.a. The Garden of Exotic Delights.

If for some reason the tax and license office and the county clerk can't help, you may want to check with the state. Millions of people, from exterminators to embalmers, must register with one or another office in Sacramento. So, if your beef is with a teacher, architect, smog control device installer, holder of a beer or wine license, etc., you will very likely be able to learn who and where they are with a letter or phone call. Check the Sacramento County phone book under the listing for the State of California. When you find an agency that looks like they should have jurisdiction over the type of business you wish to sue, call their public information number and explain your problem. It may take a little persistence, but eventually you should get the help you need.

D. Suing Partnerships

All partners in a business are individually liable for all the acts of the business. List the names of all the business partners even if your dispute is only with one (Patricia Sun and Farah Moon d.b.a. Sacramento Gardens). See Section C just above for information on how to learn just who owns a particular business. Never assume that you know without checking.

Example: You go to a local cleaners with your new, sky blue suit. They put too much cleaning fluid on it with the result that a small grey cloud settles on the right rear shoulder. After unsuccessfully trying to get the cleaners to take responsibility for improving the weather on the back of your suit, you start thinking about a different kind of suit. When you start filling out your court papers (see Chapter 10), you realize that you know only that the stores says "Perfection Cleaners" on the front and that the guy who has been so unpleasant to you is named Bob. You call the city business tax and license people and they tell you that Perfection Cleaners is owned by Robert Johnson and Sal De Benno. You should sue both and also list the name of the business.

Note: It is wise to get a judgment against more than one person if possible. When it comes to trying to collect, it's always nice to have someone in reserve if one defendant turns out to be an artful dodger.

E. Suing A Corporation

Corporations are legal people. This means that you can sue, and enforce a judgment against, a corporation itself. You should not sue the owners of the corporation or its officers or managers as individuals unless you have a personal claim against them that is separate from their role as part of the corporation. In most situations the real people who own or operate the corporation aren't themselves liable to pay for the corporation's debts. This concept is called "limited liability" and is one reason why many people choose to incorporate their businesses.

Be sure to list the full name of the corporation when you file suit (John's Liquors, Inc., a Corporation). Here again, the name on the door or the top of the stationery may not be the real name. Corporations, too, sometimes do business using fictitious names. Check with the city or county business license people where the corporation does business. In addition, the California Secretary of State's office, Corporate Status Unit, 1230 "J" Street, Sacramento, California 95814 maintains a complete list of all California corporations, and all out-of-state corporations "qualified" to do business in California. You may sue a corporation in California even if their headquarters are in another state, as long as they do business here.

F. Suing On A Motor Vehicle Accident

Here there are some special rules. If your claim arises from an accident with an automobile, motorcycle, truck or R.V., you should name both the driver of the vehicle and the registered owner as part of your suit. Most times you will have gotten this information at the time of the accident. If a police accident report was made, it will also contain this information. You can get a copy of any police report from the police department for a modest fee. If there was no police report, contact the Department of Motor Vehicles. For a small fee, they will tell you who owns any vehicle for which you have a license number.[1]

Remember, when you sue more than one person (in this case the driver and the owner if they are different), serve papers on both. When a business owns a vehicle, sue both the driver and the owners of the business.

G. Special Procedures For Suits Against Minors

It is very difficult to sue a minor for breach of contract because minors can disavow (back out of) any contract they sign as long as they do it before they turn eighteen, unless the contract was for a necessity of life, i.e., food, in which case the parents are responsible.[2] You can sue minors for damage to your person or property. If you wish to do so, you must also list a parent or legal guardian on the court papers. Do it like this:

"John Jefferey, a minor, and William Jefferey, his father."

---

[1] The DMV will ask you why you want this information. Simply tell them "to file a lawsuit based on a motor vehicle accident." This is a legitimate reason and you will get the information you need. The owner of the car will,however, be notified of your request.

[2] There are exceptions to this general rule . Minors who are on active duty in the armed services, are legally married or who have been emancipated by court order must stand behind their contracts as if they were adults. C.C. Secs. 60-70.

It is very difficult to collect from minors themselves as most don't have money or income. Of course, there are exceptions to this rule, but most minors are, almost by definition, broke. Thus, it often doesn't pay to bother with suits against minors unless you can collect from the minor's parents. Normally a parent is not legally responsible to pay for damages by his or her children. However, when a child is guilty of "willful misconduct," a parent can be liable up to $10,000 per act (up to $60,000 if a gun is involved). Parents are also liable for damage done by their minor children in auto accidents when they authorized the child to drive.

Example 1: John Johnson, age 17, trips over his shoelace while delivering your newspaper and crashes through your glass door. Can you recover from John's parents? Probably not, as John is not guilty of "willful misconduct."

Example 2: John shoots out the same glass door with a slingshot after you have repeatedly asked his parents to disarm him. Can you recover from the parents? Probably.

H. Special Rules For Suits Against Government Agencies

Before you can sue a city because your car was illegally towed away or a city employee caused you damage, or for any other reason involving personal injury or property damage, you must first file a claim with the city and have it denied. Get a claim form from the city clerk. Your claim must be filed within 100 days from the date of the incident. The city attorney will review your claim and make a recommendation to the City Council. Sometimes the recommendation will be to pay you—most often it will be to deny your claim. Once the City Council acts, you will receive a letter. If it's a denial, take it with you when you file your Small Claims action. The clerk will want to see it.

The rules for suits against counties and districts (e.g., school districts) are basically the same. Get your complaint form from the clerk of the Board of Supervisors (or the Board governing the district). Complete and file it within 100 days of the incident. Within a month or so after filing, you will be told whether your claim is approved or denied. If your claim is denied, you can then proceed to file in Small Claims Court.

Claims against the State of California must also be filed within 100 days for personal injury and property damage. Claims should be filed with the State Board of Control, Suite 300, 926 J Street, Sacramento, California 95814.

Suits against the federal government, a federal agency, or even against a federal employee for actions relating to his or her employment should not be brought in Small Claims Court. as the federal government may not be sued in this court without its consent. Suits against the federal government normally must be filed in Federal District Court. Unfortunately, there are no federal Small Claims procedures available except in Federal Tax Court.

I.   Suing Contractors And Their Bonding Companies

Whenever you sue a contractor for anything relating to work she had done improperly (or not at all), you may find that she is "bonded" by a "surety" or "guaranty" company. You can sue and collect a judgment from this kind of company, based on the contractor's poor workmanship or failure to abide by the agreement. However, to do this you must also sue the contractor and succeed in serving your papers on her (see Chapter 11). If you don't sue the contractor, or even if you do but can't serve your papers on her (perhaps because she has skipped town), your case against the surety company will be transferred to the formal court system where, again, lawyers and formal procedure are the norm (CCP Sec.117.6).

CHAPTER 9

Where Can You Sue?

Small Claims Courts are local. This makes sense because the amounts involved aren't large enough to make it worthwhile to require people to travel great distances. A Small Claims Court judicial district covers an individual city, several cities, or a county. The next city or county will have its own similar, but separate, Small Claims Court. Normally, your dispute will be with a person or business located nearby. You can sue in the judicial district where the defendant resides or, if a corporation is involved, where its main place of business is located. Sometimes though, it is not so easy to understand where to file your suit. This might be the case if the person you wish to sue lives 100 (or 500) miles away, or has moved since the dispute arose. As long as the person you want to sue lives in California, or does business here, however, you can bring suit in a California Small Claims Court. If the person you want to sue has no contacts with

California, however, you almost surely can't sue here, but must sue in the state where the defendant is located.[1]

On the first page of the first chapter we asked you to get a copy of the rules for your local Small Claims Court.[2] Refer to them now. The first thing you will wish to understand are the geographical boundaries of the Small Claims Court judicial district. If this information is not set out in the information sheet, call the clerk of the court and ask. You may be able to sue in more than one judicial district. If this is the case, choose the one that is most convenient to you.

SUMMARY OF CALIFORNIA RULES AS TO WHERE YOU CAN SUE

You can sue in any judicial districts where:

• The defendant resides;

• A corporate defendant does business;

• Injury to persons or personal property occurred;

• Defendant entered into a contract (does not apply to retail installment or to auto sales contracts);

• An obligation (contract) was to be performed (does not apply to retail installment or auto sales contracts or those to furnish goods, services, or loans intended for personal or household use);

• At the time of the contract was entered into the defendant resided or a corporate defendant did business (does not apply to a retail installment or auto finance sale).

---

[1] Under some circumstances, you can sue an out-of-state business if that business sells goods or services in California and you find a representative of the business present in this state and are able to serve them. Trying to do this, however, is seldom worth the cost, given the $1,500 Small Claims Court limit and the difficulty in collecting from an out-of-state business, even if you get a valid judgment.

[2] Small Claims Court is usually held on a weekday, often at 8:30 or 9:00 A.M. All larger areas must also provide for either Saturday or evening sessions.

SPECIAL RULES FOR
RETAIL INSTALLMENT CONTRACTS[3]

On a retail installment contract you can sue in the judicial district where:

- The buyer signed the contract;
- The buyer resided at the time the contract was signed;
- The buyer resides at time of suit;
- The goods are attached to real property.

SPECIAL RULES FOR AUTOS SUBJECT TO THE
AUTOMOBILE SALES FINANCE ACT[4]

On an auto purchase contract you can sue in the judicial district where:

- The buyer signed the contract;
- The buyer resided at the time the contract was signed;
- The vehicle is permanently garaged.

---

[3] This act covers the retail installment sales of most goods and services for personal, family or household use (not for business use), not including motor vehicles. Also it does not cover the services of physicians and dentists or services regulated by the federal government.

[4] This act covers the installment sale and long term lease of new and used motor vehicles (but not trailers or mobile homes) purchased primarily for personal (not business) use.

A. You Can Sue a Person Where He Resides/Or a Corporation Where It Does Business

This rule makes good sense, doesn't it? If a suit is brought where the defendant is located, he or she can't complain that it is unduly burdensome to appear. Books have been written about the technical definition of residence. Indeed, I remember with horror trying to sort out a law school exam in which the professor had given a person with numerous homes and businesses "contact" with six different judicial districts. The point of the examination was for us students to figure out where he could be sued. Thankfully, you don't have to worry about this sort of nonsense. If you believe a business or individual to be sufficiently present within a particular judicial district so that it would not be a hardship for them to appear in court there, go ahead and file your suit. The worst that can happen—and this is highly unlikely—is that the judge or clerk will tell you to start over someplace else or transfer your case to another judicial district.

Example: Downhill Skier lives in the city, but also owns a mountain cabin where he spends several months a year. Late one snowy afternoon, Downhill drives his new Porsche from the ski slopes to his ultra-modern, rustic cabin. Turning into his driveway, he skids and does a bad slalom turn right into Woodsey Carpenter's 1957 International Harvester Pickup. Where can Woodsey sue? He can sue in the city where Downhill has his permanent address. He can probably also sue in the county where the cabin is located, on the theory that Downhill also lives there. But read on—as you will see under Section C below, it isn't necessary for Woodsey to even get into the residence question, as he can also sue in the mountain county on the theory that the damage occurred there.

Note: You can sue multiple defendants in any judicial district in which one resides even though the other(s) live in another part of the state.

B. The Contract Which Is the Basis of Your Suit Was Entered Into in a Particular Judicial District

In addition to suing where the defendant resides, you can also sue at the place where an obligation (contract) was signed. This, too, is good common sense as the law assumes that, if people enter a contract at a certain location, it is probably reasonably convenient to both. If, for example, Downhill gets a telephone installed in his cabin, or has the fender on his Porsche fixed, or has a cesspool put in, or agrees to sit for a portrait in the mountain county, he can be sued there if he fails to keep his part of the bargain. Of course, as we learned above, Downhill might also be sued in the city where he resides permanently.

Example: John Gravenstein lives in Sonoma County, California, where he owns an apple orchard. He signs a contract with Acme Mechanical Apple Picker Co., an international corporation with offices in San Francisco, New York, Paris and Guatemala City. John signs the contract in Sonoma County. The parts are sent to John from San Francisco via U.P.S. They turn out to be defective. After trying and failing to reach a settlement with Acme, John wants to know if he can sue them in Sonoma County. Yes. Even though Acme doesn't have a business office in Sonoma County and they performed no action there in connection with their agreement to sell John the spare parts, the contract was signed there.

Reminder: You should now realize that there are often several reasons why it can be okay to bring a suit in a particular place. You only need one, but it never hurts to have more. Also, as you should now understand, there may be two, three or more judicial districts in which you can file your case. In this situation, simply choose the one most convenient to you. If you choose the wrong one your action will either be transferred or dismissed. If it is dismissed, you can refile in the correct district.

Contract Note: It isn't always easy to know where a contract has been "entered into" in a situation where the people making the contract are at different locations. If you enter a contract over the phone, for example, there could be an argument that the contract was entered into either where you are or where the other party is.[5] Rather than trying to learn all the intricacies of contract law, your best bet is probably to sue in the place most convenient to you. On the other hand, if someone sues you at the wrong end of the state and you believe they have not met any of the requirements set out in the Summary above, write the court as soon as you have been served and ask that the case be transferred to a court closer to you. Either way, if in doubt let the judge decide.

---

[5] To vastly oversimplify, a contract needs both an offer and an acceptance to exist. If I call you and order two widgets and you say okay, the contract was probably entered into at your location. However, if you write me and order the widgets and I fill the order, the contract very likely was entered into where I am.

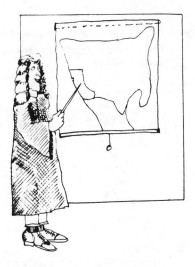

C. An Injury to a Person or to His/Her Property Occurred Within A Particular Judicial District

This means, quite simply, that, if you are in a car accident, a dog bites you, a tree falls on your noggin, or a neighbor floods your cactus garden, etc., you can sue in the judicial district where the injury occurred.

Example: Downhill is returning to his home in San Francisco. He is driving his Porsche carefully, still thankful that no one was injured when he hit Woodsey. At the same time, John Gravenstein is rushing to the city to try and get spare parts for his still broken apple picker. John jumps a red light and crumples Downhill's other fender. The accident occurs in Marin County, a county in which neither John nor Downhill live. After parking his car and taking a taxi home, Downhill tries to figure out where he can sue if he can't work out a fair settlement with John. Unfortunately for him, he can't sue in San Francisco as John doesn't reside there and the accident occurred in Marin. Downhill would have to sue either in Marin County, where his property was damaged, or in Sonoma County, where John lives. Luckily for Downhill, Marin County adjoins San Francisco. Had the accident occurred in Los Angeles County, however, Downhill would have been put to a lot more trouble if he wished to sue (presumably he would have chosen Sonoma County, which is much closer to his home than is L.A.).

D. Retail Installment Sales Contracts And Motor Vehicles Finance Sales

If your case involves a motor vehicle or a major piece of property such as a television or appliance that you bought on time, you may file suit where you presently live, where the vehicle or goods are permanently kept, where you lived when you entered into the contract or where you signed the contract.

Example: Downhill buys a major appliance on time subject to the Retail Installment Sales Act while he lives in San Francisco. Later he moves to Fresno and stops paying his bill. Can he be sued for the unpaid balance in San Francisco? Yes, he can.

CHAPTER 10

Plaintiff's and Defendant's Filing Fees, Court Papers and Court Dates

A. How Much Does It Cost?

For people who have filed 12 or fewer claims in any given Small Claims Court over the past 12 months, the Small Claims filing fee in California is $6, both for filing a "Claim of Plaintiff" and a "Claim of Defendant." For more frequent filers, the fee is $12.[1] There is an additional $3 fee for serving papers by certified mail on each defendant. You can recover your filing and service costs if you win (see Chapter 15).

B. Filling Out Your Court Papers and Getting Your Court Date

Now let's look at the initial court papers themselves to be sure that you don't trip over a detail. Forms in use in California

---

[1] CCP Sec. 117.14.

are all substantially the same although there are differences in detail in the different judicial districts. You should have little trouble filling out your papers by following the examples printed here but, if you do, simply ask the clerk for help. Small Claims clerks are required by law to give you as much help as possible short of practicing law (whatever that is). A friendly, courteous approach to the clerk can often result in much helpful information and advice. If for any reason the clerk can't help you, inquire about the availability of the free Small Claims advisor (see Chapter 13D).

Step 1. "The Plaintiff's Statement"

To start your case in Small Claims Court, go to the Small Claims clerk's office and fill out the form entitled "Plaintiff's Statement." If you have carefully read the first nine chapters of this book, this should be easy. Be particularly careful that you are suing in the right judicial district (Chapter 9) and that you are properly naming the defendant (Chapter 8).

Step 2. "The Claim of Plaintiff"

When you have completed your "Plaintiff's Statement," give it to the county clerk, who will then use it to type out your official "Plaintiff's Claim and Order to Defendant" form and assign your case a number. All parties bringing suit will be asked to sign this form under penalty of perjury. A copy of the "Claim of Plaintiff" will go to the judge and another must be served on the defendant (see Chapter 11). Here is a sample of the "Claim of Plaintiff."

Andrew Printer   Plaintiff(s) vs.

Acme Illusions, Inc.   Defendant(s)

SMALL CLAIMS CASE NUMBER

PLAINTIFF'S STATEMENT

1. Please read carefully the instructions appearing below before filing out this form:
   a. If you are suing one or more individuals, give full name of each.
   b. If you are suing a business owned by an individual, give the name of the owner and the name of the business he owns.
   c. If you are suing a partnership, give the names of the partners and the name of the partnership.
   d. If you are suing a corporation, give its full name.
   e. If you claim arises out of a vehicle accident, the driver of the other vehicle must be named, and the registered owner of the other vehicle should also be named.

2. State your name and residence address, and the name and address of any other person joining with you in this action. If this claim arises from a business transaction, give the name and address of your business.

   a. Name ___ Andrew Printer ___
      Address ___ 1800 Marilee St., Fremont, CA ___ Phone No. ___ 827-7000 ___

   b. Name _____
      Address _____ Phone No. _____

3. State the name and address of each person or business firm you are suing.

   a. Name ___ Acme Illusions, Inc. ___
      Address ___ 100 Primrose Road, Oakland, CA ___ Phone No. ___ 654-1201 ___

   b. Name _____
      Address _____ Phone No. _____

   c. Name _____
      Address _____ Phone No. _____

4. State the amount you are claiming. $ _950.00_____

5. Describe briefly the nature of your claim:

   Failure to pay for printing and typesetting

6. If your claim does not arise out of a vehicle accident, give address below where obligation was entered into or was to be performed or where injury was incurred.

   1800 Marilee St., Fremont, CA
   (street address)   (city or locality)

7. Fill out this section if your claim arises out of a vehicle accident:
   a. Date on which accident occurred: _____, 19_____.
   b. Street or intersection and city or locality where accident occurred: _____

   c. If you are claiming damages to a vehicle, were you on the date of the accident the registered owner of that vehicle? _____
      (yes or no)

8. I have received and read the form entitled "Information to Plaintiff".

9. I declare, under penalty of perjury, that I have filed ☒ 1 to 11 small claims cases in this court during the past 12 months.
   ☐ 12 or more

Date _April 27, 1987_   Signed _Andrew Printer_

PLAINTIFF'S STATEMENT, SMALL CLAIMS

Name and Address of Court: Alameda County Municipal
Oakland-Piedmont
600 Washington St.
Oakland, CA.

SMALL CLAIMS CASE NO.

— NOTICE TO DEFENDANT — YOU ARE BEING SUED BY PLAINTIFF	— AVISO AL DEMANDADO — A USTED LO ESTAN DEMANDANDO
To protect your rights, you must appear in this court on the trial date shown in the table below. You may lose the case if you do not appear. The court may award the plaintiff the amount of the claim and the costs. Your wages, money, and property may be taken without further warning from the court.	Para proteger sus derechos, usted debe presentarse ante esta corte en la fecha del juicio indicada en el cuadro que aparece a continuación. Si no se presenta, puede perder el caso. La corte puede decidir en favor del demandante por la cantidad del reclamo y los costos. A usted le pueden quitar su salario, su dinero, y otras cosas de su propiedad, sin aviso adicional por parte de esta corte.

PLAINTIFF / DEMANDANTE (Name and address of each):

Andrew Printer
1800 Marilee St.
Fremont, California 94536

DEFENDANT / DEMANDADO (Name and address of each):

Acme Illusions, Inc.
100 Primrose Road
Oakland, California 94602

☐ See attached sheet for additional plaintiffs and defendants.

PLAINTIFF'S CLAIM

1. Defendant owes me the sum of $ 950.00 , not including court costs, because (describe claim and date):
   he failed to pay for a printing and typesetting job which was completed on March 15, 198 .

2. I have asked defendant to pay this money, but it has not been paid.

3. This court is the proper court for the trial because ☐ A (In the box at the left, insert one of the letters from the list marked "Venue Table" on the back of this sheet. If you select D, E, or F, specify additional facts in this space.)

4. ☐ I have filed more than 12 claims in this court, including this claim, during the previous 12 calendar months.

5. I understand that
   a. I may talk to an attorney about this claim, but I cannot be represented by an attorney at the trial in the small claims court.
   b. I must appear at the time and place of trial and bring all witnesses, books, receipts, and other papers or things to prove my case.
   c. I have no right of appeal on my claim, but I may appeal a claim filed by the defendant in this case.
   d. If I cannot afford to pay the fees for filing or service by a sheriff, marshal, or constable, I may ask that the fees be waived.

6. I have received and read the information sheet explaining some important rights of plaintiffs in the small claims court.

I declare under penalty of perjury under the laws of the State of California that the foregoing is true and correct.

Date: (fill in date)

Andrew Printer
(TYPE OR PRINT NAME)   ►   (SIGNATURE OF PLAINTIFF)

ORDER TO DEFENDANT

You must appear in this court on the trial date and at the time LAST SHOWN IN THE BOX BELOW if you do not agree with the plaintiff's claim. Bring all witnesses, books, receipts, and other papers or things with you to support your case.

TRIAL DATE / FECHA DEL JUICIO		DATE	TIME	PLACE	COURT USE
	1.				
	2.				
	3.				
	4.				

Filed on (date):   Clerk, by _____ , Deputy

— You have a right to a small claims advisor free of charge. Read the information sheet on the reverse. —

Form Adopted by the
Judicial Council of California
SC 100 (Rev. July 1, 1987)

PLAINTIFF'S CLAIM AND ORDER TO DEFENDANT
(Small Claims)

Rule 982.7

Step 3. Getting A Hearing Date

One of the great advantages of Small Claims Court is that disputes are settled quickly. This is important. Many people avoid lawyers and the regular courts primarily because they take forever to get a dispute settled. Business people, for example, increasingly rely on private arbitration, caring more that a dispute be resolved promptly than that they win a complete victory. Anyone who has had to wait for two years for a case to be heard in some constipated state trial court knows through bitter experience that the old cliche, "justice delayed is justice denied," is all too true.

Section 116.4(b) of the Code of Civil Procedure requires that, if the defendant resides in the same county in which the action is brought, the hearing should be held no sooner than 10 days, or longer than 40 days from the time the papers are filed. If the defendant lives outside of the county where you bring suit, the case will be heard not less than 30, nor more than 70 days from the date you file your complaint. If there is more than one defendant, and one or more lives in the county where you file and one or more in another county, the case will be treated as if all defendants live within your county: that is, the case will be heard within 30 days of the time the papers are filed.

When you file your papers, you should also arrange with the clerk for a court date. Get a date that is convenient for you. You need not take the first date the clerk suggests. Be sure to leave yourself enough time to get a copy of the "Claim of Plaintiff" form served on the defendant(s). (This is five days if the defendant resides in the conty where you bring suit and 15 days if she resides in another county—see Chapter 11 for service instructions.) If you fail to properly serve your papers on the defendant in time, there is no big hassle—just notify the clerk, get a new court date, and try again.

Small Claims Courts are most often held at 9:00 A.M. on working days. Larger counties are required to hold at least one evening or Saturday session per month. Ask the clerk for a schedule.

Filing Your Papers By Mail: It is possible to file papers by mail in Small Claims Court. I recommend it only if you are a

long distance from the court you must sue in (see Chapter 9).
Send double first class postage to the court clerk with your
request for the forms necessary to file by mail. The clerk will
return the Plaintiff's Statement and Claim of Plaintiff forms.
Fill out the former and sign the latter. Return both to the clerk
with your filing fee and money for certified mail service if you
wish to follow this service approach. The details of all this
can get confusing and you will probably want to call the clerk to
review them.

C. The Defendant's Forms

No papers need be filed to defend a case in Small Claims
Court. You just show up on the date and at the time indicated,
ready to tell your side of the story. If you need to get the
hearing delayed, see Section E below. It is proper, and advis-
able, for a defendant to call or write the plaintiff and see if a
fair settlement can be reached without going to court (see
Chapter 6).

Sometimes someone sues you in a situation where you were
planning to sue them (i.e., a traffic accident where you each
believe the other is at fault). As long as your grievance stems
from the same incident, you can file a "Claim of Defendant" for
up to $1,500 in Small Claims Court and have it heard by a judge
at the same time that the plaintiff's claim against you is con-

sidered.[2] However, if you believe that the plaintiff owes you money as the result of a different injury or breach of contract, you must file your own separate case.

But what happens if you wish to make a claim against the plaintiff for more than $1,500? First reread Chapter 4 and decide whether you want to scale down your claim to fit into Small Claims. If you don't you must file your claim in either Justice or Municipal Court (up to $25,000) or Superior Court (over $25,000) and pay all necessary filing fees. Then you must file an affidavit with the Small Claims Court clerk notifying the court that you have filed the higher court action. This must be done prior to the hearing date for the Small Claims Court case and costs $1. In addition, a copy of this affidavit must be served on the plaintiff in person. Now it's up to the judge as to whether to transfer the case.

Section 116.8 of the Code of Civil Procedure states:

"The Small Claims Court shall not transfer the Small Claims Court action to the court set forth in the affidavit until a judgment is rendered in the Small Claims Court action, unless the ends of justice would be served by such a prejudgment transfer of the proceedings ... If the Small Claims matter is transferred prior to judgment, both actions shall be tried together in the transferred court."

Note: If you have a claim against a plaintiff for an amount less than the Small Claims Court maximum which arises out of the same transaction or situation that forms the basis of his suit against you, you should file it prior to the time that the plaintiff's case is heard. If you fail to file and let the case be decided, you will have a tougher time convincing the judge of the merits of your case later on.

---

[2] When you file a "Claim of Defendant," you become a plaintiff as far as this claim is concerned. This means that, if you lose, you can't appeal, because plaintiffs can't appeal. Of course, if you lose on the original plaintiff's claim, you can appeal that portion of the judgment (see Chapter 22 for more on appeal rules).

Name and Address of Court
Alameda County Municipal
Oakland-Piedmont
600 Washington St.
Oakland, CA

SMALL CLAIMS CASE NO.

— NOTICE TO PLAINTIFF — YOU ARE BEING SUED BY DEFENDANT	— AVISO AL DEMANDANTE — A USTED LO ESTA DEMANDANDO EL DEMANDADO
To protect your rights, you must appear in this court on the trial date shown in the table below. You may lose the case if you do not appear. The court may award the defendant the amount of the claim and the costs. Your wages, money, and property may be taken without further warning from the court.	Para proteger sus derechos, usted debe presentarse ante esta corte en la fecha del juicio indicada en el cuadro que aparece a continuación. Si no se presenta, puede perder el caso. La corte puede decidir en favor del demandado por la cantidad del reclamo y los costos. A usted le pueden quitar su salario, su dinero, y otras cosas de su propiedad, sin aviso adicional por parte de esta corte.

PLAINTIFF DEMANDANTE (Name and address of each)

Andrew Printer
1800 Marilee St.
Fremont, California 94536

DEFENDANT DEMANDADO (Name and address of each)

Acme Illusions, Inc.
100 Primrose Path
Oakland, California 94602

☐ See attached sheet for additional plaintiffs and defendants.

DEFENDANT'S CLAIM

1. Plaintiff owes me the sum of $ 300.00 , not including court costs, because (describe claim and date):

    of delays and poor workmanship in a printing job he performed for me in April of 198_.

2. I have asked plaintiff to pay this money, but it has not been paid.

3. I understand that
    a. I may talk to an attorney about this claim, but I cannot be represented by an attorney at the trial in the small claims court.
    b. I must appear at the time and place of trial and bring all witnesses, books, receipts, and other papers or things to prove my case.
    c. I have no right of appeal on my claim, but I may appeal a claim filed by the plaintiff in this case.
    d. If I cannot afford to pay the fees for filing or service by a sheriff, marshal, or constable, I may ask that the fees be waived.

4. I have received and read the information sheet explaining some important rights of defendants in the small claims court.

I declare under penalty of perjury under the laws of the State of California that the foregoing is true and correct.

Date: (fill in date)

Waldo Fergus
(TYPE OR PRINT NAME)

► Waldo Fergus President
(SIGNATURE OF DEFENDANT)

ORDER TO PLAINTIFF

You must appear in this court on the trial date and at the time LAST SHOWN IN THE BOX BELOW if you do not agree with the defendant's claim. Bring all witnesses, books, receipts, and other papers or things with you to support your case.

TRIAL DATE FECHA DEL JUICIO		DATE	TIME	PLACE	COURT USE
	1.				
	2.				
	3.				

Filed on (date):

Clerk, by _____ , Deputy

— You have a right to a small claims advisor free of charge. —

Form Approved by the
Judicial Council of California
SC 120 (Rev. January 1, 1985)

DEFENDANT'S CLAIM AND ORDER TO PLAINTIFF
(Small Claims)

Rule 982.7

D. Changing a Court Date

It is sometimes impossible for a defendant to be present on the day ordered by the court for the hearing. It can also happen that the plaintiff will pick out a court date and get the defendant served only to find that an unexpected emergency makes it impossible for him to be present.

It is normally not difficult to get a case delayed. To arrange this, call the other party and see if you can agree on a mutually convenient date. Don't call the clerk first they don't know what days the other party has free. Sometimes it is difficult to face talking to someone with whom you are involved in a lawsuit, but you will just have to swallow your pride. Once all parties have agreed to a new date, notify the court clerk in a written statement signed by both parties. Here is a sample:

---

11 South Street
San Diego, CA
January 10, 19__

Clerk of the Small Claims Court
San Diego, California

Re: SC 4117 Rodriguez v. McNally

Mr. Rodriguez and I agree to request that you postpone this case to a date after March 1, 19__.

JOHN MCNALLY

JOHN RODRIGUEZ

If you speak to the other party(ies) and find that he is completely uncooperative, put your request for a delay (continuance) in writing, along with the circumstances that make it impossible for you to keep the first date. Send your letter to the clerk of the Small Claims Court.

Here is a sample:

---

37 Birdwalk Blvd.
Occidental, Calif.

January 10, 19__

Clerk
Small Claims Court
City Hall
San Francisco, Calif.

Re: Small Claims No. 374-628

Dear Clerk:

I have been served with a complaint (No. 374-628) by John's Laundry, Inc. The date set for a hearing, February 15, falls on the day of my son's graduation from Nursing School in Oscaloosa, Oklahoma, which my husband and I plan to attend.

I called John's Laundry and asked to have the case delayed one week. They just laughed and said that they would not give me any cooperation.

I feel that I have a good defense to this suit. Please delay this case until any date after February 22, except March 13, which is my day for a medical check-up.

Thank you,

Sally Wren

E. If One Party Doesn't Show Up

If one party to a case doesn't appear in court on the proper day at the proper time, the case is normally decided in favor of the other. Depending on whether it is the plaintiff or defendant who fails to show up, the terms used by the judge to make his decision are different. If the plaintiff appears, but the defendant doesn't, a "default judgment" is normally entered in favor of the plaintiff (see Chapters 12 and 15 for more information on defaults). Occasionally, although it happens far less frequently, it is the plaintiff who fails to show up. In this situation, the judge may either dismiss the case or decide it on the basis of the defendant's evidence. The defendant will usually prefer this second result, especially if a Claim of Defendant has been made. Unfortunately, however, if the case is simply dismissed, the plaintiff can bring it again.

1. Setting Aside A Default (Defendant's Remedy)

Under Code of Civil Procedure Section 117.8, a defendant has 30 days to move to set aside (vacate) a default judgment.[3] To do this, get a Notice of Motion to Vacate Judgment form from the clerk, file it, and serve it on the plaintiff. She then must either appear at a hearing and explain (or submit written

---

[3] If the defendant was not properly served and did not appear at the hearing in the Small Claims Court, the defendant has 180 days to move to vacate after he discovers or should have discovered the judgment was entered against him. CCP Sec. 117.8(d)

justification) for her original failure to appear. The judge will then decide whether or not to vacate the default and grant a new trial. Some judges will routinely vacate defaults on the basis of almost any hard luck story ("I overslept," "I forgot what day it was," "My sister was sick"), while others are extremely unsympathetic to the idea of vacating a default judgment unless the defendant can show that the original papers were not properly served on her and that she didn't know about the hearing.

As th judge has great legal discretion as to whether or not to vacate a default, it's impossible to predict what any particular one will do. For this reason, defendants should move to set aside as soon as they realize they missed the original trial. It's a mistake to wait until the end of the 30-day period established by CCP 117.8 as this may be considered a negative factor by the judge. The defendant should also be prepared to convince the judge he had a very good reason to miss the original hearing.

Plaintiffs who are the beneficiaries of a default judgment and don't want it set aside should emphasize the fact that they played by the rules and showed up, while the defendant failed to do so. If the plaintiff had witnesses ready to testify at the original trial which led to the default being entered and these people will be difficult to produce a second time, this too should be emphasized.

Note: You can't appeal from a default judgment even if you have a great case. You must try to get the default set aside or the judgment will be final. If the Small Claims Court denies your motion to vacate the judgment after you have appeared in court or submitted a written justification, you may appeal this denial within 10 days. While it is fairly unlikely that this appeal will be granted, if it is and the default is vacated, the Superior Court has the authority to go ahead and hear the case on the spot (CCP 117.8). This means both sides should be prepared to argue the case on its merits in Superior Court in case the default is set aside.

Name and Address of Court

SMALL CLAIMS CASE NO.

PLAINTIFF DEMANDANTE *(Name and address of each)*

DEFENDANT DEMANDADO *(Name and address of each)*

☐ See attached sheet for additional plaintiffs and defendants.

NOTICE TO *(Name)*:

One of the parties has asked the court to CANCEL the small claims judgment in your case. If you disagree with this request, you should appear in this court on the hearing date shown below. If the request is granted, ANOTHER TRIAL may immediately be held. Bring all witnesses, books, receipts, and other papers or things with you to support your case.	*Una de las partes en el caso le ha solicitado a la corte que DEJE SIN EFECTO la decisión tomada en su caso por la corte para reclamos judiciales menores. Si usted está en desacuerdo con esta solicitud, debe presentarse en esta corte en la fecha de la audiencia indicada a continuación. Si se concede esta solicitud, es posible que se efectúe otro juicio inmediatamente. Traiga a todos sus testigos, libros, recibos, y otros documentos o cosas para presentarlos en apoyo de su caso.*

NOTICE OF MOTION TO VACATE JUDGMENT

1. A hearing will be held in this court at which I will ask the court to **cancel** the judgment entered against me in this case. If you wish to oppose the motion you should appear at the court on

HEARING DATE FECHA DEL JUICIO	DATE	TIME	PLACE

2. I am asking the court to cancel the judgment for the reasons stated in item 5 below. My request is based on this notice of motion and declaration, the records on file with the court, and any evidence that may be presented at the hearing.

DECLARATION FOR MOTION TO VACATE (CANCEL) JUDGMENT

3. Judgment was entered against me in this case on *(date)*:

4. I first learned of the entry of judgment against me on *(date)*:

5. a. ☐ I did not appear at the trial of this claim because *(specify facts)*:

   b. ☐ Other *(specify facts)*:

6. I understand that I must bring with me to the hearing on this motion all witnesses, books, receipts, and other papers or things to support my case.

I declare under penalty of perjury under the laws of the State of California that the foregoing is true and correct.

Date: ▶

....
(TYPE OR PRINT NAME)   *(SIGNATURE)*

CLERK'S CERTIFICATE OF MAILING

I certify that I am not a party to this action. This Notice of Motion to Vacate Judgment was mailed first class, postage prepaid, in a sealed envelope to the responding party at the address shown above. The mailing and this certification occurred at *(place)*: , California, on *(date)*:

Clerk, by _____ , Deputy

— You have a right to a small claims advisor free of charge. —

Form Approved by the Judicial Council of California SC-135 (Rev. January 1, 1985)	NOTICE OF MOTION TO VACATE JUDGMENT AND DECLARATION (Small Claims)	Rule 982.7

Writ of Execution Note: If a motion to vacate a default judgment is filed in a situation where a "writ of execution" to collect a Small Claims judgment has already been issued by the court, the writ of execution must be recalled by the court until a decision on the motion to vacate the default judgment is made. If the writ of execution has already been served on the judgment debtor, this person must file a motion to stay or quash the execution of the judgment, pending the decision on the motion to vacate the default judgment. For more information on how to do this, consult your Small Claims Court clerk.

2. Vacating A Judgment Of Dismissal (Plaintiff's Remedy)

If a plaintiff does not show up in court at the appointed time, the judge will do one of two things, dismiss the case, or enter a judgment in favor of the defendant. If the case is dismissed, the plaintiff can refile it. If a judgment is entered, it must be vacated before the plaintiff can have the dispute considered on its merits. Vacating a judgment entered against a plaintiff who does not appear can be difficult. By law, the plaintiff must file a motion to vacate the judgment within 30 days after the clerk has mailed a notice of entry of judgment. However, notice should be filed with the clerk as soon as possible.

Normally, what will happen next is that the clerk will set a hearing before the judge as to whether the default judgment should be set aside. (The plaintiff must serve a notice on any defendant(s) who received a judgment in their favor.) At the hearing, the judge will inquire as to why the plaintiff missed the original hearing. If the plaintiff can't make the hearing, she may submit her excuse in the form of a written affidavit, but I don't advise it. As the judge will only set aside the default if she finds "good cause" for the original failure to appear, it's best to show up with a good story. Remember, the plaintiff is the one who initiated the case and established the court date, so no one is going to have a great deal of sympathy for her failure to show up.

If the motion to set aside the judgment is granted, and all parties are present and agree, the case may be heard on the spot. If the judgment is set aside, but the defendant is not present, or it is otherwise inconvenient to proceed, the clerk will establish a new hearing date.

If your motion to set aside the default is denied, you may appeal to the Superior Court within 10 days, but only as to the decision not to grant the motion.

CHAPTER 11

Serving Your Papers

After you have filed your "Claim of Plaintiff" form with the clerk following the instructions in Chapter 10B, a copy must be served on the person, persons, or corporation you are suing. This is called "service of process." Your lawsuit is not complete without it. The reason that you must serve the other side is simple—the person(s) you are suing are entitled to be notified of the general nature of your claim and the day, time and place when they can show up to defend themselves.

A. Who Must Be Served

All defendants that you list on your Claim of Plaintiff should be served. It is not enough to serve one defendant and assume that he will tell the other(s). This is true even if the defendants are married, or living together. If you don't serve a particular defendant, the court can't enter a judgment against that person. If you sue more than one person and can serve only one, a judge can only enter a judgment against the person served, in effect dismissing your action against the other defendant(s). You can refile against these defendants if you wish.

B. How To Serve Your Papers

There are several approved ways to serve papers. All depend on your knowing where the defendant is. If you can't find the defendant and do not know where he lives or works, you can't serve him and it makes little sense to file a lawsuit.

Method 1: Personal Service

Any person who is eighteen years of age, or older, except the person bringing the suit, may serve the defendant by handing him the Claim of Plaintiff anyplace in California.[1] Any person means just that—you can hire the county sheriff or marshal (often good for its sobering effect), or a private process server (listed in the Yellow Pages), or you can have a friend or relative do the service. Again, the only person 18 years or older who can't serve the papers in your lawsuit is you.

The Claim of Plaintiff must be handed to the defendant personally. You can't simply leave the paper at her job, or home, or in the mailbox. A person making a service who doesn't know the person involved should make sure that he is serving the right person. If a defendant refuses to take the paper, acts hostile or attempts to run away, the process server should simply put the paper down and leave. Valid service has been accomplished. The process server should never try to use force to get a defendant to take any papers.

---

[1] Small claims papers cannot validly be served out-of-state (CCP Sec. 116.4).

Method 2: By Certified Mail

You can also serve your Claim of Plaintiff by certified mail. The clerk of the court does the mailing for you. There is a modest fee in California for each defendant. This is recoverable if you win (see Chapter 15). The mail method is both cheap and easy, but it depends for its success on the defendant signing for the letter. Most businesses and many individuals routinely sign to accept mail. However, some people never do, knowing instinctively, or perhaps from past experience, that nothing good ever comes by certified mail. I have asked several court clerks for an estimate as to the percentage of certified mail services that are accepted. The consensus is 50%. If you try using the mail to serve your papers and fail, simply get a process server. Chances are the defendant will end up paying for it.

Note: Never assume that your certified mail service has been accomplished and show up in court on the day of the court hearing. If the defendant didn't sign for the paper, you will be wasting your time. Call the clerk a couple of days in advance and find out if the service of process has been completed. This means the certified letter has been signed for by the defendant, not by someone else at the address.

Method 3: Substituted Service

Often it is hard to serve particular individuals. Some people have developed their skill at avoiding process servers into a high (but silly) art. In the long run this rarely works, as there is now a procedure which allows "substituted service if you try to serve a defendant and fail."[2] It works like this:

If a person can't be served with "reasonable diligence," the papers may be served by leaving a copy of the summons and complaint at the person's dwelling place in the presence of a competent member of the household who is at least eighteen years of age and who must be told what the papers are about and thereafter mailing a copy of the summons and complaint by first class mail to the person served. Service is complete ten days after mailing. Be sure that all steps are carried out by an adult who is not named in the lawsuit. Because some Small Claims Court clerks interpret the requirement for "reasonable diligence" differently, you will wish to run through the substituted service procedure with your local clerk before trying it. If your suit is against a corporation, the substituted service procedure is easier, as there is no "diligence" requirement before using it. Papers may be served by leaving a copy of the summons and complaint at the defendant's office with a person apparently in charge of the office during normal business hours and then mailing another copy of the summons and complaint to the person to be served at the same address by first class mail. Service is accomplished ten days after mailing.

After service is accomplished, you must return a "proof of service" form to the court clerk stating that all proper "service" steps have been completed. See Section F below.

Method 4: For Serving Subpoenas Only

In Chapter 14 we discuss subpoenaing witnesses and documents. Subpoenas can't be served by mail. They must be served by personal service. The rules as to who can do the serving, etc., are the same as those set forth above in Method 1 with one important difference: any person, including the person bringing the suit, can serve the subpoena. The person making the service

---

2 See CCP Sec. 415.20.

must be ready to pay the person subpoenaed a witness fee if it is requested. (See Chapter 14A for details.)

C. Costs of Personal Service

Professional process servers commonly charge from $16-$25 per service depending on time and mileage involved.[3] You can usually get your costs of service added to your judgment if you win, but be sure to remind the judge to do this when you conclude your court presentation. However, a few courts, such as the Berkeley Small Claims Court, will not give the successful party an award of costs for a process server unless they have first tried to have the papers served by the cheaper certified mail approach (Method 2 above). Other judicial districts, such as Los Angeles, prefer that you don't use the mail approach at all because they feel that too often the mail isn't accepted. Ask the Small Claims clerk in your district how they prefer that you accomplish service and how much the judge will allow as a service of process fee.

D. Time Limits in Which Papers
Must Be Served

The defendant is entitled to receive service of the Claim of Plaintiff form at least five days before the date of the court hearing, if he or she is served within the county in which the

---

3 County officials such as sheriffs and marshals will only serve papers in the county in which they are located. Call them to ask about fees.

courthouse is located. If the defendant is served in a county other than the one where the trial is to take place, he must be served at least 15 days before the trial date.

If the defendant is served less than the required number of days before the trial date, he can either go ahead with the trial anyway, or request that the case be delayed (continued) for 10 to 30 days. If it is impossible to show up in person to ask for a delay, call the court clerk (telegraph if you can't call) and point out that you weren't served in the proper time and that you want the case put over. The clerk will see that a default judgment is not entered against you (see Chapter 10E). But just to be sure, get the clerk's name.

To count the days to see if service has been accomplished in the correct time, do not count the day the service is made, but do count the day of the court appearance. Also count weekends and holidays.[4] Thus, if Jack served Julie on July 12 in Los Angeles County, with a "Declaration and Order" listing a July 17 court date in the same county, service would be proper. This is true even if Saturday and Sunday fell on July 14 and 15. To count the days you would not count July 12, the day of service, but you would count July 13, 14, 15, 16, and 17 for a total of five days. If you are unable to serve the defendant(s) within the proper time, simply ask the court clerk for a new court date and try again.

Defendant's Note: If you are improperly served either because you are not given adequate time, or the papers weren't handed to your personally, or a certified letter wasn't signed for by you, it is still wise for you to call the court clerk or show up in court on the day in question. Why should you have to do this if service was improper? Because the plaintiff may succeed in getting the case heard as a default if you fail to show up. While this is improper, the fact remains that it is often more trouble to get a default judgment set aside than to protect yourself from the start. But isn't this a Catch-22? You are entitled to proper service, but if you don't get it, is it a good idea to show up in court anyway? Perhaps, but as Catch-22's go, this one is mild. You can call the clerk or show up in court and request that

---

4 CCP Sec. 12.

the judge grant you a continuance to prepare your case. If the original service was in fact improper, your request will be honored. Of course, if you were improperly served and simply want to get the hearing out of the way, you can show up and go ahead with your case.

E. Serving A Business

If you are suing someone who owns his own business, or is a partner in a business, you must serve the person individually using the rules set out above. However, if you are suing a corporation, the rules are different.

Although a corporation is a legal person for purposes of lawsuits, you will still need to have your papers served on someone who lives and breathes. This is true whether you have the papers served personally, or use certified mail.[5] The flesh and blood person should be an officer of the corporation (president, vice-president, secretary or treasurer). Simply call the corporation and ask who, and where, they are. If they won't tell you, the city or county business tax and license people should be able to, at least for local corporations (see Chapter 8). If they can't, the California Secretary of State will supply a "Last Statement of Officers" for a small fee. If you have trouble getting someone at a large national corporation to accept service, call or write the California Secretary of State, Corporate Status Unit, 1230 "J" Street, Sacramento, California 95814. They will be able to tell you who is authorized to accept service for the company in California. You can do this by phone:

---

5 In some California judicial districts, the clerks insist that you use personal service to serve a corporation.

(916) 445-2900.[6] If you are suing a corporation in a situation where you know that the officers (or general manager) of the corporation work out of a local office, it is easy to use substituted service, as set out in Method 3 above.

F. Serving a Public Agency

As discussed in Chapter 8H, before you can sue a city, county or other government body, you must first file a claim against that agency within 100 days of the incident that gives rise to your claim. Once your claim is denied, you can sue in Small Claims Court. To serve your papers, call the governmental body in question and ask them who should be served. Then proceed following the rules set out in Method 1 or 2 above.

G. Notifying the Court That Service Has Been Accomplished ("Proof of Service")

Where certified mail is involved, you need do nothing. The court clerk sends out the certified mail for you and the signed post office receipt comes back directly to the clerk if service is accomplished. It's as simple as that.

However, a court has no way of knowing whether or not papers have been successfully filed by personal service unless

---

6 If a corporation has no authorized agent and you can find no corporate officer authorized to accept service in California, there is a procedure under which you can still accomplish valid service by "substituted service on the Secretary of State." To do this you must get a court order from the Small Claims Court clerk. Send this paper to the Secretary of State with a fee. Unfortunately, while this accomplishes legal service, it is rarely warranted. Why? Because if you can't find anyone to serve, it's unlikely you can find assets to collect from.

you tell them. This is done by filing a piece of paper known as a "Proof of Service" with the court clerk after the service has been made. The Proof of Service is a small, perforated, tear-off form that is part of the "Declaration and Order" package which must be signed by the person actually making the service. A Proof of Service is used both by the plaintiff and by the defendant if he files a "Claim of Defendant." It must be returned to the clerk's office not less than 48 hours before the trial. A Proof of Service is used when any legal documents are served by personal service. We will refer back to this example several times in future chapters. Frequently there isn't time after a defendant is served for her to properly complete service of a Claim of Defendant. In this situation, the defendant should simply file her Claim of Defendant and bring up the service problem in court. The plaintiff may well waive the time of service requirement and agree to proceed. Or, the plaintiff may request that the judge continue the case to a later date. The judge will normally grant the continuance if there is a good reason.

H. Serving A Claim of Defendant

As you will remember from our discussion in Chapter 9, a Claim of Defendant is the form that the defendant files when he wishes to sue the plaintiff for money damages arising out of the same incident that forms the basis for the plaintiff's suit. A Claim of Defendant should be filed with the clerk and served on the plaintiff at least five days prior to the time that the court has set for the hearing on the plaintiff's claim, unless the plaintiff has served the defendant less than 10 days before the date of the court hearing. In this event, the claim of defendant need only be served on the plaintiff one day prior to the hearing. CCP 116.8.

There will not be time to serve the Claim of Defendant by mail, so you will have to use personal service, returning a Proof of Service form to the court clerk. If you are a defendant who has filed a claim and you are unable to serve the plaintiff, simply show up at the court hearing date with your papers and serve the plaintiff in the hallway (not the courtroom if possible). Then explain to the judge why it was impossible to locate the plaintiff earlier. The judge will either delay the whole case over a few days, or allow you to proceed with your claim that day. Either way, she will accept your Claim of Defendant as validly served.

I. Serving Someone In the Military— Declaration of Non-Military Service

It is proper to serve someone who is on active duty in the armed forces. If she shows up, fine. If she doesn't, you have a problem. We learned in Chapter 10 that as a general rule, if a properly served defendant doesn't show up, you can get a "default judgment" against her. This is not true if the person you are suing is in the military (the reserves don't count).

Default judgments cannot normally be taken against people on active duty in the armed forces because Congress has given our military personnel special protections. To get a default judgment against any defendant a statement must be filed under penalty of perjury that he or she is not in the military. The "Declaration of Non-Military Service" is part of your Claim of Plaintiff package and is routinely filled out and signed as part of every case, unless, of course, the defendant is on active duty in the military. Fortunately, if a defendant is on active duty all is not lost. A California Attorney General's Opinion [34 Ops. Att. Gen. 60 (1959)] has been interpreted in many counties to mean that if a soldier/sailor would not be unduly prejudiced by having to appear, he or she must do so. The plaintiff can accomplish this by contacting an officer who has knowledge of the military person's duty schedule and, assuming it's true, getting a statement that no military necessity prevents them from appearing in court. Then, if the military person doesn't appear, a default judgment will probably be granted. In fact, contacting the superior officer often results in the person agreeing to show up.

CHAPTER 12

The Defendant's Options

This chapter is devoted to a review of the concerns of the defendant. Most of this material has already been discussed in the first eleven chapters, but it will be helpful to pull it all together in one place. Let's start by assuming that you are the person being sued. How do you approach what's happening to you? First, when you receive the plaintiff's papers, you will have to make one of several decisions. There is no one correct course of action—it all depends on your circumstances and desires.

A. Improper Service

You may conclude that the service was not proper (see Chapter 11). Perhaps the "Claim of Plaintiff" was left with your neighbors, or maybe you didn't have the correct number of days in which to respond. You may be tempted not to show up in court, figuring that since you weren't served properly, the case can't be heard. As noted, this is not a smart idea. The judge can easily be unaware of, or overlook, the service problem and issue a default judgment against you. If this happens, you will have to go to the trouble of requesting that the default be set aside. You are better off to contact the clerk, explain the problem with the service and ask that the case be continued to a date that is convenient to you. If the clerk can't help, write the judge or show up on the day in question and request a continuance.

B. No Defense

Now let's assume that the service was okay, but you have no real defense, or don't have the time to defend yourself, or for some other reason don't feel like going to court.[1] A decision not to show up will very likely result in a default judgment being entered against you. It will most probably be for the dollar amount demanded by the plaintiff, plus his or her filing fee and costs to serve you. We discuss default judgments and how you can try to settle them if you take action immediately in Chapters 10 and 15.

If you do not dispute the plaintiff's claim, but cannot afford to pay it all at once and want to make payments in install-ments, your best bet is to show up in court and explain your situation to the judge. If you can't be present, write a letter to the court prior to the court hearing (be sure to properly identify the case, using the number from the Claim of Plaintiff form) explaining why it would be difficult or impossible to pay any judgment all at once. For example, if you are on a fixed income, have recently been unemployed and have a lot of debts, or have

---

[1] Many people are tempted not to show up and defend a case in Small Claims Court because they have no money and figure that even if they lose, the plaintiff can't collect. This is "grasshopper thinking." The sun may be shining today and the judgment may cause you no immediate problem. But remember, judgments are good for ten years and can be renewed for another ten. You may put a few nickels together sometime in the future and you probably won't want them taken away by an industrious little ant holding a Small Claims judgment in his mouth. So wake up and defend yourself while you can.

a low or moderate income and a large family, explain this to the judge. Just state the facts; there is no need to tell a long sob story. When the judge enters a judgment against you, she will very likely order you to pay in reasonable monthly installments.

C. Try to Compromise

If you feel that perhaps the plaintiff has some right on his side, but that you are being sued for too much, contact the plaintiff and try to work out a compromise settlement. Any settlement you make should be set down in writing along the lines outlined in Chapter 6. It should also include a specific statement that the plaintiff will forever drop his pending lawsuit. Simply add a clause like the following to the sample agreement outlined in Chapter 6:[2]

"As part of this settlement, __(name of plaintiff)__ hereby agrees to drop the lawsuit, number __(insert number)__ filed in Small Claims Court in the _____ judicial district on __(date)__ against __(name of defendant)__ and that no further court action(s) will be filed regarding the subject matter of this agreement."

As a practical matter any lawsuit that is not actively pro-secuted will be dropped by the clerk. The reason that you want to have a settlement agreement written out is to cover the unlikely possibility that the other party will accept money from you and then try to go ahead with his suit too. If this

---

[2] Also an assortment of tear-out, fill-in-the-blank releases are available for this purpose in *Make Your Own Contract*, Elias (Nolo Press).

happens, you need only show your written settlement agreement to the judge.

D. Fight Back

Now we get to those of you who feel that you don't owe the plaintiff a dime. You will want to actively fight. This means that you must show up in court on the date stated in the papers served on you unless you get the case continued (see Chapter 10). A defendant need not file any papers with the court clerk; showing up ready to defend yourself is enough. The strategies to properly argue a case, including the presentation of witnesses, estimates, diagrams, etc. are discussed in Chapters 13-22 and apply equally to defendants and plaintiffs. You will wish to study this information carefully and develop a strategy for your case. You will also want to see whether the plaintiff has brought the case within the time allowed by the Statute of Limitations (Chapter 5) and whether he has asked for a reasonable amount of money (Chapter 4). If you simply show up without thinking out a coherent presentation, you are likely to lose.

E. File A "Claim of Defendant"

Finally, there are those of you who not only want to dispute the plaintiff's claim, but also want to sue him. This involves promptly filing a "Claim of Defendant" for up to $1,500 in Small Claims Court, or for a larger amount in Municipal or Superior Court. See Chapters 10C and 11G for more details.

CHAPTER 13

Getting Ready for Court

Once you have your papers on file and the defendant(s) served, the preliminaries are over and you are ready for the main event—your day in court. Movies, and especially T.V., have done much to make court proceedings false. Ask yourself, what was a trial like before every lawyer fancied himself Raymond Burr or Charles Laughton and judges acted "father-ly," or "stern," or "indignantly outraged" in the fashion of "People's Court's" Judge Wopner?

There are people whose lives revolve around courthouses, and who have been playing movie parts for so long that they have become caricatures of one screen star or another. Lawyers are particularly susceptible to this virus. All too often they substitute posturing and theatrics for good hard preparation. Thankfully though, most people who work in our courts quickly recover from movieitis and realize that the majestic courtroom is in truth a large, drafty hall with a raised platform at one end: His honor is only a lawyer dressed in a black shroud who knew the right politician and that they themselves are not bit players in "Witness For The Prosecution," "Inherit the Wind" or "The Verdict."

I mention movieitis because it's a common ailment in Small Claims Court. Cases that should be easily won are often lost because somebody goes marching around the courtroom antago- nizing everyone with comic opera imitations of E. G. Marshall. And don't assume that you are immune. Movieitis is a subtle disease because people often don't realize they have it. Ask yourself a few self-diagnostic questions. Have you watched courtroom scenes on T. V. or in the movies? Have you ever imag- ined that you were one of the actor-lawyers? How many times have you been in a real courtroom in comparison to watching movie set courtrooms?

My purpose here is not to lecture you on how to present your- self in court. But perhaps I can get you to remember something that you already know—you don't need to be false to yourself to succeed in Small Claims Court. You don't need to put on fancy clothes or airs, or try to appear more polished, intelligent or sophisticated than you are. Be yourself and you will do just fine. If you have a chance, go to the court a few days before your case is heard and watch for an hour or two. You may not learn a great deal that will be helpful in your case, but you will be a lot more relaxed and comfortable when your turn comes. Watch- ing a few cases is a particularly good thing to do if you feel anxious about your court appearance. For those of you who love to act, who simply can't pass up an opportunity to perform, at least act real. That's right, go ahead and act if you must; but make your performance that of a person—not a personality.

Movietis aside, most people I have watched in Small Claims Court have done extremely well. Many mornings I have been inspired, feeling that for the first time in years I have seen honesty and truth put in an appearance before the Bar of Justice. When I first witnessed this phenomenon as part of doing research for this book, I was surprised. I had stopped taking clients several years before, in part, because I hated the dis- honest sham that goes on in the courtroom—hated the endless natterings between lawyers about logic-chopping technicalities while clients paid and paid and paid. It was wonderful to see that once the lawyers were removed and people began communicating directly, there was much about our court system that made sense.

Commonly a judge must decide a case, at least in part, on the basis of who seems to be the most believable. This is because there isn't enough hard evidence to be conclusive either way. Different judges have varying prejudices, hunches, feelings, etc., about who is, or isn't telling the truth. Often they themselves can't explain the many intangibles that go into making this sort of decision, but most agree that a person who presents herself in a simple, straightforward way is more likely to be believed than is a person who puts on airs. For example, a house painter who shows up in his overalls and puts his lunchbox under the chair will probably be much more convincing (and comfortable) than he would be if he came painfully squeezed into his blue wedding and funeral suit. As one judge told me, "A pimp being a pimp has as good a chance as anyone else in my courtroom, but a pimp who tries to act like Saint Paul better watch out."

Before we get into a discussion of how to prepare and present different types of cases, here are a few general suggestions:

A. Interpreter Services

The Small Claims Court clerk is required to maintain and make available a list of interpreters in as many languages as possible who are willing to aid parties for no fee or a reasonable fee. However, failure to have an interpreter for a particular language on the list shall not invalidate any proceedings. (CCP Sec. 117.16).

B. Court Times

Small Claims courts can schedule cases any time they wish on business days. Most commonly court is held at 9:00 A.M. In larger judicial districts, Saturday or evening sessions must also be held. If it is not convenient for you to go to court during business hours, request that your case be scheduled at one of these other sessions.

C. Free Small Claims Advice

Every county must provide a program of free advice to Small Claims litigants on how to present their claims or defenses in Small Claims Court. CCP Sec. 117.18 requires an "advisory service" be provided "in person, by telephone, or by any other means reasonably calculated to provide timely and appropriate assistance." Some counties such as Marin and San Francisco take this mandate seriously and provide a thorough service with convenient hours. Others provide little help. Ask the clerk about times and places for your local advisory programs. Advisors can be particularly helpful if you can't answer any of the following questions:

1. Do I have a good case?

2. Is the legal theory on which my case is based sound? (I discuss this in detail in Chapter 2)

3. How can I organize my testimony and that of my witnesses in order to have the best chance to convince the judge to rule in my favor.

D. Getting to The Courthouse

Before you get to the right courtroom, you have to get to the right building. Small Claims courts are often not in the main courthouse, but like a half forgotten stepsister, are housed wherever there's an empty room. The point is, don't assume that you know where to go if you haven't been there before. Plaintiffs have already had to find the clerk's office to file their papers, so they probably know where the courtroom is, but defendants should check this out. Be sure too, that your witnesses know exactly where and when to show up. And do plan to be a few minutes early—people who rush in flustered and late start with a strike against them.

Note: San Francisco and some other counties use an insulting hurry-up-and-wait technique that would make the Army blush. They have everyone show up at 8:15 A.M. in one large room. At this time the judges are still home having coffee. Court is supposed to start at 9:00, although 9:15 is normal, and 9:30 is all too common. Can you imagine the court making lawyers show up an hour early for no reason? Courts sometimes begin at 8:30, but far more often at 9:00 in the morning—if they tell you an earlier time, call them up and ask what time the judge really gets there.

E. Understanding The Courtroom

Most Small Claims proceedings are conducted in standard courthouses that are also used for other purposes. Indeed, sometimes you will have to sit through a few minutes of some other type of court proceeding before the Small Claims calendar is called.

Most judges still sit on high in their little, wooden throne boxes and most still wear those depressing black judicial robes that trace their history back to England at a time when courts were largely controlled by king, nobility and clergy. There are court rules requiring these out-of-date traditions, although a few judges conduct their court more informally anyway. In addition to the judge, a clerk and a bailiff will normally be present. They sit at tables immediately in front of the judge. The clerk's job is to keep the judge supplied with necessary files and papers, and to make sure that proceedings flow smoothly. A clerk is not the same as a court reporter who keeps a word-by-word record of proceedings. No such record is kept in Small Claims Court, and no court reporter is present.

Courtrooms are divided about two-thirds of the way toward the front by a little fence. This fence is known to initiates as the "bar." The public must stay on the opposite side of the bar from the judge, clerk, bailiff, attorneys, etc., unless invited to cross. This invitation occurs when your case is called by the clerk. At this point you come forward and sit at the long table (known as the counsel table) just inside the fence.[1] You and your witnesses sit facing the judge with your backs to the rest of the courtroom. In Small Claims Courts, you will have been sworn (or affirmed, if you wish) to tell the truth before the judge arrives. If this has not already been done, the oath will be administered at this time. In the great majority of Small Claims Courts you, your opponent and your witnesses will present the entire case from the long table. This means that you do not sit in the witness box next to the judge. Many people feel that it is polite to stand when addressing the judge, but you should do what feels most comfortable to you.

When your case is called and you come forward to take your turn at the counsel table, have all your papers with you ready to present to the judge. This can include bills, receipts, estimates, photographs, contracts, letters to or from your opponent, etc. When the time comes to show these to the judge, you simply hand them to the clerk who will pass them on to the judge. As I have said before, documentation is a great aid to your case, but don't go overboard. Judges are a little like donkeys—load them too heavily and they are likely to lie down and go to sleep.

---

[1] In a few courtrooms judges try to hurry things by asking everyone to stand in front of the judges bench. The idea seems to be if people can't sit down they will present their cases faster. This might be okay if the judge would stand too. As it is, I feel it's insulting.

F. Dealing With Your Opponent

Before you get to the courtroom, you should do a little thinking about your opponent. Perhaps you can guess what sort of presentation she will make. If so, ask yourself how you can best deal with these arguments. This may be a good way to take the negative energy you may feel (frustration, annoyance, anger) and turn it into creative planning and preparation. In court, always be polite. You will gain nothing, and may lose the respect of the judge, if you are obviously hostile or sarcastic. Don't interrupt your opponent when she is speaking—you will get your chance. When you present your case, lay out the facts to the judge; don't conduct an argument with the other side.

G. Dealing With The Judge
Or Commissioner

It is hard to generalize about judges—each is an individual. I have seen more good than bad, but that doesn't help if your case comes up before an idiot. Unlike higher courts, no great intellectual ability is required to be a good Small Claims Court judge— indeed, most of the judges sitting on the United States Supreme Court would probably be lousy at it. What is required is a liking for people, open-mindedness and, above all, patience. Everyone who comes to Small Claims Court should have the feeling that they got a fair chance to have their say.

Most Small Claims Court judges are judges in the more formal Municipal Courts who also hear the Small Claims calendar. This is a mistake. The last thing that is needed in Small Claims Court is the "me judge, you peasant" philosophy of our formal court system. Hopefully as Small Claims Court expands in the future, it will be staffed by people (not necessarily lawyers) specifically trained to meet its needs (see Chapter 24).

One hopeful change in this direction is that court-appointed commissioners are now hearing Small Claims cases in many districts. Commissioners are lawyers appointed by local courts who normally hear Small Claims and traffic court cases exclusively. By and large, they are dedicated and competent, and often care more about Small Claims Court than does the average judge. As far as you are concerned, commissioners have the same legal standing as judges.

In addition, lawyers are often appointed as temporary judges in Small Claims. The legal slang for a temporary judge is "Judge, pro tem." If your case comes up on a day when there is a "Judge, pro tem," you have the option of refusing to accept that judge and asking that your case be heard by a regular judge. If your case is contested and you feel it involves fairly complicated legal issues, I recommend you do this. Pro tem judges are not paid, not trained and often do not have much practical experience in the legal areas that are commonly heard in Small Claims Court. While some are excellent, a fair number are seriously substandard and as a general rule they are best avoided.

What if it's a regular judge—or commissioner— you don't like after having seen a few cases before yours? A little-known law (Code of Civil Procedure (CCP) Sec. 170.6) allows you to "disqualify" a judge simply on your honest belief that he is "prejudiced" against you. No one will ask you to prove it. To disqualify a judge, you can simply say, when your case is called (after you've been "sworn in"), something like this: "Your Honor, I believe you are prejudiced against my interest, and I request a trial before another judge."

When thinking about presenting your case to a judge, there is one constructive thing that you can do. Imagine yourself in the judge's shoes. What would you value most from the people appearing before you? Before I ever sat as a judge, my answer was politeness, good organization of the material to be presented, and reasonable brevity. After experiencing Small Claims Court from the judge's chair, I would only add—documented testimony. By this, I mean testimony that consists of more than the word of the person bringing, or defending, the case. Witnesses, written statements, police accident reports, photographs—all these give the judge a chance to make a decision on something more than who tells the best story. And one final thing. Remember, the judge has heard thousands of stories very much like yours and will either cease paying attention or get annoyed if you try repeating your story three times. Judges are particularly annoyed by people who have obviously watched People's Court on TV and insist on using a full 15 minutes to present their case. In the real world judges will usually insist that you be as brief as possible and get angry if you try to turn a case involving a defendant's simple failure to repay you $1,000 into something that uses up half a morning.

H. Organizing Your Testimony And Evidence

It's essential that you organize what you have to say and the physical evidence you wish to show the judge. I recommend that you divide your testimony into a list of the main points you want to make. Under each heading, list any items of physical evidence you wish to show the judge. If your evidence consists of a number of items, make sure that you have put them in order and can find each quickly when you need it.

Example: In cases based on a hotel's failure to return your deposit when you cancelled a wedding reception three months before the event was to be held, your list might look like this:

- General Explanation of Lawsuit: "Hotel refused to return my $500 deposit when I cancelled the wedding."

- This was true even though I cancelled 83 days before the event.

- The contract I signed with the hotel allowed full refund if cancellation occurred more than 60 days before the event.

- Show contract to the judge.

- When I cancelled the hotel told me (and then sent me a letter) stating that their cancellation policy had been changed a month ago to require 90 days in order to get a refund.

- This was the first time I was notified of this policy change.

- The change should not affect my contract, and anyway, 90 days in advance is an unreasonably long cancellation policy.

- In any event, under contract law principles (mitigation of damages), the hotel has a duty to try and rerent the banquet room to minimize damages and they had plenty of time to do so.

- Present the judge with a list of short cancellation policies of five other hotels in the area, all of which allow a full refund on much shorter notice than 83 days.

Note: In Chapter 2 I discuss the mitigation of damages point mentioned above. In Chapters 14-21, you will find lots more about how to prepare for court and what to do once you get there.

CHAPTER 14

Witnesses

It is often helpful to have someone in court with you who has a first hand knowledge of the facts of your case and who can support your point of view. In many types of cases, such as car accidents, or disputes concerning whether or not a tenant left an apartment clean, witnesses are particularly valuable. In other fact situations, they aren't as necessary. For example, if a friend borrowed $500 and didn't pay it back, you don't need a witness to prove that your friend's (ex-friend's?) signature on the promissory note is genuine unless you expect him to base his defense on the theory that his signature was forged.

A good witness should have first hand knowledge of the facts in dispute. This means that either she saw something that helps establish your case (e.g., the car accident, or dog bite, or dirty apartment, etc) or is an expert you have consulted about an important aspect of your case (e.g., a car mechanic who testifies your engine wasn't fixed properly). The judge will not be interested in the testimony of a person who is repeating second hand or generalized information such as "I know Joe is a good, safe driver and would never have done anything reckless," or "I didn't see Joe's apartment before he moved out, but both Joe and his mother, who couldn't be here today, told me that they worked for two days cleaning it up."

A good witness is believable. This isn't always an easy quality to define. For example, a police officer may be a symbol of honesty to some people, while others will automatically react to him with hostility and fear. But remember, it's the judge you are trying to convince and judges tend to be fairly establishment folk (they make comfortable salaries, own their own homes and generally tend to like the existing order of things). Most judges I know would tend to believe a police officer.

In many types of cases such as a car accident, you won't have much choice as to witnesses. You will be lucky to have one. But in other disputes (was the house properly painted, or the work on the car engine competently completed?), you have an opportunity to plan ahead. When you do, try to get an expert witness who is particularly knowledgeable about the dispute in question. Thus, in a dispute over whether car repairs were properly done, it's preferable to bring a working car mechanic rather than your neighbor "who knows a lot about cars."

Unfortunately, in some types of disputes, close friends and family are often your only witnesses. There is no rule that says that you can't have these people testify for you. Indeed, I have often seen a person's spouse, or the friend that she lives with, give very convincing testimony. But, given a choice, it is usually better to have a witness who is neither friend nor kin. A judge may discount testimony of people to whom you are close on the theory that they would naturally be biased in your favor. One little trick to dispell this judicial cynicism is to have a closely-related witness bend over backwards to treat the other party as fairly as possible. Thus, if your brother is your only witness to the fact that ABC Painting splashed paint on your boat, he might point out to the judge not only that he saw them to do it, but that it was a very windy day and they were having a hard time painting the breakwater.

I will talk more about witnesses as I go through the various case examples (Chapters 16-21), but let's outline a few basic rules here:

• Prepare your witness thoroughly as to what your position is, what your opponent is likely to say and what you want the witness to say. In court, the witness will be on her own and you want to be sure that the story comes out right. It is completely legal to thoroughly discuss the case with your witness beforehand;

• Never bring a witness to court who is hostile to you or hostile to the idea of testifying;

• Do not ask a witness to testify unless you know exactly what he will say. This sounds basic, but I have seen people lose cases because their witnesses got mixed up, and in one instance, where the witness actually supported the other side;

• It's not illegal to pay an expert witness a reasonable fee (say a car mechanic who has examined your engine). In addition, a subpoenaed witness is entitled to a small witness fee (see A below);

• Never use a subpoena form to require a witness to be present unless you have made sure that it is okay with the witness (more in A below).

Important: In court a witness will be pretty much on her own when it comes to giving testimony. The witness will sit with you at the table facing the judge and talk to the judge from there.[1] Normally a witness doesn't take the witness stand in

---

[1] In a few courtrooms, the judge may ask all parties and witnesses to approach the judge's bench and stand there in a little group. Everyone will present their testimony in a conversational tone from there.

Small Claims, but I generally recommend that he stand when addressing the judge. Most judges prefer that you don't pretend to be a lawyer and ask your witness questions. Simply let the witness explain what happened as he saw it (and hopefully as you rehearsed it). The judge is likely to ask the witness questions. If you feel that the witness has left something out, ask a question designed to produce the information you want.

A. Subpoenaing Witnesses

In California, you can require that a witness be present if that person resides within the state. To do this, go to the clerk's office and get a "Subpoena" form. Fill it out, and have it served on the person who you wish to have present. But remember, you never want to subpoena a person unless you have talked to her first and gotten an okay. The very act of dragging someone into court who doesn't want to come may set her against you. A subpoenaed witness is entitled to a fee of $35 and 20¢ per mile each way from home to court. If you win your case, you will probably be able to recover your witness fees from the other side. The judge has discretion as to whether to grant you your witness fees. Most judges are strict about this, making the loser pay the winner's witness fees only if he finds that the sub-poenaed witness was essential to the preparation of the case. This means that, if your case is so strong that you don't need a witness but you subpoena one anyway, you may well have to pay the witness fee even though you win the case.

Here is the standard California subpoena form available at the Small Claims Court clerk's office. You will need to prepare an original and two copies. Once prepared, take the subpoena form to the clerk who will issue it. Service must be made per-sonally and the "Proof of Service," which is on the back of the subpoena, returned to the clerk's office. Rules for service are discussed in Chapter 11.

ATTORNEY OR PARTY WITHOUT ATTORNEY (NAME AND ADDRESS)   TELEPHONE   FOR COURT USE ONLY

John O'Gara
15 Scenic St.
Albany, CA

ATTORNEY FOR (NAME)   In Pro Per

Insert name of court, judicial district or branch court, if any, and post office and street address

MUNICIPAL COURT, COUNTY OF ALAMEDA
STATE OF CALIFORNIA
BERKELEY-ALBANY JUDICIAL DISTRICT
2000 CENTER ST., BERKELEY, CA. 94704

PLAINTIFF

Public Library

DEFENDANT

John O'Gara

CIVIL SUBPENA   ☒ COURT ☐ DEPOSITION   CASE NUMBER
☐ **DUCES TECUM**   ☐ OTHER (specify):   (Fill in number)

THE PEOPLE OF THE STATE OF CALIFORNIA, TO (NAME):

1. **YOU ARE ORDERED TO APPEAR AS A WITNESS** in this action as follows unless you make a special agreement with the person named in item 3:

   a. Date: Time: ☐ Dept.:   ☐ Div.:   ☐ Room:
   b. Address:

2. and you are
   a. ☒ ordered to appear in person.
   b. ☐ not required to appear in person if you produce the records described in the accompanying affidavit in compliance with Evidence Code sections 1560 and 1561.
   c. ☐ ordered to appear in person and to produce the records described in the accompanying affidavit. The personal attendance of the custodian or other qualified witness and the production of the original records is required by this subpena. The procedure authorized pursuant to subdivision (b) of section 1560, and sections 1561 and 1562, of the Evidence Code will not be deemed sufficient compliance with this subpena.
   d. ☐ ordered to designate one or more persons to testify on your behalf as to the matters described in the accompanying statement. (Code of Civil Procedure section 2019(a)(6).)

3. **IF YOU HAVE ANY QUESTIONS ABOUT WITNESS FEES OR THE TIME OR DATE FOR YOU TO APPEAR, OR IF YOU WANT TO BE CERTAIN THAT YOUR PRESENCE IS REQUIRED, CONTACT THE ATTORNEY REQUESTING THIS SUBPENA, NAMED ABOVE, OR THE FOLLOWING PERSON, BEFORE THE DATE ON WHICH YOU ARE TO APPEAR:**

   a. Name: b. Telephone number:

4. **WITNESS FEES:** You are entitled to receive witness fees and mileage actually traveled, as provided by law, if you request them **BEFORE** your scheduled appearance. **Request them from the person named in item 3.**

5. If this subpena requires your attendance at proceedings out of court and you refuse to answer questions or sign as required by law, you must attend a court hearing at a time to be fixed by the person conducting such proceedings.

6. You are ordered to appear in this civil matter in your capacity as a peace officer or other person described in Government Code section 68097.1.

   Date: Clerk of the Court, by _____, Deputy

DISOBEDIENCE OF THIS SUBPENA MAY BE PUNISHED AS CONTEMPT BY THIS COURT. YOU WILL ALSO BE LIABLE FOR THE SUM OF FIVE HUNDRED DOLLARS AND ALL DAMAGES RESULTING FROM YOUR FAILURE TO OBEY.

For Court Use Only: Dated: _____   _____
                                              (Signature of person issuing subpena)

                                              _____
                                              (Type or print name)

                                              _____
                                              (Title)

(See reverse for proof of service)

Form Adopted by Rule 982
Judicial Council of California
Revised Effective January 1, 1982   **CIVIL SUBPENA**

B. Subpoenaing Police Officers

You have probably already noticed that on the subpoena form there is a special box to use if you wish to subpoena a police officer. The box is easy to fill out, but hard to pay for. The deposit to subpoena a police officer is at least $125. This money must be paid to the clerk at the time the subpoena is issued. Depending on the amount of the officer's time that is used, you may eventually get a refund of some of your deposit.

C. Subpoenaing Documents

In addition to witnesses, you can also subpoena documents. It is rare that this is done in Small Claims Court, but it may occasionally be helpful. Someone (police department, phone company, hospital, corporation) may have certain books, ledgers, papers or other documents that can help your case. To get them, you must prepare a form entitled "Subpoena Duces Tecum." This is very similar to the standard subpoena form, except that there is a space to describe the papers or other documents that you want brought to court. To get a "Subpoena Duces Tecum" issued, you must attach an affidavit stating why you need the written material. Prepare three copies of all papers and, after you get the clerk to issue the subpoena, serve it on the witness using personal service as described in Chapter 11. To comply with the subpoena, the custodian of the records may mail them to court unless you demand the custodian show up personally. See CCP Sec.1985; Evidence Code Secs. 1560-1566.[2]

A Subpoena Duces Tecum must be directed to the person who is in charge of the documents, books or records that you want. It may take a few phone calls to find out who this is. Be sure you get this information accurately. If you list someone on the "Sub-

---

[2] Evidence Code Sec. 1563 establishes fees for subpoenaing documents. These include photocopy fees, compensation for the time of the record gatherer and a witness fee if you require the custodian of the documents to appear in court personally.

poena Duces Tecum" who has nothing to do with the documents, you won't get them. When dealing with a large corporation, public utility, municipal government, etc., it is wise to list the person who is in overall charge of the department where the records are kept. Thus, if you want records from a public library having to do with library fines, or from the city tax and license department having to do with business license fees, you should not list the city manager or the mayor, but should list the head librarian or the director of the tax and license office.

Example: Let's take a hypothetical case. You are being sued by the city on behalf of the public library for $300 for eight rare books which they state you failed to return. You know that you did return the books, but can't seem to get that across to the library which insists on treating you like a thief. You learn that each April the library takes a yearly inventory of all books on their shelves. You believe that if you can get access to that inventory, you may be able to figure out where the library misplaced the books, or at least show that a significant percentage of the library's other books are not accounted for, raising the implication that they lost the books, not you. Your first step is to ask the library to voluntarily open the inventory to you. If they refuse, you may well want to subpoena it. Here's how:

1. Check the "Duces Tecum" box on the Subpoena form. Check either box 2b or 2c.

2. Prepare a Declaration using a form available from the court. See sample below. It should be brief. Describe the documents you need and why they are necessary to prove issues involved in the case. If you want the custodian to show up in person give a reason. Don't argue the merits of your case.

3. Have the subpoena issued by the Small Claims clerk. Then have the subpoena served, being sure that the "Proof of Service" (see Chapter 11F) is properly filled out and returned to the clerk.

Name and Address of Attorney: Telephone: John O'Gara 15 Scenic St., Los Angeles, CA 90011 Attorney for: IN PRO PER	For court use only:
Plaintiff: Public Library	
Defendant: John O'Gara	

DECLARATION FOR:
          SUBPENA DUCES TECUM [X]
          SUBPENA DUCES TECUM RE: DESPOSITION [ ]
	Case Number:
	(Fill in number)

I hereby declare, under penalty of perjury, that I am ~~the attorney of record for~~

 appearing in pro per _____ in the above entitled action;

____ That the deposition of _____not applicable_____ is noticed for

hearing before _____

on _____ at _____.m., at _____

_____ in the city of _____, California.

____ That said action is set for trial on (fill in dates etc.)_____ at _____.m.,

at _____ in the city of _____,

California.

That _Robert Riwgle_____ is a material witness in said action.

and has under his control the following books, documents, or other thing(s):

    Book inventory information collected by the main branch of the public
    library during the calendar year 19___.

That said matters or things are material to the issues involved in said action by

reason of the following facts:*   My contention is that I returned the books which the

  library is suing me for. The inventory should back me up on this.

Request is made that Subpena Duces Tecum issue accordingly.

Executed on _____ at _____, California.

_____

*Materiality must be set forth in full detail

Note: The person who you have subpoenaed the documents from should mail them to the court. If you need an opportunity to examine the documents, request it from the judge. He or she may well let you do your examining right there in the courtroom while other cases go ahead, or, if necessary, he may continue the case for a few days and arrange to have you make your examination at the place of business of the owner of the records.

D. Written Evidence

In Small Claims Court, there are no formal rules of evidence requiring that a witness testify in person. While it is best to have a witness appear in court, this isn't always possible and a judge will accept written statements from both eye witnesses ("I was there and saw the filthy apartment") and expert witnesses ("I examined the transmission and found that it was not the original one, but a rebuilt part installed improperly"). If you do present the written statement of a witness, make sure the witness states the following facts:

* The date of the event.

* If she is an eye witness, what she saw and where she saw it from.

* If he is an expert witness, the credentials that make him an expert ("I am a state certified T.V. repairperson and have run my own repair business for 12 years"), as well as his relevant opinion.

* Any other facts that have a bearing on the dispute.

A letter that accomplishes this, written by an eye witness to an automobile accident, would look like this (see Chapter 17 for a written statement by an expert witness):

37 Ogden Court
Ukiah, CA
September 30, 19__

Presiding Judge
Small Claims Court
Ukiah, California

Re: John Swift vs. Peter Petrakos
Small Claims Case No. 11478

Your Honor:

On September 15, 19__, I witnessed an auto accident a little after 7:30 a.m., involving John Swift and Peter Petrakos. I clearly saw Mr. Petrakos' Toyota, which was heading north on South Dora, go through a red light and hit Mr. Swift's blue van, which was proceeding south on West 7th, well inside the 25 MPH speed limit. I noticed that the traffic light facing Mr. Petrakos did not turn to green for ten seconds or so after the accident, so it is clear to me that this was not a case of Mr. Petrakos just being a little early or late getting through an intersection at a light change.

Sincerely,
Victor Van Cleve

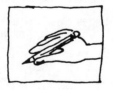

E. Judges as Witnesses

CCP Sec. 117 states, "The judge may consult witnesses informally and otherwise investigate the controversy." In practice this means as much, or as little, as an individual judge wants it to mean. But it clearly does allow the conscientious judge great discretion to climb down off the bench to check out an important fact.

Using a judge as a witness is a valuable technique in many situations. This is done routinely in many types of disputes, such as clothing cases in which you bring the damaged garment into court for the judge's examination. Always bring to the courtroom any physical evidence that meets these two criteria:

- Showing it to the judge will help your case;
- It will fit through the door.

But what if your evidence is impossible to bring into the courtroom (a car with a poor paint job or a supposedly pedigreed puppy that grew up looking as if Lassie were the mother and Rin Tin Tin the father)? Why not ask the judge to accompany you outside the building to examine the car, or the dog, or whatever else is important to your case? Many (but not all) judges are willing to do so if they feel that it is necessary to a better understanding of the dispute and won't take too long. But never ask a judge to take time to leave her court to view evidence if you can prove your case just as well by other means, such as witnesses and pictures. A good approach is to do as much as you can in court, and to ask the judge to view evidence outside of court only if it is essential. Sometimes it clearly is. For example, one excellent judge I know was disturbed one morning when two eye witnesses gave seriously contradictory testimony about a traffic accident. He questioned both in detail and then took the case under submission. That evening, he drove over to the relevant corner. Once there, it was clear that one of the witnesses couldn't possibly have seen the accident from the spot on which she claimed to be standing (in front of a particular restaurant). The judge decided the case in favor of the other.

F. Testimony by Telephone

A Small Claims Court judge has the power to take testimony or otherwise investigate a case over the phone. Many judges don't like to do this, but a number will if a witness cannot be present because he or she is ill, disabled, out-of-state, or can't take off from work. While procedures vary, some courts will set up conference calls so that the opposing party has the opportunity to hear what is being said and to respond.

Don't just assume that a particular judge will allow information to be presented over the phone. Ask the clerk. If you get a negative response, don't give up—ask the judge when you get into the courtroom. It is also an extremely good idea to have a letter from the witness who you want to reach by phone, explaining what he or she will testify to (e.g., your opponent's car ran a red light and broadsided you) and explaining why it is impossible for him to be in court. Such a letter should look like the one in Section D above, except the witness should add:

"Mr. Swift has asked me to testify on his behalf, and normally I would be happy to do so. However, I will be in New York City on business during the months of October, November and December 19__ and cannot be present.

"I have asked Mr. Swift to let me know the day and approximate time of the court hearing and have told him that I will give him a phone number where I can be reached. If you think it desirable, I will be pleased to give my testimony by phone."

CHAPTER 15

Presenting Your Case
to the Judge

A. Uncontested Cases—Getting A Judgment By Default

Surprisingly often, presenting your case will be easy—your opponent will simply not show up. If this occurs, you will normally be asked to present the facts of your case briefly. The judge will then check to see that your opponent was properly served. She will not want you to present a long argument or lots of evidence.[1] After all, the other side hasn't shown up, so if your statement of the facts entitles you to relief, you will get it.

If a defendant doesn't show up to argue his case, he can't appeal to the appellate division of the Superior Court (see Chapter 22) unless he first gets the Small Claims Court judge to reopen the case by "setting aside the default judgment." If the

---

[1] CCP Sec. 117(a)

defaulting party makes a motion to set aside the default within 30 days, the judge may—but does not have to—set it aside. (See Chapter 10E for a discussion.) If the Small Claims judge refuses to set aside the default, the defendant can appeal the judge's refusal (not the case itself) to Superior Court. If the Superior Court does set it aside, the case will be reheard right there.

B. Contested Cases

Assuming now that both sides show up and step forward when the case is called by the clerk, what happens next? First, the judge will establish everyone's identity. Next, he will ask the plaintiff to briefly state his case.

The plaintiff should tell the judge what is in dispute and then briefly outline his position. It is critical that the judge know what the case is about before you start arguing it. For example, if your case involves a car accident, you might start by saying, "This case involves a car accident at Cedar and Rose Streets in which my car suffered $372 worth of damage," not "It all started when I was driving down Rose Street after having two eggs and a danish for breakfast." Only occasionally have I seen a case where the plaintiff's initial presentation should take longer than five minutes. As part of his statement the plaintiff should present any relevant papers, photos or other documentary evidence. These should be handed to the clerk and explained. If the plaintiff has done any legal research and believes that a California statute or court decision supports his position, he should call it to the attention of the judge. One good way to do this is to write the statute and the name of the court decision, along with its citation, on a piece of paper and hand it to the judge.

Example: Assume you are slightly injured when a portion of the ceiling in your rented apartment falls. You miss a couple of days work (you are out $200 per day) and have doctor's bills of $200. You decide to sue for $1,200 to include the pain and discomfort you experienced. However, you are worried about one thing—was the defendant negligent (the ceiling looked fine before it fell). You go to the law library and find that there is a California Supreme Court case which states that landlords are "strictly liable" to tenants for injuries caused by defective rental premises, whether negligence can be shown or not (see Chapter 2D for more on strict liability). To tell the judge about this case, prepare a memo like this:

John Tenant, Plaintiff v. Tillie Landlord, Defendant
Small Claims Case #123456

Memorandum of Legal Authority
Supporting Plaintiffs' Position

A main issue of my case is whether I need to prove that defendant was negligent. I contended that the law only requires me to show that a defect in defendant's building caused me to be injured. I base this assertion that the doctrine of "strict liability" applies on decision in the case of *Becker v. I.R.M.* 38 Cal.3d 454 (1985).

Respectfully Submitted,
John Tenant
4/7/___

The plaintiff should also be sure to indicate the presence of any witnesses to the judge.

When the plaintiff is finished, the judge may wish to ask questions. He may or may not wish to hear from the plaintiff's witnesses before the defendant speaks. Each judge will control the flow of evidence differently. It's best to go with the judge's energy, not against it. Just be sure that, at one time or another, you have made all of your points. If you feel rushed, say so. The judge will normally slow things down a little.

Sooner or later the defendant will get his chance. Defendants often get so angry at something the plaintiff has said ("lies! lies!") that when their turn comes, they immediately attack. This is silly and usually counter-productive. The defendant should calmly and clearly present his side of the dispute to the judge. If the plaintiff has made false or misleading statements, these should be answered, but at the end of the presentation, not at the beginning. Tell your story first, then deal with the plaintiff's testimony if this seems necessary.

Here are a few tips that you may find helpful. These are not rules written on golden tablets, but only suggestions. You may want to follow some and ignore others.

1. Stand when you make your initial presentation to the judge. Standing gives most people a sense of presence and confidence at a time when they may be a little nervous. But this doesn't mean that you have to jump to your feet every time the judge asks you a question.

2. Don't read your statement. Reading in court is almost always a bore. Some people find it helpful to make a few notes on a card to serve as a reminder if they get nervous or forget something. If you decide to do this, list the headings of the various points you want to make in an outline form. Be sure your list is easy to read at a glance and that the topics are in the correct order. (I give a sample list in Chapter 13H.)

3. Be as brief as you can and still explain and document your case thoroughly.

4. Never interrupt your opponent or any of the witnesses no matter how outrageous their "lies." You will get your chance to respond.

5. Be prepared to present any section of your case that is difficult to get across in words, in another way. This means

bringing your used car parts, damaged clothing or other exhibits, such as photographs or cancelled checks with you, and having them organized for easy presentation.

6. There will be a blackboard in court. If a drawing will be helpful, as is almost always true in cases involving car accidents, be sure to make one. You will want to draw clearly and legibly the first time, so it's wise to have practiced in advance. If you wish to make a drawing and the judge doesn't ask you to, simply request permission to do so.

A SAMPLE CONTESTED CASE

Now let's take a typical case and pretend that someone has made written record of it (in fact, no transcript is made in Small Claims Court)

Clerk: "The next case is John Andrews v. Robertson Realty. Will everyone please come forward?" (Four people come forward and sit at the table facing the judge.)

Judge: "Good morning. Which one of you is Mr. Andrews? Okay, will you begin, Mr. Andrews?"

John Andrews: (stands) "This is a case about my failure to get a $400 cleaning deposit returned, your Honor. I rented a house from Robertson Realty at 1611 Spruce St. in Fresno in March of 19_ on a month-to-month tenancy. On January 10, 19_, I sent Mr. Robertson a written notice that I was planning to move on March 10. In fact, I moved out on March 8 and left the place extremely clean. All of my rent was properly paid. A few days after I moved out, I asked Mr. Robertson to return my $400 deposit. He wrote me a letter stating that the place was dirty and he was keeping my deposit.

I have with me a copy of a letter I wrote to Mr. Robertson on March 15 setting out my position in more detail. I also have some photographs that my friend Carol Spann, who is here as a witness, took on the day I moved out. I believe the pictures show pretty clearly that I did a thorough clean-up. (John Andrews hands the letter and pictures to the clerk who hands them to the judge.)

Your Honor, I am asking not only for the $400 deposit, but also for $200 in punitive damages plus 2% monthly interest that the law allows a tenant when a landlord improperly refuses to return a deposit."[2]

Judge: "Mr. Andrews, will you introduce your witness."

Andrews: "Yes, this is Carol Spann. She helped me clean up and move on March 7 and 8."

Judge: (looking at the pictures) "Ms. Spann, were you in the apartment the day John Andrews moved out?"

Carol Spann: (standing) "Yes, I was and the day before too. I helped clean up and I can say that we did a good job. Not only did we do the normal washing and scrubbing, but we waxed the kitchen floor and shampooed the rugs."

Judge: (turning to Mr. Robertson) "O.K., now it's your turn to tell me why the deposit wasn't returned."

---

[2] The legal rules on returning deposits and punitive damages for the failure to do so are contained in Section 1950.5 of the California Civil Code and are discussed in Chapter 8 of *The California Tenants' Handbook*, Moskovitz & Warner, Nolo Press.

Harry Robertson: (standing) "I don't' know how they could have cleaned the place up, your Honor, because it was filthy when I inspected it on March 9. Let me give you a few specifics. There was mildew and mold around the bathtub, the windows were filthy, the refrigerator hadn't been defrosted and there was dog—how shall I say it—dog manure in the basement. Your Honor, I have brought along Clem Houndstooth as a witness. Mr. Houndstooth is the tenant who moved in three days after Mr. Andrews moved out. Incidentally, your Honor, the place was so dirty that I only charged Mr. Houndstooth a $200 cleaning deposit, because he agreed to clean it up himself."

Judge: (looking at Clem Houndstooth) "Do you wish to say something?"

Clem Houndstooth: (standing) "Yes, I do. Mr. Robertson asked me to come down and back him up and I am glad to do it because I put in two full days cleaning that place up. I like a clean house, your Honor, not a halfway clean, halfway dirty house. I just don't think that a house is clean if the oven is full of gunk, there is mold in the bathroom, and the insides of the cupboards are grimy. All these conditions existed at 1611 Spruce St. when I moved in. I just don't believe that anyone could think that that place was clean."

Judge: "Mr. Andrews, do you have anything to add?"

John Andrews: (standing up) "Yes, I sure do. First, as to the mildew problem. The house is forty years old and there is some dampness in the wall of the bathroom. Maybe there is a leaky pipe someplace behind the tile. I cleaned it a number of times, but it always came back. I talked to Mr. Fisk in Mr. Robertson's office about the problem about a month after I moved in and he told me that I would have to do the best I could because they couldn't afford to tear the wall apart. As to the cupboards and stove, they are both old. The cabinets haven't been painted in ten years, so, of course, they aren't perfect, and that old stove was a lot dirtier when I moved in than it is now."

Judge: "What about the refrigerator, Mr. Andrews? Was that defrosted?"

John Andrews: "No, your Honor, it wasn't, but it had been defrosted about three weeks before I moved out and I thought that it was good enough the way it was."

Judge: "Okay, if no one else has anything to add, I want to return your pictures and letters. You will receive my decision by mail in a few days."

Now, I have a little surprise for you. This was a real case taking place not in Fresno, but in Small Claims Court in San Francisco. As they used to say on Dragnet, "Only the names have been changed to protect the innocent." And I have another surprise for you. I spoke to the judge after the court session and I know how the case came out. The judge explained his reasoning to me as follows.

"This is a typical case in which both sides have some right on their side. What is clean to one person may be dirty to another. Based on what I heard, I would have to guess that the old tenant made a fairly conscientious effort to clean up and probably left the place about as clean as it was when he moved in, but that the new tenant, Houndstooth, had much higher standards and convinced the landlord that it was filthy. The landlord may not have needed too much convincing since he probably would just as well keep the deposit. But I did hear enough to convince me that Andrews, the old tenant, didn't do a perfect job cleaning up. My decision will be that Andrews gets a judgment for the return of $250 of the $400 deposit, with no punitive damages. I believe that $150 is more than enough to compensate the landlord for any damages he suffered as a result of the apartment "being a little dirty.""

I then asked the judge if he felt that the case was well presented. He replied substantially as follows:

"Better than average. I think I got a pretty good idea of what the problems were. The witnesses were helpful and the pictures gave me an idea that the place wasn't a total mess. Both sides could have done better, however. Andrews could have had a witness to talk about the condition when he moved in if it was truly dirtier than when he left. Another witness to testify to the apartment's cleanliness when he moved out would have been good too. His friend, Carol Spann, seemed to be a very close friend and I wasn't sure that she was objective when it came to judging whether the place was clean. The landlord, Robertson, could also have done better. He could have presented a more disinterested witness, although I must say that Houndstooth's testimony was pretty convincing. Also he could have had pictures documenting the dirty conditions and an estimate from a cleaning company for how much they would have charged to clean the place up. Without going to too much trouble, I think that either side could have probably done somewhat better with more thorough preparation."

C. Don't Forget to Ask for Your Costs

When you finish your presentation to the judge, you should be sure he realizes that you have incurred certain costs. These can be added to the judgment amount. As I have mentioned, you can't recover for such personal expenses as taking time off from work to prepare for or attend court, paying a babysitter, or photocopy charges. You can recover for:

• Your court filing fee

• Service of process costs (In some districts, you must try and fail to serve papers by certified mail as a condition of the court awarding you the fees of a process server—see Chapter 11)

• Subpoenaed witness fees must be approved by the judge. Fees for subpoenaing witnesses and documents are only likely to be approved if absolutely necessary.

• The cost of obtaining necessary documents, such as verification of car ownership by the D.M.V.

If you forget to get your costs added to the judgment in court and want to go to the trouble, you can file a "Memorandum of Costs" with the Small Claims clerk within five days after judgment. Forms are available at the clerk's office. For information on recovering costs incurred after judgment when your opponent won't voluntarily pay the judgment, see Chapter 23C.

CHAPTER 16

Motor Vehicle Repair Cases

Most Small Claims Court cases fall into a dozen or so broad categories with perhaps another dozen subcategories. In the next six chapters, we look at the most common types of cases and discuss strategies to handle each. Even if your fact situation doesn't fit neatly in one of these categories, read them all. By picking up a few hints here and a little information there, you should be able to piece together a good plan of action. For example, many of the suggestions I make to handle motor vehicle repair disputes can also be applied to cases involving major appliances such as televisions, washers, and expensive stereos.

Let's start by imagining that you go to the auto repair shop to pick up your trusty, but slightly greying, steed after a complete engine overhaul. The bill, as agreed to by you in advance, is $1,225. This always seemed a little steep, but the mechanic had talked you into it based on his claim that he would do a great job and that the engine should last another

50,000 miles. At any rate, you write out a check and drive out of the garage in something approaching a cheerful mood. One of life's not so little hassles has been taken care of, at least temporarily.

You're right—temporarily can sometimes be a very short time. In this case, it lasts only until you head up the first hill. What's that funny noise, you think? Why don't I have more power? "Oh shit," you say (you never swear, but there are some extreme provocations where nothing else will do). You turn around and drive back to the garage. Not only are you out $1,225, but your car runs worse than it did when you brought it in.

Funny, no one seems as pleasant as they did before. Funny, no one seems to have time to listen to you. Finally, after several explanations and a bit of foot stomping, you get someone to say that they will look the car over again. You take a bus home, trying not to be paranoid. The next day you call the garage. Nothing has been done. You yell at the garage owner and then call your bank to stop payment on the check. You are told that it has already been cashed. The next day the garage owner tells you that the problem is in a part of the engine that they didn't work on. You only paid for a "short block job" they tell you. "Give us another $300 and we can surely solve this new problem," they add.

In disgust, you go down and pick up your handicapped friend and drive it home—slowly. You are furious and decide to pursue every legal remedy, no matter what the trouble. How do you start?

First, park your car, take a shower and have a glass of wine. Nothing gets decided well when you're mad. Now, going back to the reasoning we used at the beginning of this book, ask yourself some basic questions:

A. Have I Suffered a Loss?

That's easy. Your car doesn't work properly, you paid out a lot of money and the garage wants more to fix it. Clearly, you have suffered a loss.

B. Did the Negligence of the Garage Cause My Loss?

Ah ha, now we get to the nitty gritty. In this type of case you can almost always expect the garage to claim that they did their work properly and that the car simply needs more work. Maybe the garage is right—it's your job to prove that they aren't. Doing so will make your case; failing to do so will break it. You better get to work.

Step 1. Collect Available Evidence

First, get all evidence together where time is of the essence. In this fact situation, this means getting your used parts (it's a good idea to do this anytime you have major work done.) If the garage will not give them to you, make your request by letter, keeping a copy for your file. If you get the parts, fine—if you don't, you have evidence that the garage is badly run or has something to hide.

Step 2. Have The Car Checked

Before you drive many miles, have your car checked by an established local mechanic or mechanics. Sometimes it is possible to get a free estimate from a repair shop if they think they will get the job of fixing it. In this situation, however, you may be better off paying for someone to look at the engine thoroughly, as you want to be sure that at least one of the people who looks the car over is willing to come with you to Small Claims Court if the need arises, or at the very least, write a convincing letter stating what's wrong with the engine. One way to try and accomplish this is to take your car to a garage that someone you know already has a good personal relationship with.

Step 3. Try to Settle Your Case

By now you should have a pretty good idea as to what the first garage did wrong. Call them and ask that either the job be redone, or that they give you a refund of part or all of your money. Often the repair shop will agree to do some, or all, of the work over to avoid a further hassle. If they agree to take the car back, insist on a written agreement detailing what they will do and how long it will take. Also, talk to the mechanic who will actually work on the car to be sure he understands what needs to be done. Naturally, you may be a little paranoid about giving your car back to the garage that screwed it up, but unless they have been outrageously incompetent, this is probably your best approach at this stage. If you sue and the garage owner shows up in court and says he offered to work on the car again but you refused, it may weaken your case.

Step 4. Write A Demand Letter

If the garage isn't cooperative, it's time to write them a formal demand letter. Remember our discussion in Chapter 6. Your letter should be short, polite and written with an eye to a judge reading it. In this situation you could write something like this:

Haig Mackey
15 Orange St.
Laguna Beach, CA

Happy Days Motors
100 Speedway
Corona Del Mar, CA.

Dear People:

On August 13, 19_, I brought my 1978 Dodge to your garage. You agreed to do a complete engine rebuild job for $1,225. You told me, "Your car will be running like a watch when we're through with it." The car worked well when I brought it in, but was a little short on power. Two days later, when I picked up my car, it barely moved at all. The engine made such a clanging noise that I have been afraid to drive it.

I have repeatedly asked you to fix the car or to refund my money. You have refused. Shortly after the work was done, I asked for my used parts to be returned. You refused to give them to me, even though it is a violation of state law.

I have had several mechanics look my car over since you worked on it. They all agree that you did your job improperly and even installed some used parts instead of new ones. The work you did on the engine rings was particularly badly done.

After receiving no response from you, I had the work redone at a cost of $900. My car now works well. Please refund my $1,225. Should you fail to do so, I will exhaust all my legal remedies, including complaining to interested state and local agencies and taking this dispute to Small Claims Court. I hope to hear from you promptly.

Haig Mackey

cc: California Dept. of Consumer Affairs
    Bureau of Automotive Repair
    3116 Bradshaw Road
    Sacramento, CA

Note: Most small independent garages don't make any written warranty or guaranty of their work. However, if you were given any promises in writing, mention them here in your letter. Also, if you were told things orally about the quality of the work the garage planned to do and you relied on these statements as part of your decision to have the work done, you should call attention to this express verbal warranty (see Chapter 2E).

Step 5. File Your Court Papers

If you still get no satisfactory response from the garage, file your papers at the Small Claims clerk's office of your local Small Claims Court. Reread Chapters 7-10.

Step 6. Prepare for Court

If you want a third person (a judge) to understand your case, you must understand it yourself. Sounds simple, doesn't it? It does to me too until I get involved with machinery. My opinion of cars (and most other mechanical devices) is low—they are supposed to work without trouble, but most of us know better.

For me to argue a case in Small Claims such as the one we are talking about here could be a disaster unless I did some homework. This sort of disaster is repeated often in Small

Claims. I have seen many, many people argue cases about their cars knowing no more than "the car was supposed to be fixed, your Honor, and it's worse than ever." On some mornings when the roses are in bloom, the peaches are sweet and the angels are in heaven, this is enough to win—usually it isn't. Why? Because the people from the garage are likely to have a terrific sounding story about the wonderful job they did. They will talk about pistons, rings, bearings, pulling the head and turning the cam shaft. It's all likely to sound so impressive that you can easily find yourself on the defensive.

This sort of thing needn't happen if you are willing to learn a little about your car (or whatever machinery is involved). Fifteen minutes' conversation with a knowledgeable mechanic may be all you need to understand what's going on. Also, your local library will have manuals about every type of car, complete with diagrams, etc.

Remember the Judge: In Chapter 13 I mentioned that it's important to pay attention to whom you are presenting your case. Most Small Claims judges don't understand the insides of cars any better than you do. People often become lawyers because they don't like to get their hands dirty. So be prepared to deal with a person who nods his head but doesn't really understand the difference between the drive shaft and the axle. Car cases are sometimes easier to present to a woman judge. Cultural changes in the last few years notwithstanding, women still don't usually have the same ego involvement with being mechanical car experts that men do. They are often more willing to say "I don't know" and to listen.

Step 7. Appearing in Court

When you appear in court, be sure that you are well organized. Bring all the letters you have written, or received, about your car problem as well as written warranties (if any), photographs if they are helpful and your used parts if they aid in making your case. If you have a witness to any oral statements (warranties) made by the garage be sure to bring that person. Also, be sure to present any written letters by independent garage people who have examined your car. Several times in cases involving machinery, I have seen people give effective testimony by presenting a large drawing illustrating the screw-up. Also, be sure that you get your witnesses to the courtroom on time. The best way to do this is to pick them up at home or work and personally escort them.

If you are well prepared you should win the sort of case outlined here without difficulty. Judges drive cars and have to get them fixed; they tend to be sympathetic with this type of consumer complaint. Simply present your story (see Chapter 15), your documentation and your witnesses. If you feel that your opponent is snowing the judge with a lot of technical lingo, get his Honor back on the track by asking that the technical terms be explained in ordinary English. This will be a relief to everyone in the courtroom except your opponent. You will likely find that, once his case is shorn of all the magic words, it will shrink from tiger to pussycat.

CHAPTER 17

Motor Vehicle
Purchase Cases

All too often someone buys a motor vehicle, drives it a short way, and watches it fall apart. And all too often the seller won't stand behind the product sold or work out some sort of fair adjustment. There are major differences in approach between buying a new vehicle from a dealer, buying a used vehicle from a dealer and buying a used vehicle from a private party. Let's look at each situation individually.

A. New Vehicles

Here the most common problem is the lemon with major manufacturing defects. Before considering Small Claims Court, California consumers should fully understand the terms of CC Sec. 1793.2 (the lemon law). This law provides that if within one year or 12,000 miles the same nonconformity has been subject to repair four or more times by the manufacturer or its agents for a cumulative total of more than 30 calendar days, the manufacturer must either replace the goods or reimburse the buyer.

If, as part of the repair process, a dispute arises, it must first be submitted to a "qualified third party dispute resolution process if one exists" (see CC Sec. 1793.2(e) (3) for details). This is normally either an independent arbitration program run by the Better Business Bureau or a supposedly independent one established by the car company directly. If the buyer is not satisfied with this decision, he may then take the case to court.[1] The decision of the third party arbitrator shall be admissible in court, however.

Unfortunately, many disputes involving new vehicles don't fall under the lemon law. This would be the situation if the same defect didn't recur four times or if problems develop just after the warranty expires.

Sometimes it seems as though there is a little destruct switch set to flip fifteen minutes after you hit the end of the warranty period. Often too, a problem starts to surface while the car is still under warranty and a dealer makes inadequate repairs which last scarcely longer than the remainder of the warranty term. When the same problem develops again after the warranty has run out, the dealer refuses to fix it.

Not long ago I saw a case involving this sort of problem. A man—let's call him Bruno—with a new, expensive European car was suing the local dealer and the parent car company's West Coast representative. Bruno claimed that he had repeatedly brought the car into the dealer's repair shop with transmission problems while it was still under written warranty. Each time adjustments were made which seemed to eliminate the problem. But each time, after a month or so, the

---

[1] On the surface, it would seem you are limited to suing for $1,500 in Small Claims Court. This is true, but if you sue for this amount, you can also request equitable relief (see Chapter 4E). One form of equitable relief involves the judge rescinding the purchase contract and restoring you to your original position by court order (i.e., you get your money back). CCP 116.3a. I do not know of instances where this has been done, but it is possible.

same problem would reappear. A few months after the written warranty ran out, the transmission died. Even though the car was only a little over a year old, and had gone less than 20,000 miles, both the dealer and the parent car company refused to repair it. Their refusals continued even though the owner repeatedly wrote them, demanding action.

How did Bruno go about dealing with his problem? First, because he needed his car, he went ahead and had the repairs made. Then, although the repairs cost slightly in excess of $1,500—the Small Claims limit—he decided that because it was too expensive to hire a lawyer and sue in Municipal Court, he would scale down his claim and sue for the Small Claims maximum. Because the dealer was located in the same city as Bruno was, he sued locally.[2] In this situation it would have been adequate to sue only the local dealer and not the car company, but it didn't hurt to sue both following the general rule, "when in doubt, sue all possible defendants."

In court, Bruno was well prepared and had a reasonably easy time. Both he and his wife testified as to their trials and tribulations with the car. They gave the judge copies of the several letters they had written the dealer, one of which was a list of the dates they had taken the car to the dealer's shop. They also produced a letter from the owner of the independent

---

2 Only one defendant need be local to sue in a particular judicial district. The fact that the car company's West Coast headquarters was in a different part of the state didn't cause a problem with bringing the suit where the dealer was located (see Chapter 9).

garage which finally fixed the transmission stating that, when he took the transmission apart, he discovered a defect in its original assembly. The new car dealer simply testified that his mechanics had done their best to fix the car under the written warranty. He then contended that, once the written warranty had run out, he was no longer responsible. The dealer made no effort to challenge the car owner's story, nor did he bring his own mechanics to testify as to what they had done while the car was still under warranty. Bruno won. He presented a convincing case to the point that the defect had never been fixed when it should have been under the written warranty. The dealer did nothing to rebut it. As the judge noted to me after the hearing, a $18,000 car should come with a transmission that lasts a lot longer than this one did. Bruno would have had an even stronger case if he had brought the independent garage man to court, but the letters, along with his own testimony and that of his wife, were adequate in a situation where the dealer didn't put up much of a defense.

Note: In this sort of case it is very convincing to have documentation of all the trips you have made to the dealer's repair shop. You may be able to find copies of work orders you signed, or your cancelled checks. If you don't have this sort of record, sit down with a calendar and do your best to make an accurate list. Give the list to the judge in court. He will accept it as true unless the car dealer disputes it.

Even if your car is no longer covered by a written warranty when trouble develops, you may have a case. When a relatively new car falls apart for no good reason, many Small Claims Court judges bend over backwards to give you protection over and above the actual written warranty period that comes with the vehicle. Thus, if the engine on your properly maintained car burns out after 25,000 miles, you will stand a good chance of recovering some money even if the written warranty has expired.

In other words, many judges will not follow the strict letter of the law when doing so would produce a clearly unfair result. You may also wish to consider other remedies in addition to Small Claims Court such as trying to enlist the help of state regulatory agencies. One strategy of last resort if you don't have much equity in the car is to simply drive it to the dealer and leave it there, refusing to make any more payments until it is fixed. This is an extreme remedy and should only be considered in an extreme situation. It does have the beauty of shifting the responsibility to take action, legal or otherwise, to the other side. If you do this, be sure to set forth in writing all the circumstances surrounding the mechanical deficiencies and your efforts to remedy the situation, and send a copy to both the car dealer and the bank or other financial institution to whom you pay your loan.

Note: Particular models of cars are prone to particular problems. After a car has been in production for awhile, a pattern develops. Manufacturers are extremely sensitive to complaints in "high problem" areas and may even have issued an internal memo telling dealers to fix certain types of problems upon request. One reason for this is that they want to avoid Federal Government-required recalls. How can knowing this benefit you? By giving you the opportunity to pressure the company where it is most vulnerable. If your car which is no longer covered by a written warranty develops a serious problem before it should, talk to people at independent garages that specialize in repairing this type of car. If they tell you the problem is widespread and that the company has fixed it for some persistent customers, write a demand letter to the car dealer and manufacturer (see Chapter 6). Mention that if your problem is not taken care of you will sue in Small Claims Court and you will subpoena all records having to do with this defect (see Chapter 14). This may well cause the company to settle with you. If not, do both.

B. Used Vehicle Dealers

Recovering from used vehicle dealers can be tricky for several reasons. Unlike new vehicle dealers who are usually somewhat dependent upon their reputation in the community for honesty, used vehicle dealers commonly have no positive reputation to start with and survive by becoming experts at self-protection. Also (and don't underestimate this one), judges almost never buy used vehicles and therefore aren't normally as sympathetic to the problems used vehicle owners encounter. Chances are a judge has had a problem getting her new car fixed under a warranty, but has never bought a ten year old Plymouth in "tip-top shape," only to have it die two blocks after leaving Honest Al's.

The principal self-protection device employed by used vehicle dealers is the "as is" designation in the written sales contract. The salesperson may promise the moon, but when you read the fine print of the contract, you will see it clearly stated that the seller takes absolutely no responsibility for the condition of the vehicle and that it is sold "as is."

Time and again I have sat in court and heard hard luck stories like this:

"I bought the car for $1,200 two months ago. The man at 'Lucky Larry's' told me that it had a completely reconditioned engine and transmission. I drove the car less than 400 miles and it died. I mean really died— it didn't roll over and dig itself a hole, but it may as well have. I had it towed to an independent garage and they told me that, as far as they could see, no engine or transmission work had ever been done. They estimated that to put the car right would cost $800. I got one more estimate which was even higher, so I borrowed the $800 and had the work done. I feel I really got took by Lucky Larry. I have with me the cancelled check for the $800 in repairs, plus the mechanic who did the work who can testify as to the condition of the car when he saw it."

Unfortunately, this plaintiff will probably lose. Why? Because going back to the sort of issues we discussed in Chapter 2, he has proven only half of his case. He has shown his loss (he bought a $1,200 car that wasn't worth $1,200), but he has not dealt with the issue of the defendant's responsibility to make the loss good ("liability"). Almost surely the used car dealer will testify that he "had no way of knowing how long a ten year old Plymouth would last and that, for this very reason, sold the car 'as is.'" He will then show the judge a written contract that not only has the "as is" designation, but which will say someplace in the fine print that "this written contract is the entire agreement between the parties and that no oral statements or representations made by the dealer or any salesperson are part of the contract."

How can you fight this sort of cynical semi-fraud? It's difficult to do after the fact. The time for self-protection is before you buy a vehicle when you can have it checked by an expert and can insist that any promises made by the salesperson as to the condition of the car or the availability of repairs, be put in writing. Of course, good advice such as this, after the damage has been done, "isn't worth more than a passle of warm spit" as former Vice-President John Nance Garner so graphically put it. If you have just been cheated on a used car deal, you want to know what, if anything, you can do now. Here are some suggestions.

1. If the car broke almost immediately after you took it out of the used car lot, you can file in Small Claims and argue that you were defrauded. Your theory is that, no matter what the written contract said, there was a clear implication that you purchased a car, not a junk heap. When the dealer produces the "as is" contract you signed, argue that it is no defense to fraud. I discuss fraud in more detail in Chapter 2F.

2. If the dealer made any promises either in writing or orally about the good condition of the vehicle, he may be required to live up to them. Why? Because, as noted in Chapter 2E, statements about a product that you rely on as part of deciding whether to purchase constitute an express warranty. This is true even if the seller had you sign an "as is" statement which disclaims all warranties. The key to winning this sort of case is to produce a witness to the dealer's laudatory statements about the vehicle, copies of ads which state the car is in good shape, plus anything else which will back up your story.

3. If the seller of a used car provides any warranty at all (e.g., a 30-day warranty on parts only), the buyer is automatically entitled to the implied warranty of fitness (see Chapter 2 for more on this).[3] This implied warranty cannot be disclaimed. The duration of the implied warranty is the same as the written warranty, but not less than 30 days or more than 90 days. The point of knowing all of this is, of course, that if a used car breaks soon after purchase and you have received any warranty at all, you should tell the judge this and argue that the defects in the car constitute a breach of the implied warranty of general fitness and merchantability. In other words, the car you bought was so defective that it didn't meet the reasonable standards expected of even a used car.

4. You may want to consider having the car towed back to the lot and refusing to make future payments. This puts the burden on the bank or finance company to sue you, at which point you can defend on the basis of fraud. If you take this approach, be sure you have excellent documentation that the car was truly wretched. Of course, you will probably have made some down payment, so even in this situation you may wish to initiate action in Small Claims Court.

5. Have your car checked over by someone who knows cars and will be willing to testify if need be. If this person can find affirmative evidence that you were cheated, you will greatly improve your Small Claims case. They might, for example, find that the speedometer had been tampered with in violation of state law, or that a heavy grade of truck oil had been put in the

---

3 CC Secs. 1793, 1795.5

crank case so that the car wouldn't belch smoke. Also, this is the sort of case where a Subpoena Duces Tecum (subpoena for documents) might be of help (see Chapter 13). You might wish to subpoena records the car dealer has pertaining to his purchase price of the car, or its condition when purchased. It might also be helpful to learn the name of the car's former owner with the idea of contacting him. With a little digging you may be able to develop information that will enable you to convince a judge that you have been defrauded.

6. Consider other remedies besides Small Claims Court. These can include checking with your state Department of Consumer Affairs, or the local Department of Motor Vehicles to see if used car lots are regulated. In California and many other states, the Department of Motor Vehicles licenses used car dealers and can be very helpful in getting disputes resolved, particularly where your complaint is one of many against the same dealer for similar practices. Also, contact your local District Attorney's office. Most now have a consumer fraud division which can be of great help. If you can convince them that what happened to you smells rotten, or your complaint happens to be against someone they have already identified as a borderline criminal, they will likely call the used car dealer in for a chat. In theory, the D.A.'s only job is to bring a criminal action which will be of no direct aid in getting your money back, but in practice, negotiations often go on which can result in restitution. In plain words, this means that the car dealer may be told, "Look buddy, you're right on the edge of the law here (or maybe over the edge). If you clean up your act, which means taking care of all complaints against you and seeing that there are no more, we will close your file. If you don't, I suggest you hire a good lawyer because you are going to need one."

C. Used Vehicles From Private Parties

Normally it is easier to win a case against a private party than it is a used vehicle dealer. This runs counter to both common sense and fairness, as a private party is likely to be more honest than a dealer. But fair or not, the fact is that a non-dealer is usually less sophisticated in legal self-protection than is a pro. Indeed, in most private party sales the seller does no more than sign over the title slip in exchange for the agreed upon price. No formal contract is signed that says the buyer takes the car "as is."

If trouble develops soon after you purchase the vehicle and you are out money for unexpected repairs, you may be able to recover. Again, the problem is usually not proving your loss, but convincing the judge that the seller of the vehicle is responsible ("liable") to make your loss good. To do this, you normally must prove that the seller represented the vehicle to be in better shape than in fact it was, and that you relied on these promises when you made the deal.

Recently, I watched Barbara, a twenty-year-old college student, succeed in proving just such a case. She sued John for

$1,150, claiming that the B.M.W. motorcycle she purchased from him was in far worse shape than he had advertised. In court, she ably and convincingly outlined her conversations with John around the purchase of the motorcycle, testifying that he repeatedly told her that the cycle was "hardly used." She hadn't gotten any of his promises in writing, but she did a creative job of developing and presenting what evidence she had. This included:

• A copy of her letter to John which clearly outlined her position, such as the letter below:.

---

14 Stockton St.
Corte Madera, Calif.
January 27, 19__

John Malinosky
321 South Zaporah
Albany, Calif.

Dear Mr. Malinosky:

This letter is a follow-up to our recent phone conversation in which you refused to discuss the fact that the 19__ B.M.W. motorcycle I purchased from you on January 15 is not in the "excellent condition" that you claimed.

To review: on January 12, I saw your ad for a motorcycle that was "almost new— hardly used—excellent condition" in the local flea market newspaper. I called you and you told me that the cycle was a terrific bargain and that you would never sell it except that you needed money for school. I told you that I didn't know much about machinery.

The next day, you took me for a ride on the cycle. You told me specifically that:

1. The cycle had just been tuned up.

2. The cycle had been driven less than 10,000 miles.

3. The cycle had never been raced or used roughly.

4. That if anything went wrong with the cycle in the next month or two, you would see that it was fixed.

I didn't have the cycle more than a week when the brakes went out. When I had them checked, the mechanic told me that the carburetor also needed work (I confirmed this with another mechanic—see attached estimate). The mechanic also told me that the cycle had been driven at least 50,000 miles (perhaps a lot more) and that it needed a tune-up. In addition, he showed me caked mud and scratches under the cycle frame which indicated to him that it had been driven extensively off the road in rough terrain and had probably been raced on dirt tracks.

The low mechanic's estimate to do the repairs was $1,150. Before having the work done, I called you to explain the situation and to give you a chance to arrange for the repairs to be made, or to make them yourself. You laughed at me and said, "Sister, do what you need to do—you're not getting dime one from me."

Again I respectfully request that you make good on the promises (express warranty) you made to me on January 15. I relied on the truth of your statements (express warranty) when I decided to buy the bike. I enclose a copy of the mechanic's bill for $1,150, along with several higher estimates that I received from other repair shops.

Sincerely,
Barbara Parker

• Copies of repair bills (and estimates) dated within two weeks of her purchase of the cycle, the lowest of which came to $1,150.

• A copy of John's newspaper ad which she answered. It read: "B.M.W. 500 c.c., almost new—hardly used—excellent condition—$3,500."

• Finally, Barbara presented the judge with this note from the mechanic who fixed the cycle.

To Whom It May Concern:

It's hard for me to get off work, but if you need me, please ask the judge to delay the case a few days. All I have to say is this: the B.M.W. that Barbara Parker brought to me was in fair shape. It's impossible to be exact, but I guess that it had been driven at least 50,000-75,000 miles and I can say for sure that it was driven a lot of miles on dirt.

>   Respectfully submitted,
>   Al "Honker" Green
>   February 3, 19__

Barbara quickly outlined the whole story for the judge and emphasized that she had saved for six months to get the money to make the purchase.[4]

Next, John had his turn. He helped Barbara make her case by acting like a weasel. His testimony consisted mostly of a lot of vague philosophy about machinery. He kept asking "how could I know just when it would break?" When the judge asked him specific questions about the age, condition and previous history of the cycle, he clammed up as if he was a mafioso called to testify by a Senate anti-racketeering committee. When the judge asked him if he had, in fact, made specific guarantees about the condition of the bike, John began a long explanation about how when you sell things, you "puff them up a little" and that "women shouldn't be allowed to drive

---

4 This sort of testimony isn't relevant, but it never hurts. As an old appeals court judge who had seen at least 75 summers told me when I graduated from law school and was proud of my technical mastery of the law, "Son, don't worry about the law—just convince the judge that truth and virtue are on your side and he will find some legal technicality to support you." No one ever gave me better advice.

motorcycles anyway." Finally, the judge asked him to please sit down.

Important: In this type of case, absent a written warranty such as an ad that states the vehicle is in great shape, it's often one person's word against another's. Any shred of tangible evidence that the seller has made an express verbal warranty as to the condition of the goods can be enough to shift the balance to that side. Of course, if you have a friend who witnessed or heard any part of the transaction, his or her testimony will be extremely valuable. Getting a mechanic to check over a vehicle and then testify for you is also a good strategy. Sometimes you can get some help from the blue book that lists wholesale and retail prices for used cars. Several times I have seen people bring this book (car dealers have them) into court and show the judge that they paid above the bluebook price for a used car "because the car was represented to be in extra good shape." This doesn't constitute much in the way of real proof that you were ripped off, but it is helpful to at least show the judge that you paid a premium price for unsound goods.

Note on Written Warranties: As mentioned above in Section B3, if a seller makes any written warranty about the condition of a used car (or other goods), the buyer is also automatically entitled to the implied warranty that the vehicle is fit for its purpose (CC Secs. 1793, 1795.5). The duration of the implied warranty is the same as the written warranty, but not less than 30 days or more than 90 days. If the written warranty contains no time limit, argue that 90 days applies.

CHAPTER 18

Cases Where Money Is Owed

The most common type of Small Claims case involves the failure to pay money. Let's look at how these disputes commonly develop from both the debtor's and creditor's point of view.

A. From the Creditor's Point of View

The job of the plaintiff in a case where he or she is suing for non-payment of a debt is to prove that a valid debt exists and that it has not been paid. Here are a few suggestions.

1. Sue Promptly

When you are owed money, be sure you sue promptly. You will find a discussion of the Statutes of Limitations applicable to different sorts of debts in Chapter 5. But even when there is no danger that the limitation period will run out, it makes sense to proceed as soon as reasonably possible. Another reason to bring your case promptly is that judges just aren't as sympathetic to old claims. Several times when I have sat as judge, I have wondered why someone waited three years to sue for $500. Was it because she wasn't honestly convinced that her suit was valid? Perhaps the best reason to sue right away is that you will get your money faster. Indeed you may be pleasantly surprised that a considerable number of people who said they would never pay will, in fact, pay up when you demonstrate you are serious enough to go to court.

2. Written Contracts

If the debt is based on a written contract, be sure that your paperwork is in order. Bring to court the original copy of any written note proving the indebtedness so that the court can cancel it when the judgment is entered. Also bring any ledger sheets or other documentation as to any payments made, interest charged, etc. Often I have seen otherwise sensible looking business people show up with botched records and become flustered when closely questioned by the judge. The courtroom is not the place to straighten out a poor accounting system.

Note: If you provide goods or services, it's wise to include in all letters and bills to people who owe you money a request that they notify you if the goods are defective, or the services substandard. Bring copies of these notices to court. If the debtor shows up with a story about not paying because of some problem or defect, produce your documents. The fact that you requested to be informed about any problems with the product or service long ago and that no complaints were made previous to your court hearing will pretty clearly imply that the defendant is fabricating or at least exaggerating his current complaint.

3. Oral Contracts

A debt based on an oral contract is legal as long as the contract could have been carried out in one year. However, you may face a problem proving that the debt exists if the defendant denies that he borrowed the money, or bought the goods. Your best bet is to come up with some written documentation that your version of the story is true. If you have no written evidence (cancelled checks, letters or notes asking for more time to pay, etc.), your next step is to try to think of any person who knows about the debt and who is willing to testify. For example, if you asked the defendant to pay you and he said in the presence of your friend, "I'll pay you next month," or "You will never get your money back," or anything to indicate that a loan existed, bring your friend as a witness.

Of course, in many situations, no direct written or verbal evidence sufficient to prove the existence of a contract exists. If this is your situation, you will have to try and establish the existence of the contract by reference to the conduct of the parties. For example, if Richard, a professional painter, paints Tara's house, and Tara refuses to pay him, a judge will almost surely use what is known in law as the "quantum meruit doctrine"[1] to presume that an oral contact exists between the two calling for Tara to pay Richard a reasonable amount for his

---

[1] See Chapter 2 for a brief discussion of *"quantum meruit,"* which basically means that if a person receives goods or services in a situation where payment is normally expected, they are liable to pay.

work. (Judges, like everyone else, know that professional painters don't work for free.) However, it will be much harder for Richard to establish the amount and terms of the contract using this approach. Thus, if Richard says he was to be paid $20 per hour and Tara says he agreed to work for $15, Richard may have a hard time convincing the judge to award him the higher amount.

4. Proving Your Case

When it comes to establishing that money is owed, any business, whether incorporated or not, can send a bookkeeper to court (see Chapter 7D for detailed rules.) This works well if the defendant defaults (doesn't show up) or appears in court but doesn't dispute the amount owed. Unfortunately, a bookkeeper is not competent to testify if the defendant shows up and defends on the basis that the goods or services were defective, delivered late, etc. For example, if you own a TV repair business and are suing on an unpaid repair bill in a situation where you expect the defendant may show up in court and claim (whether falsely or not) that you did lousy work, you will need to have someone in court who knows the details of the particular job. If your business is not incorporated, this means you or a co-owner must appear (again, see Chapter 7). And unless you did the work personally, you will also find it necessary to bring the person who did as a witness. However, if you are incorporated, you have another valuable choice; your Board of Directors can authorize any employee not employed for the sole purpose of representing the corporation in Small Claims Court to appear in court d(you do not have to go yourself). This can be the employee who knows firsthand all the facts of the situation. In the context of this example, this would be the person who repaired the TV.

But what happens if you or your bookkeeper find yourself in Small Claims Court suing on what you think is a routine debt in a situation where you do not expect the defendant to show up and contest, and you are surprised by the presence of a fire-eating defendant who raises all sorts of substantive claims that you (or your bookkeeper) have no firsthand knowledge about?

Your best bet is to ask the judge to delay (continue) the case for a few days to give you the opportunity to get the right witness (or at least the person's written testimony) to court. Many judges will do this if they feel you made a sincere effort to be ready in the first place.

Note: Many businesses, and especially professionals such as doctors, dentists and lawyers, don't use Small Claims Court to collect unpaid bills because they think it takes too much of their own time, or is "undignified." You will have to worry about your "dignity" yourself, but I can tell you that Small Claims Court actions can be handled with very little time and expense once you get the hang of it. This is especially true when you consider that the alternative is to turn the bill over to a collection agency or not to collect it at all. As long as the suit simply involves getting a judgment for an unpaid bill, you can send your bookkeeper to court. Wait until you have several cases and schedule them on the same day. You will find that, once your bookkeeper understands the system, he or she can often be in and out of court in fifteen minutes to a half hour. Once you get your judgment, your secretarial staff should be able to handle the collection activities described in Chapter 23.

B. From the Debtor's Point of View

While there are an increasing number of private individuals using Small Claims Court, most plaintiffs are business people or employees of government entities, such as a library, hospital or city tax office, trying to collect debts. When I first watched debt collection cases, I did so with scant attention. I assumed that individuals being pursued by large institutions were bound to lose, especially since I assumed they mostly did owe the money. I even wondered why a lot of folks bothered to show up—knowing in advance that they had no defense, and no money. I thought it unjust that our society divided its bounty so unfairly and sad that the poor had no better defense than their inability to pay.

But then a curious thing happened. Many of the "downtrodden" I had dismissed so easily refused to play their docile parts. Instead of shuffling in with heads down and nothing constructive to say, they argued back, stamped their feet and acted like the proud and dignified people they were. I realized suddenly that I was the only person in the courtroom that had dismissed them. I learned that morning, and on dozens of later mornings, that there are lots of ways to constructively defend non-payment of debt cases. Here are some examples.

• A local hospital sued an unemployed man for failure to pay an emergency room bill for $478. It seemed an open and shut case—the person from the hospital had all the proper records, and the defendant hadn't paid. Then the defendant told his side of it. He was taken to the emergency room suffering from a superficial but painful gunshot wound. Because it was a busy night and he was not about to die, he was kept waiting two hours for treatment. When treatment was given, it was minimal and he suffered later complications that might have been avoided if he had been treated more promptly and thoroughly. He said he didn't mind paying a fair amount, but that he didn't feel he got $478 worth of care for seeing a doctor for less than twenty minutes. The judge agreed and gave judgment to the hospital for $150, plus court and service of process costs. After the defendant explained that he had only his unemployment check, the judge ordered that he be allowed to pay off the judgment at the rate of $10 per month.

• A large tire company sued a woman for not paying the balance on a tire bill. She had purchased eight tires for two pickup trucks and still owed $512.50. The tire company properly presented the judge with the original copy of a written contract along with the woman's payment record, and then waited for judgment. They are still waiting. The woman, who ran a small neighborhood gardening and landscaping business, produced several advertising flyers from the tire company which strongly implied that the tires would last at least 40,000 miles. She then testified and presented a witness to the fact that the tires had gone less than 25,000 miles before wearing out. The defendant also had copies of four letters written over the past year to the headquarters of the tire company in the Midwest complaining about the tires. Both in the letters, and in court, she repeatedly stated that the salesperson at the tire company told her several times that the tires were guaranteed for 40,000 miles. Putting this all together, the judge declared the tires should be pro-rated on the basis of 40,000 miles and gave the tire company a judgment for only $210, instead of the $512.50 requested. The woman wrote out a check on the spot and departed feeling vindicated.

• A rug company sued a customer for $686 and produced all the necessary documentation showing that the carpet had been installed, but no payment received. The defendant testified that the rug had been poorly installed with an uneven seam running down the center of the room. He had pictures that left no doubt that the rug installer was either drunk or blind. The defendant also presented drawings that illustrated that there were obviously several better ways to cut the carpet to fit the room. The rug company received nothing.

The point of these examples is not the facts of the individual situations—yours will surely differ. The point is that there are all sorts of defenses, and partial defenses, and that it makes good sense to defend yourself creatively if you feel that goods or services you received were worth less than you are being sued for (see Chapter 2 for information on warranties and fraud). It is usually not enough to tell the judge that you were dissatisfied with what you received. A little more imagination is required. If shoddy goods are involved, show them to the judge. If you received bad service, bring a witness or other supporting evidence. If, for example, you got roof repairs done that resulted in more holes than you had before, take pictures of the rain leaking in, and get an estimate from another roofer.

There is often a tactical advantage for the debtor in the fact that the person who appears in court on behalf of the creditor is not the same person that he had dealings with. If, for example, you state that a salesperson told you X, Y and Z, that person probably won't be present to state otherwise. This may tilt a closely balanced case to you. It is not inappropriate for you to point out to the judge that your opponent has only books and ledgers and no first hand knowledge of the situation. The judge may sometimes continue the case until another day to allow the creditor to have the employee(s) you dealt with present, but often this is impossible because the employee in question will have left the job, or be otherwise unavailable.

A Little More Time To Pay: In California (CCP 117) and in many other states, the judge has considerable discretion to order that a judgment be paid in installments. Thus, a judge could find that you owe the phone company $200, but allow you to pay it off at $20 per month, instead of all at once. Time payments can be particularly helpful if you don't have the money to pay all at once, but fear a wage attachment or other collection activity by the creditor. Don't be afraid to ask the judge for time payments—he or she won't know that you want them if you don't.

CHAPTER 19

Vehicle Accident Cases

It is a rare Small Claims session that does not include at least one fender bender. Usually these cases are badly prepared and presented. The judge commonly makes a decision at least partially by guess. I know from personal experience when I sat as a "pro tem" judge that it sometimes would not have taken much additional evidence for me to completely reverse a decision.

The average vehicle accident case that ends up in Small Claims Court doesn't involve personal injury, but is concerned with damage to one, or both, parties' car, cycle, R.V., moped or whatever.[1] Because of some quirk of character that seems to be deeply embedded in our overgrown monkey brains, it is almost impossible for most of us to admit that we are bad drivers, or

---

[1] Cases involving all but the most minor personal injuries don't belong in Small Claims Court as they are worth far more than the small claims maximum.

were at fault in a car accident. We will cheerfully acknowledge that we aren't terrific looking or geniuses, but we all believe that we drive like angels. Out of fantasies such as these are lawsuits made.

In Chapter 2, I discuss the concept of negligence. Please re-read this material. To recover in a vehicle accident case, you have to either prove that the other person was negligent and you were not or, if both of you were negligent, that you were less so. Normally dealing with concepts of negligence in a vehicle accident is a matter of common sense; you probably have a fairly good ideal of the rules of the road. If you are in doubt, however, consider whether either you or the other party violated any Vehicle Code provision relating to highway safety which contributed to the accident (see Section B below).

A. Who Can Sue Whom?

The owner of a vehicle is the correct person to file a claim for damage to the vehicle, even if he wasn't driving when the damage occurred. Suit for damage to the vehicle should be brought against the negligent driver of the other car. If that driver is not the registered owner, suit should also be brought against that person. In other words, both the driver and the registered owner are liable. To find out who owns a car, contact the Department of Motor Vehicles. As long as you can tell them the license number, they can tell you the registered owner.

B. Was There a Witness to the Accident?

Because the judge has no way of knowing what happened unless one or more people tell her, a good witness can make or break your case. It is better to have a disinterested witness than a close friend or family member, but any witness is better than no witness. If the other guy is likely to have a witness and you have none, you will have to work extra hard to develop other evidence to overcome this disadvantage. Re-read Chapter 14 for more information on witnesses. If you can't get a witness to show up in court, bring a written statement.

C. Police Accident Reports

When you have an accident and believe the other person was more at fault than you were, it is almost always wise to call the police so that a police report can be prepared. A police report is admissible as evidence in Small Claims Court.[2] The theory is that a cop investigating the circumstances of the accident at the scene is in a better position to establish the truth of what happened than is any other third party. So, if there was an accident report, buy a copy for a few dollars from the police station. If it supports you, bring it to court. If it doesn't, be prepared to refute what it says. This can best be done with the testimony of an eye witness. If both an eye witness and a police report are against you, try prayer.

Note: Many of you will be reading this book some considerable period of time after your accident. Obviously, my advice to call the police and have an accident report prepared will be of no use. Unfortunately, if the police are not called at the time of the accident, it's too late.

---

[2] *Davies v. Superior Ct.*, 36 CA3d 219 (1984).

D. Determining Fault

In Chapter 2 I discussed the general concept of negligence. While that discussion is fully applicable to motor vehicle cases (go back and read it if you haven't already), negligence can also be determined in these types of cases by a showing that the other driver caused the accident (in whole or in part) as a result of Vehicle Code violation. For instance, if Tommy runs a red light (prohibited by the Vehicle Code) and hits a car crossing the intersection, Tommy is negligent (unless he can offer a sufficient excuse for his action). On the other hand, if Tommy is driving without his seatbelt on (also prohibited by the Vehicle Code) and has an accident, the violation cannot be said to have caused the accident and therefore can't be used to determine negligence.

If there is a police report, the reporting officer may have noted any vehicle code violations which occurred relative to the accident. The report may even conclude that a vehicle code violation caused the accident. If there is no police report, or the report does not specify any violations, you may wish to do a little research on your own. The Vehicle Code is available in most large public libraries, all law libraries, and sometimes at the Department of Motor Vehicles. You can use its index to very quickly review dozens of driving rules which may have been violated by the other driver. If you discover any violations that can fairly be said to have contributed to the accident, call them to the attention of the judge. Congratulations, you have gone far towards establishing your negligence claim.

E. Diagrams

With the exception of witnesses and police accident reports, the most effective evidence is a good diagram. I have seen a good case lost because the judge never properly visualized what happened. All courtrooms have blackboards, and it is an excellent idea to draw a diagram of what happened as part of your presentation. If you are nervous about your ability to do this, you may want to prepare your diagram in advance and

bring it to court. Use crayons or magic markers and draw on a
large piece of paper about three feet square. Do a good job with
attention to detail. Here is a sample drawing that you might
prepare to aid your testimony if you were going eastbound on
Rose St. and making a right hand turn on Sacramento St. when
you were hit by a car that ran a stop sign on Sacramento. Of
course, the diagram doesn't tell the whole story—you have to
do that.

F. Photos

Photographs can sometimes be of aid in fender bender cases.
They can serve to back up your story about how an accident
occurred. For example, if you claimed that you were sideswiped
while you were parked, a photo showing a long series of
scratches down the side of your car would be helpful. It is also a
good idea to have pictures of the defendant's car if you can
manage to get them as well as photos of the scene of the
accident.

G. Estimates

It is important that you obtain several estimates for the cost of repairing your vehicle. Three is usually a good number. If you have already gotten the work done, bring your cancelled check or receipt from the repair shop, along with the estimates you didn't accept. Be sure to get your estimates from reputable shops. If, for some reason, you get an estimate from someone you later think isn't competent, simply ignore it, and get another. You have no responsibility to get your car fixed by anyone suggested to you by the person who caused the damage. Common sense normally dictates that you don't. Unfortunately, you can't recover money from the other party to cover the time you put in to get estimates, take your car to the repair shop, or to appear in court.

In addition to damage to your car, you can also recover for the fair market value of anything in your car that was destroyed. You must be prepared not only to establish the fact of the damage, but the dollar amount of the loss (see Chapter 5 for a discussion of what is involved in doing this). You can also recover for alternate transportation while your car is disabled. However, you can only recover for the minimum reasonable time it should take to get your car fixed. Thus, if you could arrange to get a fender fixed in two days, you are only entitled to rent a car for two days, even if an overworked mechanic takes four.

Defendant's Note: Sometimes plaintiffs dishonestly try to get already existing damage to their car fixed as part of getting the legitimate accident work done. If you think the repair bill is high, try developing your own evidence that this is so. If you have a picture of the plaintiff's car showing the damage, this can be a big help. Also, remember that the plaintiff is only entitled to get repairs made up to the total value of the car before the accident. If the car was worth only $500 and the repairs would cost $750, the plaintiff is only entitled to $500 (see Chapter 5).

H. Your Demand Letter

Here again, as in almost every other type of Small Claims Court case, you should write a letter to your opponent with an eye to the judge reading it. See the examples in Chapter 6. Here is another:

18 Channing Way
Fullerton, California

August 27, 19__

R. Rigsby Rugg
27 Miramar Crescent
Anaheim, California

Dear Mr. Rugg:

On August 15, 19__ I was eastbound on Rose Street in Fullerton, California at about 3:30 on a sunny afternoon. I stopped at the stop sign at the corner of Rose and Sacramento and then proceeded to turn right (south) on Sacramento. As I was making my turn, I saw your car going southbound on Sacramento. You were about 20 feet north of the corner of Rose. Instead of stopping at the stop sign, you proceeded across the intersection and struck my car on the front right fender. By the time I realized that you were coming through the stop sign, there was nothing I could do to get out of your way.

As you remember, after the accident the Fullerton police were called and cited you for failure to stop at a stop sign. I have gotten a copy of the police report from the police and it confirms the facts as I have stated them here.

I have obtained three estimates for the work needed on my car. The lowest is $612. I am proceeding to get this work done as I need my car fixed as soon as possible.

I will appreciate receiving a check from you as soon as possible. If you wish to talk about any aspect of this situation, please don't hesitate to call me, evenings at 486-1482.

Sincerely,
Sandy McClatchy

In court Sandy would present her case like this:

Clerk: "Next case, McClatchy v. Rugg. Please come forward."

Judge: "Please tell me what happened, Ms. McClatchy."

Sandy McClatchy: "Good morning. This dispute involves an auto accident that occurred at Rose and Sacramento Streets on the afternoon of August 15, 19_. I was coming uphill on Rose (that's east) and stopped at the corner. There is a four-way stop sign at the corner. I turned right, or south, on Sacramento Street, and as I was doing so, Mr. Rugg ran the stop sign on Sacramento and crashed into my front fender. Your Honor, may I use the blackboard to make a quick diagram?"

Judge: "Please do, I was about to ask you if you would."

Sandy McClatchy: (makes drawing like the one in D above, points out the movement of the cars in detail and answers several questions from the judge) "Your Honor, before I sit down, I would like to give you several items of evidence. First, I have a copy of the police accident report from the Fullerton police which states that Mr. Rugg got a citation for failing to stop at the stop sign in question. Second, I have some photos which show the damage to the front fender of my car. Third, I have my letter to Mr. Rugg, trying to settle this case and finally I have several estimates as to the cost of repairing the damage to my car. As you can see from my cancelled check, I took the lowest one."

Judge: "Thank you, Ms. McClatchy. Now, Mr. Rugg, it's your turn."

R. Rigsby Rugg: "Your Honor, my case rests on one basic fact. Ms. McClatchy was negligent because she made a wide turn into Sacramento Street. Instead of going from the right hand lane of Rose to the right hand, or inside lane, on Sacramento Street, she turned into the center lane on Sacramento Street. (Mr. Rugg moves to the blackboard and points out what he says happened.) Now it might be true that I made a rolling stop at the corner. You know, I really stopped, but maybe not quite all the way—but I never would have hit anybody if she had kept to her own side of the road. Also, your Honor, I would like to say this—she darted out; she has one of those little foreign cars and instead of easing out slow like I do with my Lincoln, she jumped out like a rabbit being chased by a red fox."

Judge: "Do you have anything else to say, Ms. McClatchy?"

Sandy McClatchy: "I am not going to even try to argue about whether Mr. Rugg can be rolling and stopped at the same time. I think the policeman who cited him answered that question. I want to answer his point about my turning into the center lane on Sacramento St., instead of the inside lane. It is true that, after stopping, I had to make a slightly wider turn than usual. If you will look again at the diagram I drew, you will see that a car was parked almost to the corner of Sacramento and Rose on Sacramento. To get around this car, I had to drive a little farther into Sacramento before starting my turn than would have been necessary otherwise. I didn't turn into the center lane, but as I made the turn, my outside fender crossed into the center lane slightly. This is when Mr. Rugg hit me. I feel that since I had the right of way and I had to do what I did to make the turn, I wasn't negligent."

Judge: "Thank you both—you will get my decision in the mail."

(The judge decided in favor of Sandy McClatchy and awarded her $612 plus service of process and filing costs.)

Comparative Negligence Note: As I discuss in Chapter 2, you can win, or partially win, a case involving negligence even if you were not completely in the right. As long as the other person was more negligent than you were, you are entitled to some recovery.

Professional Driver Note: Be particularly wary when you are opposing a bus or truck driver. Many of these people suffer problems on their jobs if they are found to be at fault in too many accidents. As a result, they deny fault almost automatically. Judges usually know this and are often unsympathetic when a bus driver says that there has never been a time when he "didn't look both ways twice, count to ten and say the Lord's Prayer" before pulling out from a bus stop. Still, it never hurts to question the driver in court as to whether his employer has any demerit system or other penalty for being at fault in an accident.

CHAPTER 20

Landlord-Tenant Cases

Small Claims Court can be used by a tenant to sue for money damages for such things as the failure of a landlord to return a cleaning or damage deposit, invasion of the tenant's privacy, or landlord's violation of his duty to provide habitable premises, and rent control violations, to name but a few. A landlord can use Small Claims Court to sue a tenant or former tenant for damage done to the rental property. In some situations it is also possible for a landlord to use it to evict a tenant. This is an exception to the general rule that only money judgments can be handed down by Small Claims Courts. It makes great sense to use Small Claims Court for money damage cases, and a lot less sense to use it for evictions. Evictions are usually handled better in Municipal Court. Why? Because, in Small Claims Court, the defendant has an automatic right to appeal the eviction judgment and to remain living in the rental unit while the appeal is pending even though no rent is paid (see Section C below).

A. Deposit Cases

The most common landlord-tenant disputes concern the failure of a landlord to return a tenant's cleaning and damage deposits after the tenant moves out. These days, deposits can add up to many hundreds of dollars and tenants understandably want them returned. No matter what they are called (e.g., cleaning, damage, security, etc.), all deposits are refundable in full if the rental unit is left clean and undamaged.[1] Non-refundable fees and deposits for rental housing are illegal in California. The law also states that if a deposit is not returned within two weeks from the time the tenant moves out and if the landlord acted in bad faith in retaining the deposits, the tenant may be entitled to $200 in "punitive" damages, over and above the actual amount of the deposits, plus interest on the withheld deposit at 2% a month.[2] Whether or not the tenant actually gets punitive damages is a matter of judicial discretion, but it never hurts to bring your suit for an amount that includes them.

Going to court if a landlord refuses to return a deposit can be easy or difficult depending upon both the facts of the situation and on how much homework the tenant does in advance of filing suit. Many landlords are experienced with Small Claims proceedings and come to court prepared with a long list of damaged and dirty conditions that they claim the tenant left behind. All too often, the landlord's presentation leaves the tenant sputtering with righteous indignation. Unfortunately evidence, not indignation, wins cases. Think about it—if the tenant testifies the apartment was clean, and the landlord that it was dirty, the judge (unless he is psychic) is stuck making a decision that is little more than a guess. Faced with this sort of situation, most judges will split the difference.

How should a tenant prepare a case involving failure to return deposits? Ideally, preparation should start when he or she moves in. Any damaged or dirty conditions should be noted as part of the lease or rental agreement. The tenant should also

---

[1] CC Sec. 1950.5.
[2] CC Sec. 1950.5.

take photographs of substandard conditions and have
neighbors or friends look the place over. When the tenant
moves out and cleans up, he should do much the same
thing—take photos, have friends check the place over, keep
receipts for cleaning materials and once the place is cleaned up,
try and get the landlord to agree that it is in satisfactory
condition.[3]

Now let's assume that you are a tenant and have not gotten
$600 in cleaning and damage deposits returned even though you
moved out of an apartment three weeks ago, having paid all
your rent and having given proper notice. Start by writing the
landlord a letter like this:

[3] All of this is discussed in more detail in *The California Tenants'
Handbook*, Moskovitz and Warner and *The Landlord's Law Book
(Vol.1): Rights and Responsibilities*, Brown and Warner. Both of these
books contain a tear-out room-by-room inventory sheet so that the
landlord and tenant can inspect the place on moving in and moving
out and jointly record the results.

1700 Walnut Street
Costa Mesa, California
October 15, 19__

Anderson Realty Co.
10 Rose St.
Costa Mesa, California

Dear People:

As you know, until September 30, 19__, I resided in apartment #4 at 1700 Walnut Street and regularly paid my rent to your office. When I moved out, I left the unit cleaner than when I moved in.

As of today, I have received neither my $300 cleaning deposit nor my $300 damage deposit. Indeed, I have never received any accounting from you for any of my money. Please be aware that I know my rights under California Civil Code 1950.5 and that, if I do not receive my money within the next week, I will regard the retention of these deposit as showing "bad faith" on your part and shall sue you, not only for the $600 deposit, but also for the $200 punitive damages allowed by Section 1950.5 of the California Civil Code.

May I hear from you soon.

Sincerely,
Farah Shields

If you get no satisfactory response, file your case. Sometimes it is hard to know who to sue, since rent is often paid to a manager or other agent instead of the owner. Multiple occupancy buildings with 2 or more units must have ownership information posted on the premises, or list the name of the owner (or his agent for purposes of suit) on the rental agreement. If you are in doubt as to who owns your building, you are probably safe if you sue both the person to whom you pay your rent, and the person who signed the rental agreement, unless you have received notice that the building has been transferred to a new owner, in which case you would sue that person.

On court day a well-prepared tenant would show up in court with as many of the following pieces of evidence as possible:

• Photos of the apartment on moving in which show any dirt or damage that already existed.

• Photos of the apartment on moving out which show clean conditions.

• Receipts for cleaning supplies used in the final clean-up.

• A copy of your written lease or rental agreement, if any.

• A copy of a demand letter to the landlord such as the one set out above.

• One, or preferably two, witnesses who were familiar with the property and saw it after you cleaned up and who will testify that it was immaculate. People who helped in the clean-up are always particularly effective witnesses. If you also have a witness who saw the place when you moved in and who will say that it wasn't so clean (or damage already existed), so much the better.

• A copy of an inventory of conditions when moving in and moving out, signed by the landlord and tenant, if one was prepared.

Proceedings in court should go something like this:

Clerk: "Shields v. Anderson Realty. Please step forward."

Judge: "Good morning. Please tell me your version of the facts, Ms. Shields."

Farah Shields: "I moved into the apartment at 1700 Walnut St. in Costa Mesa in the spring of 19__. I paid Mr. Anderson here my first and last months' rent which totaled $400. I also paid him a $600 security deposit.

When I moved into #4 at 1700 Walnut, it was a mess. It's a nice little cottage, but the people who lived there before me were sloppy. The stove was filthy, as was the bathroom, the refrigerator, the floors and just about everything else. In addition, the walls hadn't been painted in years. But I needed a place and this was the best available, so I moved in despite the mess. I painted the whole place—everything. Mr. Anderson's office gave me the paint, but I did all of the work. And I cleaned the place thoroughly too. It took me three days. I like to live in a clean house.

Here are some pictures of what the place looked like when I moved in (hands photos to clerk who gives them to the judge). Here is a second set of photos which were taken after I moved out and cleaned up (again hands pictures to clerk). Your Honor, I think these pictures tell the story—the place was clean when I moved out. I also have receipts (hands to clerk) for cleaning supplies and a rug shampooer that I used during the clean-up. They total $18.25. I have also brought two people who saw the place the day I left and can tell you what it looked like."

Judge: (looking at one of the witnesses) "Do you have some personal knowledge of what this apartment looked like?"

John DeBono: "Yes, I helped Farah move in and move out. I simply don't understand what the landlord is fussing about. The place was a smelly mess when she moved in, and it was spotless when Farah moved out."

Judge: (addressing the second witness) "Do you have something to add?"

Puna Polaski: "I never saw 1700 Walnut when Farah moved in because I didn't know her then. But I did help her pack and clean up when she moved out. I can tell you that the windows were washed, the floor waxed and the oven cleaned because I did it. And I can tell you that the rest of the cottage was clean too, because I saw it."

Judge: "Mr. Anderson, do you want to present your case."

Adam Anderson: "Your Honor, I am not here to argue about whether the place was clean or not. Maybe it was cleaner when Miss Shields moved out than when she moved in. The reason I withheld the deposits is that the walls were all painted odd, bright colors and I have had to paint them all over. Here are some color pictures of the walls taken just after Miss Shields moved out. They show pink and purple walls, two of which are adorned with rainbows. And in one of the bedrooms, there were even animals painted on the walls. I ask you, your Honor, how was I going to rent that place with a purple bulldog painted on the wall? It cost me more than $300 to have the place painted over white."

Judge: (looks at the pictures and gives up trying to keep a straight face, which is okay, as everyone in the courtroom is laughing except Mr. Anderson) "Let me ask a few questions. Was it true that the place needed a new coat of paint when you moved in, Ms. Shields?"

Farah Shields: "Yes."

Judge: "Do you agree, Mr. Anderson?"

Adam Anderson: "Yes, that's why my office paid her paint bills although we never would have if we had known about that bulldog, not to mention the rainbows."

Judge: "How much did the paint cost?"

Adam Anderson: "$125."

Judge: "I normally send decisions by mail, but today I am going to explain what I have decided. First, the apartment needed repainting anyway, Mr. Anderson, so I am not going to give you any credit for paying to have the work done. However, Ms. Shields, even though the place looked quite— shall I say, cheerful—when you moved out, Mr. Anderson does have a point in that you went beyond what is reasonable. Therefore, I feel that it's unfair to make Anderson Realty pay for paint twice. My judgment is this: The $125 for the paint that was given to Ms. Shields is subtracted from the $600 deposits. This means that Anderson Realty owes Farah Shields $475 plus $9.00 for costs."

Note: We have focused here on deposits cases from the tenant's point of view. This is because tenants are the ones who initiate this sort of case. Landlords, who commonly must defend deposit cases, should carefully read the list of evidence that is helpful in court. Often the best witness for a landlord is the new tenant who has just moved in. This person is likely to feel that the place isn't as clean as did the person who moved out.

B. Money Damage Cases— Unpaid Rent

Landlords most commonly initiate Small Claims actions to sue for unpaid rent. Often the tenant has already moved out and doesn't bother to show up in court. If this happens, the landlord wins by default. Sometimes the tenant does show up, but presents no real defense and is only there to request the judge to allow him to make payments over time.

The landlord (or a bookkeeper who complies with rules set out in Chapter 7D) should bring the lease or rental agreement to court and simply state the time periods for which rent is due, but unpaid. Nothing else is required unless the tenant presents a defense as discussed below. Sometimes a landlord will sue for three times the amount of rent owed (triple damages) under a lease or rental agreement that states that he is entitled to them if the tenant fails to pay rent, but stays in the rental unit. Doing this will almost guarantee that the tenant will put up a fight. In my experience landlords are rarely awarded more than their actual out-of-pocket loss, and it makes little sense to request more.

There are several valid defenses to a suit based on a tenant's failure to pay rent. The principal one is where the tenant claims that rent was withheld because the condition of the premises was "uninhabitable."[4] This amounts to the tenant saying to the landlord: "I won't pay my rent until you make necessary repairs."[5] It is legal to do this in California under the authority of the court decision in *Green v. Superior Court*, 10 Cal. 3d 616. The important thing for a tenant to understand is that rent withholding is not legal where the landlord refuses to fix some minor defect. For rent to be legally withheld, the condition needing repair must be sufficiently serious as to make the home "uninhabitable," unhealthy or unsafe. In addition, the landlord must have been given reasonable notice to correct the problem. Thus, a broken furnace that a landlord refuses to fix would qualify as a condition making a home uninhabitable in the winter, but lack of heat in the summer would not.

If you are involved in a rent withholding case as a tenant, your job is to prove (pictures, witnesses, etc.) that the condition that caused you to withhold rent is indeed serious. Thus, you might call the building inspector or an electrician to testify that the wiring was in a dangerous state of decay. The landlord, of course, will probably testify that the rental unit is in fundamentally sound shape, even though there may be some minor problems. A landlord has the right to inspect the property as long as she gives the tenant reasonable notice (see Section D below for the legal rules in this area).

C. Obnoxious Behavior

Occasionally a particular landlord or tenant can get pretty obnoxious. This is also true of plumbers, physics teachers, and

---

[4] Under California law it is also legal for a tenant to have repairs done himself under some circumstances and deduct the cost from one month's rent. See California CC Secs. 1941-42. This "repair and deduct" remedy is also discussed in detail in *The California Tenants' Handbook* and *The Landlord's* Law Book (Vol.1).

[5] Often a tenant who fails to pay rent is brought to court by the landlord as part of an eviction action. If the tenant can prove that rent was withheld for a valid reason, he or she can't be evicted for exercising this right. See Section C of this chapter.

hair stylists, but since this chapter is about landlord-tenant disputes, we will concentrate on these folks.

From the start, there is a major difference between how landlords and tenants handle problems. This is because landlords have two advantages tenants don't have. First, they can charge deposits, and if a tenant fails to pay rent or damages the place, a landlord can often recover her loss by subtracting the amount in question from the deposit. In addition, the landlord usually has the right to ask a tenant to move out. (If the tenant has a lease or the unit is located in a city requiring just cause for eviction, this right is restricted.[6]) Tenants, on the other hand, have neither of these rights and, as a result, are much more likely to sue for money damages in Small Claims Court when they are seriously aggrieved.

Typically, tenants have problems with landlords who cannot stop fidgeting and fussing over their property. Smaller landlords tend to develop this problem to a greater extent than do the larger, more commercial, ones. Nosy landlords are always hanging around or coming by, trying to invite themselves in to look around and generally being pests. In addition, a tenant may also run into a manager who is on a power trip.

If a landlord or manager is difficult or unpleasant to deal with, she can make a tenant's life miserable. There is no law which protects a tenant from a landlord's disagreeable personality, and, if the tenant has no lease, she is especially unprotected from all but the most outrageous invasions of privacy or trespass. However, if the landlord's conduct is truly obnoxious, courts recognize that tenants have a right to sue for the intentional infliction of emotional distress. In the case of *Newby v. Alto Riviera Apts.*, 60 Cal.App.3d 288 (1976),[7] the

---

[6] We discuss these points in detail in the *California Tenant's Handbook*, Moskovitz and Warner and the *Landlord's Law Book (Vol. 1): Rights and Responsibilities*, Brown and Warner, both published by Nolo Press.

[7] Also see *Stoiber v. Honeychuck*, 101 Cal.App.3d 903 (1980), where a court awarded a tenant damages for the mental distress suffered from having to live in slum conditions.

court found that it was necessary to prove four things in this sort of lawsuit:

1. Outrageous conduct on the part of the landlord;

2. Intention to cause, or reckless disregard of the probability of causing, emotional distress;

3. Severe emotional suffering;

4. Actual suffering or emotional distress.

D. The Landlord's Right of Entry and The Tenant's Right of Privacy

One area where tenants are easily and understandably upset is when they feel their privacy is invaded. Landlords, on the other hand, have a legal right to enter their rental units in certain situations. Sometimes a tenant's needs to be left alone and a landlord's need to enter conflict. If they do, it is extremely important that both parties understand their rights.

Section 1954 of the California Civil Code establishes the circumstances under which a landlord can enter his tenant's home, and Section 1953 (a)(1) provides that these circumstances cannot be expanded, or the tenant's privacy rights waived or modified, by any lease or rental agreement provision. The first thing to realize is that there are only four broad situations in which a landlord may legally enter while a tenant is still in residence. They are:

1. To deal with an emergency;

2. To make needed repairs (or assess the need for them):

3. To show the property to prospective new tenants or purchasers; and

4. When you invite the landlord in.

In most instances (emergencies and tenant invitations excepted), a landlord can enter only during "normal business hours" (9:00 a.m. to 5:00 p.m.) and then only after "reasonable notice," presumed to be 24 hours.

If a landlord does not follow these rules, a tenant's first step is to politely ask him to do so. If violations persist, a letter is in order. If this doesn't help, it is possible to sue in Small Claims Court for invasion of privacy if the landlord's conduct is persistently outrageous.

E. Evictions

It is legal to do some types of evictions in Small Claims Court. This includes the situation where a tenant of residential property has a written or oral, month-to-month (or week-to-week) rental agreement and is behind in the rent. If a lease is involved giving the tenant a set term of occupancy longer than 30 days, or if the eviction is for some reason other than non-payment of rent, the eviction action cannot be brought in Small Claims Court.

Without question, landlords should have a simple and cheap way to free themselves of tenants who don't pay their rent. Unfortunately, Small Claims Court, as presently set up, isn't it. If a landlord wants to be sure to get a tenant out without ridiculous delays, an "unlawful detainer" action must be filed in Municipal Court. This is because, as noted above, if a tenant loses in Small Claims Court, she has the automatic right to remain in the premises if she appeals to Superior Court, where she is entitled to a new trial. The *California Landlord's Law Book: Evictions (Vol. II)* tells landlords how to fill out the Municipal Court papers themselves.

Because I recommend that all evictions be done in Municipal Court, I do not go into detail here about how to handle this procedure in Small Claims Court. However, if despite my advice you plan to bring an unlawful detainer in Small Claims Court, you must first serve the defendant (tenant) with a three-day notice to pay all rent currently due or leave the premises.[8] A copy of this notice should be retained to show the Small Claims Court. Only after the three-day notice has run out can an "unlawful detainer" be filed. The three-day notice must be personally served on the tenant by the landlord himself or by anyone else 18 or over.

A proof of service should be filled out. All forms and instructions necessary to prepare a three-day notice are contained in the *Landlord's Law Book (Vol 1): Rights and Responsibilities* (Brown and Warner)

The form necessary to bring an "unlawful detainer" (eviction) action in Small Claims Court looks like this.

---

8 The notice must be in the alternative (e.g., pay or move)—a notice that simply tells the tenant to get out is not legal and can be challenged later by the tenant in court. Only after a proper three-day notice has run out can the landlord legally start his eviction action.

Name and Address of Court:

SMALL CLAIMS CASE NO.

— NOTICE TO DEFENDANT — YOU ARE BEING SUED BY PLAINTIFF	— AVISO AL DEMANDADO — A USTED LO ESTAN DEMANDANDO
To protect your rights, you must appear in this court on the trial date shown in the table below. You may lose the case and YOU MAY BE EVICTED from your home if you do not appear. The court may award the plaintiff the amount of the claim and the costs. Your wages, money, and property may be taken without further warning from the court.	Para proteger sus derechos, usted debe presentarse ante esta corte en la fecha del juicio indicada en el cuadro que aparece a continuación. Si usted no se presenta, puede perder el caso, Y PUEDEN OBLIGARLO DESALOJAR SU CASA. La corte puede decidir en favor del demandante por la cantidad del reclamo y los costos. A usted le pueden quitar su salario, su dinero, y otras cosas de su propiedad, sin aviso adicional por parte de esta corte.

PLAINTIFF/DEMANDANTE (Name and address of each):

John Landlord
33 Orange
Berkeley, CA 94702

DEFENDANT/DEMANDADO (Name and address of each):

Tillie Tenant
160 11th Street
Berkeley, CA 94710

☐ See attached sheet for additional plaintiffs and defendants

PLAINTIFF'S CLAIM FOR EVICTION AND MONEY

1. I am entitled to possession of the residential property located in this judicial district at (street address, city, and county):
   160 11th Street, Berkeley, CA 94710

2. Defendant agreed to rent this property for $ 400.00 ☒ per month ☐ per other shorter period (specify):
   The rent is ☒ due on first of the month ☐ due on other day (specify):

3. Defendant owes me the sum of
   a. $ 350.00   for rent due as of (date): Dec. 25   for the months of (specify):
      plus $ 13.33   per day thereafter.
   b. ☐ and $ for (specify):

4. I have served a Notice to Pay Rent or Quit on defendant. The notice expired on (date): Dec. 25

5. Defendant has not paid the rent and is in possession of the property without my consent.

6. I have performed all conditions of the rental agreement and complied with all applicable laws and ordinances.

7. ☐ I have filed more than 12 claims in this court, including this claim, during the previous 12 calendar months.

8. I understand that
   a. I may talk to an attorney about this claim, but I cannot be represented by an attorney at the trial in the small claims court.
   b. I must appear at the time and place of trial and bring all witnesses, books, receipts, and other papers or things to prove my case.
   c. I have no right of appeal on my claim, but I may appeal a claim filed by the defendant in this case.
   d. If I cannot afford to pay the fees for filing or service by a sheriff, marshal, or constable, I may ask that the fees be waived.

9. I have received and read the information sheet explaining some important rights of plaintiffs in the small claims court.
   I declare under penalty of perjury under the laws of the State of California that the foregoing is true and correct.

Date:
   John Landlord
   (TYPE OR PRINT NAME)   (SIGNATURE OF PLAINTIFF)

ORDER TO DEFENDANT

You must appear in this court on the trial date and at the time LAST SHOWN IN THE BOX BELOW if you do not agree with the plaintiff's claim. Bring all witnesses, books, receipts, and other papers or things with you to support your case.

TRIAL DATE FECHA DEL JUICIO	DATE	TIME	PLACE	COURT USE
1.				
2.				
3.				

Filed on (date):   Clerk, by_____, Deputy

— You have a right to a small claims advisor free of charge. Read the information sheet on the reverse. —

Form Adopted by the
Judicial Council of California
SC-110 (Rev. January 1, 1987)

PLAINTIFF'S CLAIM AND ORDER
TO DEFENDANT — UNLAWFUL DETAINER
(Small Claims)

Rule 982.7

When a landlord gets to Small Claims Court, he must prove that the rent was not paid and that a correct three-day notice was properly served. Bring a copy of the three-day notice to court and a "proof of service" form filled out by the person doing the service. The fact that a tenant is suffering from some hardship such as illness, poverty, birth of a child, etc., is not a defense to failure to pay rent. Possible tenant defenses are discussed briefly in Section B of this chapter. These include rent withholding because of a condition in the rental property that makes it uninhabitable. A tenant cannot legally raise the existence of a defect for the first time on the day of the court hearing. The landlord must be given reasonable notice that a defect exists before rent is withheld, or repairs are made.

Self-Help Evictions: It is illegal in California for a landlord to try and force a tenant, no matter how obnoxious, to move without filing an unlawful detainer. For example, if the landlord causes any utility service to be cut off with intent to terminate a tenant's occupancy, a court will order the utility service restored and award the tenants out-of-pocket damages, punitive damages of up to $100 per day (but not less than $250 for each violation) plus attorney fees.[9]

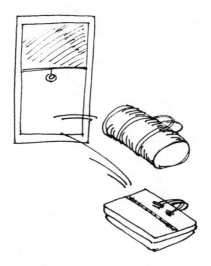

---

9 CC Sec. 789.3.

Small Business, Small Claims

More and more, people who own or manage small businesses are turning to Small Claims Court to settle business disputes that they have been unable to compromise. They have learned that Small Claims Court is a relatively fast and cost efficient way to resolve business differences.

This chapter didn't appear in the first few editions of this book because I naively assumed that Chapter 18—"Cases In Which Money Is Owed"—provided sufficient information to solve the problems of business people. It's here now because I have had so many requests from friends who own their own small businesses asking for additional information. It turned out, of course, that although many disputes between small business people involve a simple failure to pay money, a significant number are more complicated. Commonly these more complex disputes involve people who have had a continuing business relationship and find themselves in the midst of a major misunderstanding that goes beyond the refusal to pay a bill. Often both parties are in court because they feel badly used—perhaps even "ripped off" or "cheated" by the other.

I have been asked for advice on preparing Small Claims Court cases by a surprising variety of business people. For example, requests for help have come from a dentist furious at a dental equipment wholesaler, an industrial designer who hadn't been paid for drawing preliminary plans, a typesetter being sued by his former accountant in a dispute involving the value of the latter's services, a landscape architect who was trying to enforce a verbal agreement that he could increase his bid after a client asked for changes in final plans, and an author who claimed that her publisher had taken too long to publish her book. Although these disputes seem quite different from one another at first impression, they all turned out to have one thing in common—in each situation the disputants had enjoyed friendly business relationships at some time in the past. And in each case, at least part of the reason that the plaintiff brought the dispute to court was that he was mad.

A. Organizing Your Case

Business people normally have two advantages over ordinary mortals when it comes to preparing for court. First; as a matter of course, they maintain a recordkeeping system which includes files, ledgers, and increasingly, computer storage devices. Taken together, these resources normally contain considerable raw material helpful to successfully proving a case. The second advantage is more subtle, but no less real. It involves the average small businessperson's organizational skill—that is, his or her ability to take a confused mess of facts and organize them into a coherent and convincing narrative. Small business people who don't quickly develop good organizational skills commonly aren't in business long enough to even consider going to court. But the fact that business people begin with a little head start isn't usually much of an advantage when it comes to dealing with another business person. This is because two head starts have a way of cancelling one another out, with the only beneficiary being the judge, who gets to officiate a more coherent dispute.

Here are several hints that may be of real value when thinking about how to present a business case. This material is meant to supplement, not replace, the information contained in the rest of the book, particularly Chapters 2, 6, 13, 14, and 15. If you haven't already done so, I think you will find it helpful to read these chapters before continuing.

1. Contracts

Most business cases involve one person claiming that the other has broken a contract (see Chapter 2). Start by asking yourself the exact nature of the contract which was involved in your case. That is, what were your obligations and expected benefits from the deal, what was the other person supposed to do, and what was he or she going to get out of the deal?

Remember that oral contracts that can be carried out in one year (even if they actually take longer) are legal and enforceable in California. But remember, too, that oral agreements raise real problems in that they are often difficult to prove.

You should also remember that a written contract need not be a formal document written on parchment and notarized by the Dalai Lama. Any letter or writing can constitute a contract. For example, if Hubert writes to Josephine, "I would like to order 1,000 gopher traps at $14 per trap," and Josephine writes back saying, "Thank you for your order. The traps will be sent next week," there is a contract. Indeed, if Josephine didn't write back at all but simply sent the traps in a reasonable period of time, there would also be a contract implied from the circumstances of the transaction.

You should also be aware that the business usage and practices in a particular field are commonly viewed as being part of a contract and can be introduced as evidence in Small Claims Court to support your case. Thus, if Hubert ordered rodent traps in February and Josephine didn't send them until September, Hubert could present evidence in court that everyone in the rodent control business knows that traps are only saleable in the summer when rodents attack crops and that Josephine's failure to deliver the traps in the correct season constituted a breach of contract.

And keep in mind that contracts can be, and often are, changed many times as negotiations go back and forth and circumstances change. The important agreement is the last one.

2. Presenting Your Evidence In Court

In addition to the general techniques of presenting evidence efficiently in Court, here are a few more suggestions of special interest to small business people:

• In business disputes, the problem is often having too much evidence, rather than too little. If this occurs, your job is obviously to separate the material that is essential to proving your case from that which is less important. One good way to do this is to organize both your verbal presentation and the backup evidence around the central issue in dispute rather than trying to fill in all the background in an effort to work up to the point. Or, to say the same thing in a different way, you usually want to start with the end of your case rather than the beginning. For example, if Ted did interior decorating work for Alice and she called off the deal, Ted would start his testimony with the fact that a contract existed to do the work and that Alice broke it. The fact that Ted and Alice had had dealings over the last several years which cast light on the present dispute, or that Ted had turned down another job to work for Alice, or that Alice had made a number of unreasonable demands on him, might well constitute good supporting evidence, but should be alluded to only to the extent that they support the main point. All too often I have seen people tell a great but lengthy story in court that put the judge to sleep before the main point was reached.

• Many business people have employees, partners, or business associates who have intimate knowledge of the dispute. By all means, bring them to court as witnesses. A witness who is knowledgable about the transaction is almost always worth more than a stack of documentary evidence.

• In some situations, having a witness testify as to the normal business practices in a field can be helpful. Thus, if in your business payment is customarily made within thirty days after delivery of goods and the person you are having a dispute with claimed that a 120-day payment schedule was routine, you would want to present an "expert" witness who could testify as to normal business practices.

B. The Drama of the Distraught Designer

Now let's review a case that I was recently asked about. Don is a successful industrial designer who heads his own small company. He has offices in a converted factory building near the University of California and prides himself on doing highly innovative and creative work. Normally he is confident and cheerful, but one day when he stopped by the Nolo office to say hello, he looked more than a little out of sorts.

"What's up?" I asked

"Oh, a couple of late nights of high pressure work," Don replied.

"What's new about that?" I asked him.

"Well, that's not really what's bugging me. Actually, I wonder if you can give me a little advice."

"Sure, what's the problem?"

"Well, I did some design work for an outfit that wants to build a small candle factory and I'm out $2,100. They claim that we never had a contract, but that's simply not true. What really happened is that they gambled and authorized me to do some preliminary work before they got their financing assured. When interest rates went through the roof, the whole deal collapsed. I had already completed my work, but they got uptight and refused to pay."

"So what are you going to do?" I asked him.

"Well, I got Stephanie Carlin, a lawyer who has done some work for me, to write them a letter, but that didn't do any good, so I took Stephanie's advice and filed a Small Claims Court suit against them myself."

"For how much?"

"For the Small Claims maximum. I had to scale down the claim to fit it in, but it was better than paying Stephanie's $125 an hour."

"How can I help?" I asked.

"Believe it or not, I've never been to court and I'm afraid I will overlook something or do something stupid, like calling the judge 'your holiness' instead of 'your honor.' I'm not much on bowing and scraping and the whole court rigamarole has always annoyed me."

"Okay, let me show you how simple your job is. First, how did the candle people (let's call them Wickless) contact you to set up the deal?"

"They are friends of friends. They called and we talked on the phone a couple of times. There was a lot of back and forth about how much I would charge for the whole job and how much for parts of it. After a little garden-variety confusion, we decided that I would start with the preliminary drawings and be paid $1,200. If the whole job came through and we felt good about one another, I would do the whole thing."

"Did you write a contract?"

"No, that's just it. On big jobs I always do, but this one was tiny. They just stopped by the next day and we hashed out the whole thing in person."

"Did you make notes?"

"Sure. In fact, I made a few sketches and then they gave me specifications and sketches they had made."

"Do you still have those?"

"Yes, and also a couple of letters they sent later thanking me for my good ideas and making a few suggestions for changes. And of course, I have copies of the detailed drawings I made and sent them."

"Well, that's it then," I said.

"What do you mean, that's it? You mean that I don't have a case?"

"Just the contrary. I mean you have just told me that you can prove that a contract exists. The combination of the sketches they provided and the letters they wrote you pretty well prove that they asked you to do the work. There is a strong presumption in law (called "quantum meruit") that when a person is asked to do work in a situation where compensation is normally expected, she is to be paid when the work is completed.[1] Now, in this sort of situation, I suspect that Wickless will raise one of two defenses if they bother to contest your claim at all. The first is that you were doing your work on speculation—that is, that the deal was that you were to be paid for your preliminary work only if the financing went through, and/or second, that your work was substandard in some way, such as not being what was agreed on."

"But they wrote me that my design was of excellent quality."

---

[1] This *"quantum meruit"* concept is discussed briefly in Chapter 2.

"Great, then that takes care of that issue. How about the other one? Do you ever do preliminary work without expecting to be paid unless the deal goes through? And is that a common way to operate in your business?"

"Me? Never! I don't have to. I suppose some designers do, or at least prepare detailed proposals without pay, but I have more work than I can decently do and I make it clear to all potential clients that I charge for preliminary drawings. In this situation, as I said, we agreed on the price in advance."

"What about witnesses to that conversation?"

"Well, Jim, my partner, sat in on one of the early discussions. We hadn't agreed on the final price yet, but we weren't too far apart."

"Was it clear to Jim that you intended to charge and that Wickless knew you did?"

"Yes, absolutely."

"Great, bring Jim to court with you. Here is how I would proceed. Organize your statement as to what happened so that it takes you no longer than five minutes to present it to the judge. Bring your sketches, and most important, the sketch the Wickless people made, along with the letters they sent you, and show them to the judge. Then have your partner testify to being present when money was discussed. You should have no trouble. If you're nervous about being in court, go down and check it out a few days before. It's just down at Center Street and I'm sure that if you watch for half an hour, you will be raring to go!"

Note: This little scenario is a simplified version of a real case. Don was given a judgment for the entire amount he requested and Wickless paid it.

C. Old Friends Fall Out

Let's look at a typical story. Tom, a true artist when it comes to graphics, is a bit ingenuous when it comes to dollars and cents. Recognizing this, he never prepares his own tax returns.

For the past several years, he turned all of his tax affairs over to Phillip, a local C.P.A. Price was discussed the first year, but after that Tom just paid Phillip's bill when the job was done.

One spring, things went wrong. As usual, Tom's records weren't in great shape, and he was late in getting them to Phillip. Phillip was busy and put Tom's tax return together without discussing it with him in detail. When Tom saw the return, he was shocked. He felt that he was being asked to pay way too much to Uncle Sam. He called Phillip and reminded him of a number of deductions that he felt had been overlooked. There was some discussion of whether Phillip should have known about these items or not. At this time, Phillip complained about Tom's sloppy records and his delay in making them available, and Tom told Phillip that he thought that Phillip had done a hurried and substandard job. After some more grumpy talk back and forth, Phillip agreed to make the necessary corrections. In a week this was done and the return was again sent to Tom.

While his tax liability was now less, Tom was still annoyed, feeling that not all of the oversights had been corrected. Tom called Phillip again and this time they quickly got into a shouting match which ended with Phillip very reluctantly agreeing to look at the return a third time and Tom saying that he was taking his business to an accountant who could add. Tom found another accountant and, after several modifications were made which resulted in a slightly lower tax liability, the return was filed. The second accountant stated that as he needed to check all of Phillip's work to satisfy himself that it was correct, he ended up doing almost as much work as if he had started from scratch. He billed Tom for $1,000, saying that this was $250 less than if he had not had the benefit of Phillip's work.

Phillip billed Tom $1,200. Tom was furious and refused to pay. Phillip then sent Tom a demand letter stating that most of the problems were created by Tom's bad records, that he had made a number of changes when requested to do so and had offered to make the final changes at no additional charge. Tom replied with "I'll see you in court." Which is exactly what happened as Phillip went ahead with his suit.

Okay, now it's up to you. Imagine for a moment that you are Phillip. How would you prepare your case? In the spirit of not asking you questions I am afraid to answer myself, here is how I would proceed.

PHILLIP'S CASE

1. Phillip's first job is to write a clear, concise demand letter (see Chapter 7);

2. In court, Phillip will want to prove that he did work that was worth $1,200. Bringing copies of Tom's tax returns as well as his own work sheets is the simplest way to accomplish this. The returns should not be presented to the judge page by page, but as a package. The purpose is to indicate that a lot of work has been done, not go into details;

3. Phillip should then testify as to his hourly rate and how many hours he worked. He should mention that more hours were required than would otherwise have been the case because Tom did not have the raw data well organized. To illustrate his point, Phillip should introduce the raw data Tom gave him into evidence (i.e., a shoe box full of messy receipts);

4. Phillip has now presented his basic case, which is simply that he was hired to do a job, he did it, and he wasn't paid. However, Phillip would be wise to go beyond this and anticipate at least some of Tom's defenses, which will almost surely involve the poor quality of the work done, as well as a claim that Phillip is simply charging too much. Therefore, were I Phillip, I would close my testimony with a statement along these lines:

"Your honor, when I finished my work my client pointed out that several deductions had been overlooked. I believed then and believe now that this was because the data he provided me with was inadequate, but I did rework the return and corrected several items that were left out. When my client told me that he felt even the revised draft needed work, I again told him that I would work with him to make any necessary changes. It was at this point that he refused to let me see the returns and hired another accountant. In my professional opinion, very little work remained to be done at this stage—certainly nothing that couldn't be accomplished in an hour or two. Now, as to the amount charged, it took me ten hours to reconstruct what went on in the typesetting business from the mess of incomplete and incoherent records I was given. At $60 per hour, this means that $600 of my bill involved work that had to be done prior to actually preparing the return. Taking into consideration the difficult circumstances, I believe I charged fairly for the work I did, and that I did my work well."

TOM'S CASE

Okay, so much for getting into the head of an indignant accountant. Now let's see how Tom, the upset typesetter, might defend his case.

1. Tom should write a letter of his own, rebutting Phillip's demand letter point by point (see Chapter 7). He should bring this letter to court and give it to the judge.

2. Next, Tom should testify that he refused to pay the bill because he felt that Phillip's work was so poorly done that he didn't trust Phillip to finish the job. Tom should testify as to the details of several of the points that Phillip overlooked. Thus, if Tom provided Phillip with information concerning equipment purchases and Phillip forgot to claim depreciation, this would be important evidence. But Tom should be careful to make his points relatively brief and understandable. He won't gain by a long and boring rehash of his entire return.

3. Now, to really make his case, Tom should present more detailed evidence that supports his claim that Phillip poor work. The tax return as correctly prepared by the new accountant would be of some help, but far more valuable would be having the second accountant come to court to testify. Unfortunately, professionals are commonly reluctant to testify against one another, so this may be difficult to arrange. But Tom should at the very least be able to get a letter from the new accountant outlining the things that he found it necessary to do to change the return as prepared by Phillip.

4. Tom should also present to the court his cancelled checks, establishing the amounts paid Phillip for the last several years' returns, assuming, of course, that Phillip's previous bills were much less. For example, if Tom had been billed $400 and $500 in the two previous years, it would raise some questions as to whether Phillip's bill of $1,200 for the current year was reasonable.

5. Tom should also present the bill from the second accountant to the court as well as his note explaining that his $1,000 charge was $250 less than his normal bill for the whole job.

Note: After (or perhaps during) Phillip's and Tom's testimony, the judge is almost certain to ask a number of questions. In addition, he will probably give each an opportunity to rebut the statements of the other. I don't have space to discuss how this might go in detail, but in rebuttal, it's important to focus on the one or two points that you think the judge has missed or is in danger of getting wrong. This is not a time to attempt to restate your entire case.

WHAT HAPPENED?

Phillip was given a judgment for $700. The judge didn't explain his reasoning, but apparently felt that there was some right on each side and split the difference with a little edge to Tom. This sort of decision where each side is given something is common in Small Claims Court and again illustrates the wisdom of the parties' working out their own compromise. Even if Tom and Phillip had arrived at a solution where one or the other gave up a little more than the judge ordered, there would have been a saving in time and aggravation that probably would have more than made up the difference.

Bad Check Note: Every merchant is stuck with a rubber check now and then. Until recently, it usually didn't pay to take a bad check writer to court, especially for smaller checks. Now CC Sec. 1719 permits a person holding a bad check to obtain a judgment for between $100-$500 in damages in addition to the amount of the check. I discuss how to take advantage of this law in Chapter 4D.

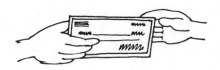

D. Damage to Real Property

There is no typical case when it comes to damage to real property, as facts vary greatly. So instead of trying to set down general rules, let's look at a situation that happened recently to a friend of mine. (Let's call her Babette.)

Babette owns a cinder-block building that houses two stores. One morning when she came to work, she noticed water pouring in through the back of her building. Because the building was set into a hill, it abutted about eight feet of her uphill neighbor's land. (Let's call her neighbor Boris.) After three days of investigation involving the use of green dye in Boris's plumbing system, it was discovered that the water came from an underground leak in Boris's sewer pipe. At this point, Babette had spent considerable effort and some money to pay helpers to get the water mopped up before it damaged anything in the stores.

Instead of fixing the leak promptly, Boris delayed for four days. All of this time, Babette and her helpers were mopping frantically. Finally, when Boris did get to work, he insisted on digging the pipe out himself, which took another four days. (A plumber with the right equipment could have done it in one.) In the middle of Boris's digging, when his yard looked as though it was being attacked by a herd of giant gophers, it rained. The water filled the holes and trenches instead of running off as it normally would have. Much of it ran through the ground into Babette's building, bringing a pile of mud with it.

When the flood was finally over, Babette figured out her costs as follows:

First three days (before the source ofthe water was discovered)	$148 (for help with mopping and cleaning)
Next four days (while Boris refused to cooperate)	$288 (for help with mopping and cleaning)
Final four days (including day it rained)	$262 (for help with mopping and cleaning)
One secondhand water vacuum purchased during rain storm	$200

Her own time, valued at $7 $500
per hour

Assuming that Boris is unwilling to pay Babette's costs, for what amount should she sue and how much is she likely to recover? If you remember the lessons taught in Chapter 2, you will remember that before Babette can recover for her very real loss, she must show that Boris was negligent or caused her loss intentionally. Probably she can't do this for the first three days. No one knew where the water was coming from, and it's probably impossible to show that Boris was negligent because he failed to replace a pipe that up until then had worked fine. However, once the problem was discovered and Boris didn't take immediate steps to fix it, he was clearly negligent, and Babette can recover at least her out-of-pocket loss ($550 for labor and $200 for the water vacuum). Can Babette also recover for the value of her own time? The answer to this question is "maybe." If she could show that she had to close her store or take time off from a job to stem the flood, she probably could recover. Were I she, I would sue for $1,250 ($550 for labor she paid for, $200 for the vacuum, and $500 for the value of her own labor) and count on getting most of it.

CHAPTER 22

Judgment and Appeal

A. The Judgment

The decision in your case will be mailed to the address on record with the clerk any time from a few days to a few weeks after your case is heard. The exception to this rule is when one side doesn't show up and the other wins by default. Default judgments are normally announced right in the courtroom.[1] The truth is that in the vast majority of contested cases the judge has already made up his mind at the time the case is heard

---

[1] In Chapters 10, 12 and 15 we discuss default judgments and the fact that people who have had defaults entered against them can often get them set aside if (1) they had a decent excuse for not being present, and (2) they notify the court clerk immediately of their desire to have the judgment set aside.

and notes down his decision before the parties leave the courtroom. Traditionally, decisions have been sent by mail because the court didn't want to deal with angry, unhappy losers, especially those few who might get violent. More recently, however, some judges have begun explaining their decisions in court, on the theory that both parties are entitled to know why a particular decision was reached. One progressive judge explained his policy in this regard as follows: "The only time I don't announce in court is when I have phoning or research to do or if I feel that the losing party will be unnecessarily embarrassed in front of the audience."

Often when a judgment is entered against a person, she feels that the judge would surely have made a different decision if he hadn't gotten mixed up, or overlooked some crucial fact, or had properly understood an argument. On the basis of my experience on the bench, I can tell you that in the vast majority of Small Claims cases, there is little likelihood that the judge would change his decision even if you had a chance to argue the whole case over. In any event, you don't.[2] You have had your chance and the decision has gone against you. It won't help you to call the judge, or go to see him, or send him documents through the mail (see Section D, below, for appeal rights).

Note: Now that a judgment has been entered, we need to expand our vocabulary slightly. The person who wins the case (gets the judgment) now becomes "the judgment creditor" and the loser is known as "the judgment debtor."

---

[2] There is one possible exception to this rule. If your case was heard by a "pro tem" judge (see Chapter 13G) and you feel it was obviously decided wrongly, it may be worthwhile to immediately send a short written statement to the presiding judge of the local Municipal Court. Title it "Motion for Rehearing" and explain why the decision was obviously wrong. This probably won't work, but I know of a few instances where it has.

B. Time Payments

I have mentioned the fact that in California a judge may order that the loser be allowed to pay the winner over a period of time, rather than all at once. The judge won't normally make this sort of order unless you request it. So, if you have no real defense to a claim, or if you have a fairly good case but aren't sure which way the judge will go, be sure that the judge knows that, if the judgment goes against you, you wish to pay in installments. You might put your request this way:

• "In closing my presentation, I would like to say that I believe I have a convincing case and should be awarded the judgment, but in the event that you rule for my opponent, I would like you to allow me time payments of no more than (whatever amount is convenient) per month."

Or, if you have no real defense:

• "Your Honor, I request that you enter the judgment against me for no more than (an amount convenient to you) per month."

If you neglect to ask for time payments in court and wish to make this request after you receive the judgment, first contact the other party to see if he will voluntarily agree to accept his money on a schedule you can afford to pay. If she agrees, it is wise to write your agreement down and each sign it. If your opponent is an all-or-nothing sort of person and refuses payments, promptly contact the court clerk and ask that the case again be brought before the judge—not as to the facts, but only to set up a payment schedule that you can live with.

1
2
3   SMALL CLAIMS COURT, FOR _____
4   JUDICIAL DISTRICT, COUNTY OF _____, STATE OF CALIFORNIA
5
6   JOHN TOLLER,
7   Plaintiff   Action Number SC._____
8   v.
                                            PETITION, NOTICE OF MOTION,
9   MILDRED EDWARDS,   AND ORDER ALLOWING JUDGMENT TO BE
                                            PAID IN INSTALLMENTS.
10   Defendant.
11
12   Comes now MILDRED EDWARDS and represents to the court that a judgment was
13   entered against her in the above entitled action in the amount of $526.00. That
14   payment of this entire judgment immediately will cause a severe hardship to
15   MILDRED EDWARDS because ___(of lack of employment, or illness or whatever)___ .
16   Petitioner can pay $25.00 per month.
17   Wherefore petitioner requests that an order by made to allow payment in
18   this amount.
19
20   DATED:_____
21   _____
                                                      PETITIONER
22
                              NOTICE OF MOTION
23
           To JOHN TOLLER. Please take note that you are ordered to appear in court
24   on ___(date)_____ at ___(time)_____ to give any legal reason why
25   it shall not be ordered that the judgment in the above entitled case be paid in
26   installments of $25.00 per month.
27
28   DATED:_____
                                            _____
                                                        JUDGE

```
1                              ORDER
2        Judgment to be paid $25.00 on the first day of each month until fully
3    paid.  Should the judgment debtor fail to make one or more payments, the
4    judgment creditor may file an affidavit so stating with this court and
5    the above order shall thereby be vacated and the clerk shall proceed as
6    if it had not been made.
7
8    DATED:_____        _____
9                                              JUDGE
10
11
12
```

C. The Satisfaction of Judgment

Once a judgment is paid, whether in installments or a lump sum, a "judgment creditor" must file a "satisfaction of judgment" form with the court (CCP Sec. 117.9). If a judgment creditor who receives payment in full on a judgment fails to do this, the judgment debtor should send a written demand that this be done. A first class letter is adequate. It's important to do this because otherwise the judgment will continue to appear on credit records as unpaid and may result in the judgment debtor being denied credit. If, after written demand, the judgment creditor doesn't file his satisfaction within 15 days and without just cause, the judgment debtor is entitled to recover all actual damages he or she may sustain by reason of such failure (i.e., for denial of a credit application) and, in addition, the sum of $50.

Here is a sample "Satisfaction of Judgment" form which is available from the Small Claims Court clerk. Again, it should be signed by the judgment creditor when the judgment is paid and filed with the court clerk. Don't forget to do this; otherwise, you may have to track down the other party later.

ATTORNEY OR PARTY WITHOUT ATTORNEY *(Name and Address):*   TELEPHONE NO.:   FOR RECORDER'S OR SECRETARY OF STATE'S USE ONLY

ATTORNEY FOR *(Name)*:

NAME OF COURT:
STREET ADDRESS:
MAILING ADDRESS:
CITY AND ZIP CODE:
BRANCH NAME:

PLAINTIFF:

DEFENDANT:

ACKNOWLEGMENT OF SATISFACTION OF JUDGMENT   CASE NUMBER:
☐ FULL   ☐ PARTIAL   ☐ MATURED INSTALLMENT

1. Satisfaction of the judgment is acknowledged as follows *(see footnote* before completing)*:   FOR COURT USE ONLY

   a. ☐ Full satisfaction
      (1) ☐ Judgment is satisfied in full.
      (2) ☐ The judgment creditor has accepted payment or performance other than that specified in the judgment in full satisfaction of the judgment.

   b. ☐ Partial satisfaction
      The amount received in partial satisfaction of the judgment is
      $

   c. ☐ Matured installment
      All matured installments under the installment judgment have been satisfied as of *(date)*:

2. Full name and address of judgment creditor:

3. Full name and address of assignee of record, if any:

4. Full name and address of judgment debtor being fully or partially released:

5. a. Judgment entered on *(date)*:
      ☐ (1) in judgment book volume no.:   (2) page no.:
   b. ☐ Renewal entered on *(date)*:
      ☐ (1) in judgment book volume no.:   (2) page no.:

6. ☐   An ☐ abstract of judgment ☐ certified copy of the judgment has been recorded as follows *(complete all information for each county where recorded)*:

      COUNTY   DATE OF RECORDING   BOOK NUMBER   PAGE NUMBER

7. ☐   A notice of judgment lien has been filed in the office of the Secretary of State as file number *(specify)*:

NOTICE TO JUDGMENT DEBTOR: If this is an acknowledgment of full satisfaction of judgment, it will have to be recorded in each county shown in item 6 above, if any, in order to release the judgment lien, and will have to be filed in the office of the Secretary of State to terminate any judgment lien on personal property.

Date: ▶
_____
                                        (SIGNATURE OF JUDGMENT CREDITOR OR ASSIGNEE OF CREDITOR OR ATTORNEY)
*The names of the judgment creditor and judgment debtor must be stated as shown in any Abstract of Judgment which was recorded and is being released by this satisfaction. A **separate notary acknowledgment** must be attached for each signature.

Form Approved by the
Judicial Council of California   **ACKNOWLEDGMENT OF SATISFACTION OF JUDGMENT**   CCP 724.060, 724.120,
EJ-100 [Rev. July 1, 1983]   724.250

Note: If either party ever needs it, the clerk, for a small fee, will provide a certified copy of this form to prove that the judgment has been paid.

Sometimes people forget to get a "Satisfaction of Judgment" form signed when they pay a judgment, only to find later that they can't locate the judgment creditor. If this happens and you need a satisfaction of judgment to clean up your credit record or for some other reason, you can get it if you present the court clerk with the following documents:

1. A cancelled check or money order written subsequent to the judgment by the judgment debtor for the full amount of the judgment, or a cash receipt for the full amount of the judgment thereof signed by the judgment creditor; and

2. A statement signed by the judgment debtor under penalty of perjury stating all of the following:

• The judgment creditor has been paid the full amount of the judgment and costs;

• The judgment creditor has been requested to file a satisfaction of judgment and refuses to do so or can't be located;

• The documents attached (e.g., the check or money order) constitute evidence of the judgment debtor's receipt of the payment.

Here is a sample:

SAMPLE STATEMENT

My name is John Elliot. On January 11, 19__ , a judgment was awarded against me in Small Claims Court in San Francisco, California (Case # 1234). On March 20, 19__ I paid Beatrice Small, the prevailing party $1,200, the full amount of this judgment [or, if payments were made in installments—"I paid Beatrice Small, the prevailing party in this action, the final installment necessary to pay this judgment in full."]

I attach to this statement a cancelled check for the full amount of the judgment endorsed by Beatrice Small.[3]

Beatrice Small did not voluntarily file a Satisfaction of Judgment. When I tried to contact her, I learned that she had moved and had left no forwarding address.[4]

Sincerely,

John Elliot

D. The Appeal

If, in the face of justice, common sense and all of your fine arguments, the judge turns out to be a big dummy and rules for your opponent, you can appeal to a higher court, right? Not necessarily. In Small Claims Court if you are the person who brought the suit (the plaintiff) and you lose, you are finished, done, through when it comes to judgments rendered on claims

---

[3] If payment was made by money order or cash (with a receipt), modify this statement as needed.

[4] If the judgment creditor refuses to sign a Satisfaction of Judgment, or is otherwise not available to do so, modify this statement as necessary.

you initiated. Plaintiffs have absolutely no right to appeal to any other court unless the defendant filed a claim of his own and the plaintiff lost on the defendant's claim. Why? Because that's how the legislature made the rules. However, if you are the defendant and lose, you can appeal to the Superior Court if you do so promptly.

Note: Losing defendants can't appeal from decisions rendered on claims they file (initiate) against the plaintiff using a Defendant's Claim. They can only appeal claims initiated by the plaintiff.

Isn't it unfair, maybe even unconstitutional, to allow appeal rights for defendants and none for plaintiffs? I will leave it to you to decide the fairness issue, but it's not unconstitutional for the simple reason that a plaintiff knows before he files that he doesn't have a right to an appeal. He has a choice of bringing his suit in Small Claims Court where there is no right for plaintiffs to appeal, or in Municipal Court where both sides can appeal. The defendant doesn't have this opportunity to pick the court and, therefore, the legislature decided that his appeal rights should be preserved.

E. Filing Your Appeal

Now let's look at the mechanics of the appeal. In California, the defendant must file a notice of appeal within 20 days of the day the court clerk mails the judgment to the parties (or hands it over, if a decision is made in the courtroom). This means if the decision was mailed, there will be less than 20 days to file an appeal from the day that the defendant receives the judgment. The date the judgment was mailed will appear on the judgment. If for some reason attributable to the magic of the U.S. Postal Service your judgment doesn't show up within 20 days after it was entered, call the Small Claims clerk immediately and request help in getting an extension of time to file your appeal.

Both sides may be represented by a lawyer on a Small Claims appeal. However, this is not generally necessary, as appeals are conducted following informal procedures similar to Small Claims Court itself. And, of course, the amount of money involved does not really justify your hiring a lawyer.

To file your notice of appeal, go to the Small Claims clerk's office and fill out a paper such as the one illustrated below. Currently, the appeal fee is close to $25. There is no charge for the original plaintiff to appear in Superior Court on the defendant's appeal. If the original Small Claims judgment is affirmed in whole or in part or the appeal is dismissed, the defendant shall not only be ordered to pay the amount of the judgment, but also interest, costs and the sum of $15 as an attorney fee. In addition, if the judge finds that the appeal was without substantial merit and not based on good faith, but intended to harass, delay or encourage plaintiff to abandon her claim, the judge may award attorney fees of up to $250 after hearing the appeal. CCP 11712.

When you file your appeal, the court will notify the other side that you have done so. You need not do this yourself. Once your appeal is on file at the Superior Court, your next step is to wait. When you are done waiting, you will probably have to wait some more. You are in the formal court system now, where traditionally very little happens, very slowly. Those who have been in the armed services will understand. All the deadlines apply to you—never to the bureaucracy. Eventually (two to six months depending on the county) you will get a notice giving you a court date in the Superior Court.

An appeal of a Small Claims judgment is not the sort of appeal that the U.S. Supreme Court hears. The Supreme Court, and the other formal appellate courts, are concerned with looking at the written record of what went on in a lower court with the idea of changing a decision when a judge has misinterpreted the law. Since no record has been made in Small Claims Court, the Superior Court has nothing to look over. They must start from scratch, as if nothing had been said in Small Claims Court. You simply argue the case over from the start, presenting all your witnesses, documents, etc. Of course, both sides should give some thought to how their presentation can be improved. This is particularly true of the defendant, who has already lost once.

Name and Address of Court

SMALL CLAIMS CASE NO.

PLAINTIFF DEMANDANTE *(Name and address of each)*

John Albertson
106 Easy Way
Inglewood, CA

DEFENDANT DEMANDADO *(Name and address of each)*

Gloria Ferdinand
66 Echo St., Apt. 4
Los Angeles, CA

☐ See attached sheet for additional plaintiffs and defendants.

NOTICE OF FILING NOTICE OF APPEAL

TO: ☐ Plaintiff *(name)*:

☐ Defendant *(name)*:

Your small claims case has been APPEALED to the superior court. Do not contact the small claims court about this appeal. The superior court will notify you of the date you should appear in court. The notice of appeal is set forth below.	*La decisión hecha por la corte para reclamos judiciales menores en su caso ha sido APELADA ante la corte superior. No se ponga en contacto con la corte para reclamos judiciales menores acerca de esta apelación. La corte superior le notificará la fecha en que usted debe presentarse ante ella. El aviso de la apelación aparece a continuación.*

Date: _____ Clerk, by _____, Deputy

NOTICE OF APPEAL

I appeal to the superior court from the small claims judgment or the denial of the motion to vacate the small claims judgment, as provided by law.

DATE APPEAL FILED *(clerk to insert date)*:

. . . . *(TYPE OR PRINT NAME)* . . . .

▶

(SIGNATURE OF APPELLANT OR APPELLANT'S ATTORNEY)

CLERK'S CERTIFICATE OF MAILING

I certify that

1. I am not a party to this action.
2. This Notice of Filing Notice of Appeal and Notice of Appeal were mailed first class, postage prepaid, in a sealed envelope to
   ☐ plaintiff
   ☐ defendant
   at the address shown above.
3. The mailing and this certification occurred
   at *(place)*: _____, California,
   on *(date)*:

Clerk, by _____, Deputy

Form Approved by the
Judicial Council of California
SC-140 (Rev. January 1, 1985)

NOTICE OF APPEAL
(Small Claims)

Rule 982.7

But what if your opponent hires an attorney on appeal? Aren't you at a disadvantage if you represent yourself? Not really, because, as mentioned, the appeal court must follow informal rules (Judicial Council Rule 155), similar to those used in Small Claims Court. This means the rules of evidence and procedure normally used in Superior Court can't be required by the judge in hearing your appeal. This should put you on a fairly equal footing with the lawyer. If you have prepared carefully, you may even have an advantage; you carry with you the honest conviction that you are right while a lawyer arguing a Small Claims appeal always seems a bit pathetic. If, despite this common sense view of the situation, you still feel a little intimidated, the best cure is to go watch a few Small Claims appeals. Ask the Superior Court clerk when they are scheduled.

Jury Trial Note: As of early 1987, the question of whether either party can ask for a jury trial for a Small Claims Court appeal, or whether there is no right to a jury, is before the California Supreme Court in the case of *Crouchman v. Superior Ct.*

Discovery Note: As this book goes to press, there is a legal argument as to whether formal pretrial methods such as depositions, written interrogatories, etc. can be used in Small Claims appeals. These can slow appeals at the same time they favor lawyers who know all the tricks. We look forward to the day when it is clear that they have been eliminated.

Appeal from the Appeal: If a defendant loses the appeal, there is no right to file a second appeal. However, it is possible to file an extraordinary writ (a special request for review based on extraordinary circumstances) to the Court of Appeal claiming that the case involves an important question of law (the Superior Court judge also may recommend that the Court of Appeal hear the case). Because of the small amounts of money involved, extraordinary writs are almost never filed, based on Small Claims judgments. When they are, they are seldom granted. For these reasons, I do not cover this procedure here.

CHAPTER 23

Collecting Your Money

You won. You are entitled to the dollar amount of the judgment from the opposing party or parties. How are you going to get it? Your first job is to be patient for a short while longer. Specifically, if the defendant showed up in court at the trial, you must legally wait 20 days after the day the notice of entry of judgment form is mailed out (or handed to the defendant) before resorting to any of the official collection techniques discussed in this chapter. If you got your judgment on the basis of the defendant's failure to show up at the trial (it's a default judgment), you must wait 30 days, which is the time allowed a defendant to ask the court to set aside the default judgment (see Chapter 10E). It is not illegal to ask for your money during this 20-day period, but it is unwise. Why? Because if you make your request for money, you may remind the defendant to take advantage of his right to appeal.

Once the 20 day period (30 days if the defendant defaulted) is up, what should you do? Try asking politely for your money.

This works in the majority of cases, especially if you have sued a responsible person or business. If you don't have a personal contact with the party who owes you money, try a note.

If you receive no response to your polite note, you will have to get serious about collecting your money or forget it. The emphasis in the previous sentence should be on the word "you." Much to many people's surprise, the court does not enforce its judgments and collect money for you—you have to do it yourself.

SAMPLE COLLECTION NOTE

P.O. Box 66
Berkeley, California
February 15, 19__

Mildred Edwards
11 Milvia Street
Berkeley, California 94706

Dear Mrs. Edwards:

As you know, a judgment was entered against you in Small Claims Court on January 15 in the amount of $457.86. As the judgment creditor, I will appreciate your paying this amount within 10 days.

Thank you for your consideration.

Very truly yours,
John Toller

A few of the ways to collect money from a debtor are relatively easy. I mentioned these briefly in Chapter 3. Hopefully you gave some thought to collection before you brought your case. If you only now realize that if your opponent doesn't have the money to buy a toothbrush and never will, you are better off not wasting more time and money trying to get him to pay up, at least for the present. Remember, though—a judgment is valid for 10 years and can be renewed for an additional ten if you can show that you have tried to collect it, but failed. In some situations you may simply want to sit on your judgment, with the hope that your "judgment debtor" will show a few signs of life in the future.

Note: In the rest of this chapter I discuss how to collect using the simplest collection techniques. Nolo Press also publishes *Collect Your Court Judgment* by Ginny Scott, which is a far more thorough book on this subject. It specifically deals with what to do if the debtor files a claim of exemption or threatens bankruptcy.

A. Levying On Wages, Bank Accounts, Business Assets, Real Property, Etc.

If a polite letter doesn't work (10 days is plenty of time to wait), and you know that the person who owes you the money (the "judgment debtor") has it, you will have to start acting like a collection agency.[1]

If you know where the judgment debtor works, you are in good shape. Federal and state laws allow you to get approximately 25% of a person's net wages to satisfy a debt.[2] Knowing where a judgment debtor banks can also be extremely valuable as you can order a sheriff, marshal or constable to levy on a bank account and get whatever it contains at the time of the levy.[3] Of course,

---

[1] It is possible to turn your debt over to a real collection agency, but this probably doesn't make too much sense as the agency will usually take 50% of what they can collect. Unless you are a regular customer, the agency probably won't treat your debt with much priority unless they believe that it is easy to collect. If it is easy for them to collect, it probably won't be hard for you to do it yourself and save the fee.

[2] If a person has a very low income, the amount you can recover can be considerably less than 25%.

[3] Bank account levies are subject to the exempt property laws. Approximately 75% of wages placed in a bank account are exempt (100% if there has been a previous wage attachment involving the same money) for 30 days after payment. Social security money in a bank account is totally exempt.

a bank account levy will only work once as the debtor is pretty sure to move his account when he realizes that you have access to it.

Other types of property are normally much more difficult to grab. Why? Because California has a number of "exemption" laws which say that, even though a person owes money, certain types of her property can't be taken to satisfy the debt. Items protected include a family house with up to $45,000 in equity, furniture, clothes, and much more.[4] Practically speaking, the only assets other than wages and bank accounts that are normally worth thinking about to satisfy a Small Claims judgment are a motor vehicle in which the judgment debtor has an equity considerably in excess of $1,200, real property other than the place where the debtor lives, and the receipts of an operating business. Theoretically, there are many other assets that you could reach, but in most cases they are not worth the time and expense involved, considering that your judgment is for the Small Claims maximum, or less.[5]

1. The Writ Of Execution

Before you can levy on a person's wages or other property, you must get a court order called a "Writ of Execution." If you have a Small Claims judgment, you are entitled to this writ. You get your Writ from the Small Claims Court clerk who will help you fill it out. There is a small fee, which is a recoverable cost (see C below).

---

[4] $60,000 in equity is exempt for elderly and disabled homeowners. Single individuals not yet 65 get equity protection in the amount of $30,000. Families qualify for a $45,000 equity exemption.

[5] You will find a complete list of exempt property and a thorough discussion of debtors' rights including bankruptcy in *Billpayers' Rights,* Warner and Elias, Nolo Press.

ATTORNEY OR PARTY WITHOUT ATTORNEY *(Name and Address)*   TELEPHONE NO   FOR RECORDER'S USE ONLY

Recording requested by and return to:

John Toller
P.O. Box 66   (415) 845-0000
Berkeley, CA 94702

ATTORNEY FOR ☐ JUDGMENT CREDITOR ☐ ASSIGNEE OF RECORD

NAME OF COURT   (fill in court)
STREET ADDRESS
MAILING ADDRESS
CITY AND ZIP CODE
BRANCH NAME

PLAINTIFF   John Toller

DEFENDANT   Mildred Edwards

CASE NUMBER

WRIT OF   ☐ EXECUTION (Money Judgment)
              ☐ POSSESSION OF ☐ Personal Property
                                ☐ Real Property   FOR COURT USE ONLY
              ☐ SALE

1. To the Sheriff or any Marshal or Constable of the County of: (fill in county where the assets are located)
   You are directed to enforce the judgment described below with daily interest and your costs as provided by law.

2. To any registered process server: You are authorized to serve this writ only in accord with CCP 699.080 or 715.040.

3. *(Name):* John Toller   is the
   ☐ judgment creditor ☐ assignee of record
   whose address is shown on this form above the court's name.

4. Judgment debtor *(name and last known address)*:

   Mildred Edwards

5. Judgment entered on *(date):* (clerk will
6. ☐ Judgment renewed on *(dates):* supply
                     this information)
7. Notice of sale under this writ
   a. ☐ has not been requested.
   b. ☐ has been requested *(see reverse)*.
8. ☐ Joint debtor information on reverse.

(SEAL)

9. ☐ See reverse for information on real or personal property to be delivered under a writ of possession or sold under a writ of sale.
10. ☐ This writ is issued on a sister-state judgment.
11. Total judgment . . . . $
12. Costs after judgment (per filed order or memo CCP 685.090) . $
13. Subtotal *(add 11 and 12)* . . . . $
14. Credits . . . . $
15. Subtotal *(subtract 14 from 13)* . $
16. Interest after judgment (per filed affidavit CCP 685.050) . . . . . . $
17. Fee for issuance of writ . . . . . $
18. Total *(add 15, 16, and 17)* . . . . $
19. Levying officer: Add daily interest from date of writ *(at the legal rate on 15)* of . . . . $

☐ additional judgment debtors on reverse

20. ☐ The amounts called for in items 11–19 are different for each debtor. These amounts are stated for each debtor on Attachment 20.

(fill in the correct amounts)

Issued on
(date)
                          Clerk, by _____, Deputy

— NOTICE TO PERSON SERVED: SEE REVERSE FOR IMPORTANT INFORMATION —

(Continued on reverse)

Form Approved by the
Judicial Council of California
EJ-130 Rev. January 1, 1983   **WRIT OF EXECUTION**   CCP 699.520, 712.010, 715.010

2. The Sheriff (Or Marshal)

Once your "Writ of Execution" form is filled out, take or send it to the sheriff, marshal or constable in the county where the assets are located. The Small Claims Court clerk will do this for you if you request it.[7] Give the officer or Small Claims clerk the following:

a. The "Writ of Execution" (original) and one to three or more copies depending on the asset to be collected;[8]

b. His fees for collecting (this will vary as to the type of asset. Call ahead to inquire);

c. Instructions on what type of asset to collect and where it is located. The sheriff, marshal, constable or Small Claims clerk may have a form they wish you to use when providing these instructions. Normally, however, they will accept your letter if it contains all the necessary information.

3. How To Levy On Wages And Bank Accounts

To seize a person's wages or bank account, you need the original and one copy of a "Writ of Execution" for the sheriff, marshal, or constable, and a letter of instruction (see below). Under the terms of CCP Sec. 700.160 you can also levy on bank accounts held jointly in the name of the judgment debtor and third persons. Under this code section it is even possible to levy on accounts held by the judgment debtor's spouse (or on a business where a fictitious business statement lists the owner as the judgment debtor or the judgment debtor's spouse). However, in both of these later instances extra paperwork must be filed. Ask the sheriff, marshal or constable what they require and see CCP Sec. 700.160 if you have any problems. The fee is $15.50 for wage garnishments and $32 for bank accounts.

---

[7] Do this right away, as the Writ of Execution expires in 180 days if it is not served by the sheriff or marshall. If this time runs out, you will have to go back to the Small Claims clerk and get another "Writ of Execution" issued.

[8] Don't forget to keep a copy of the "Writ of Execution" for your files.

P.O. Box 66
Berkeley, California
March 1, 19__

Sheriff (Civil Division),
Alameda County
Alameda County Courthouse
Oakland, California

Re: John Toller v. Mildred Edwards
Albany-Berkeley Judicial District
Small Claims Court No. 81-52

Dear Sir:

Enclosed you will find the original and one copy of a
Writ of Execution issued by the Small Claims Court for
the Oakland Judicial District in the amount of
$____(fill in total due)___. I also enclose a check for
your fee in the amount of $_____.

I hereby instruct you to levy on the wages of Mildred
Edwards, who works at the Graphite Oil Co., 1341
Chester St., Oakland, California. Please serve the Writ
on or before March 15, 19__.

Very truly yours,
John Toller

4. Levying On Motor Vehicles (Including Planes, Boats and R.V.'s)

Getting money from wages or bank accounts is fairly easy. Selling a person's motor vehicle is more difficult for several reasons, including the following:

a. $1,200 combined equity in one or more motor vehicles is exempt from your levy (CCP Sec. 704.010).

Example: A judgment debtor has two cars worth $4,000 on which he owes $3,000 to a bank. This means that his equity is $1,000—the bank owns the rest. As an equity of $1,200 is exempt under CCP Sec. 704.010, you would end up with nothing.

b. One motor vehicle is exempt from attachment up to $2,500 if it is a "tool of a person's trade" (CCP Sec. 704.060).

Example: A "judgment debtor" has a pickup truck worth $2,000 which she uses every day in her gardening business. The truck would be exempt as a tool of trade.

c. The judgment debtor may not own the car he drives. It may be in someone else's name, or he may owe a bank or finance company as much or more than the car is worth.

To find out if a judgment debtor owns the car he drives, go to the Department of Motor Vehicles and give them the license number. For a small fee, they will tell you who owns the car, including whether or not a bank or finance company is involved. Once you have this information, you can determine whether the car is likely to sell for enough to pay off any loan you discover, provide the debtor with her $1,200 exemption, cover the costs of sale, and still leave enough to pay off your judgment, or at least a substantial part of it. If you are convinced that the vehicle is worth enough to cover these costs, as would be the case if it is relatively new and owned by the debtor free and clear, have the sheriff pick up the car and sell it. But remember, the sheriff fees to do this are relatively high (usually about $350) and must be paid in advance. This money is recoverable when the vehicle is sold. Call the sheriff, marshal, or constable of the county in which the car is located to find out how much money he requires as a deposit with your

Writ of Execution and how many copies of the Writ you need.
Then write a letter such as this:

P.O. Box 66
Berkeley, Calif.
March 1, 19___

Sheriff (Civil Division)
Alameda County
Alameda County Courthouse
Oakland, California

Re: John Toller v. Mildred Edwards
Small Claims Court
Albany-Berkeley Judicial District
No. SC 81-52

Dear Sir:

You are hereby instructed, under the authority of the
enclosed Writ of Execution, to levy upon and sell all of
the right, title and interest of Mildred Edward,
judgment debtor, in the following motor vehicle:

[Type the description of the car as it appears on your
D.M.V. report, including the license number.]

The vehicle is registered in the name(s) of Mildred
Edwards, and is regularly found at the following
address(es):

[List home and work address of owner.]

Enclosed is my check for $_____ to cover your
costs of levy and sale.

Very truly yours,
John Toller

5. Real Property

The simple act of recording an "Abstract of [Your] Judgment" at the County Recorder's office in any (or all) counties where the judgment debtor owns real property gives you a lien against all of his real property in that county. When the judgment debtor wishes to sell his real property, the title will be clouded by your lien and he will have to pay you off to be able to transfer clear title to a third party. Thus, sooner or later, you will get your money.[9] This being true, it normally makes little sense to go through the complicated procedures involved actually in selling, or trying to sell, a person's real property to satisfy your relatively small judgment.

To record your judgment against real property, first get an "Abstract of Judgment" from the Small Claims clerk's office. The clerk will prepare this paper for you. Then take the "Abstract of Judgment" to the County Recorder's office in the county where the property is located, pay a fee and give the Recorder the mailing address of the judgment debtor so that he can be notified. They will do the rest.

6. Other Personal Property

Normally, it isn't worth the trouble to try to levy on small items of personal property such as furniture or appliances because they are commonly covered by one or another of the state exemption laws which state that certain possessions are exempt from being taken to satisfy debts. The exemption laws

---

[9] The only exception to this rule is that a home on which the judgment debtor has filed a homestead prior to your filing your "Abstract of Judgment" can be sold by the judgment debtor and the money (up to $45,000 in equity for a family, $30,000 for a single person under 65, and $65,000 for people over 65, the blind or disabled) used to buy another homesteaded home within six months without paying off your lien. If you wish information as to how to fill out the simple form necessary to homestead your house, see *Homestead Your House*, Warner, Sherman and Ihara, Nolo Press.

are found listed in CCP Sec. 704.010 et seq. and include furniture, clothing, and much more.

7. Business Assets

It is possible to have someone from the sheriff's or marshal's office sent to the business of a person who owes you money to collect it from the cash on hand. This can be done in two ways as follows:

a. **Eight Hour Keeper:** A deputy goes to the place of business and picks up all the money in the till. If there isn't enough to cover the judgment, he stands by the cash register and grabs the money as it comes in. The fee for this is $51.

b. **24-Hour Keeper:** Same as the eight-hour keeper, but the deputy stays three times as long as necessary. The fee is $172.

Talk to the sheriff or marshal in your area to get more details. They will want an original and three copies of your Writ of Execution as well as instructions telling them where and when to go. Fees are recoverable from the judgment debtor if enough money comes in to cover them, plus the judgment.

8. Pensions and Retirement Benefits

You can go after the money in individual or self-employment retirement plans (IRAs, KEOGHS) only if that money is in excess of the amount tax exempt under federal income tax law. In addition, the judgment debtor may try to claim that non tax exempt money is necessary for the reasonable support of her and her family. If the court agrees, you're out of luck.

Private company retirement plans and state or local government retirement plans can't be touched until the money is paid over to the employee.

Federal government payroll checks and pension and retirement benefits may not be garnished to satisfy any debts, except those for alimony and child support.

. . . . COURT, SMALL CLAIMS DIVISION

. . . . COURT DISTRICT

(Address and Telephone Number of Court)

. . . . COUNTY, CALIFORNIA

SMALL CLAIM CASE NO

PLAINTIFF (Name and address)   DEFENDANT (Name and address of each)

JUDGMENT DEBTOR'S STATEMENT OF ASSETS

The *judgment debtor* in this small claims case is the person (or business) who lost the case and owes money to the winner. The winner of the case is the *judgment creditor.*

TO THE JUDGMENT DEBTOR:

The small claims court has decided you owe money to the judgment creditor.

1. Unless you pay, appeal or move to vacate, you must fill out this form and send it to the person who won the case within **35 days** after the Notice of Entry of Judgment is mailed to you by the clerk.

2. If you file an appeal or a Motion to Vacate, you do not need to fill out this form unless you lose your appeal or motion to vacate. Then you will have 30 days to pay or complete this form and deliver it to the judgment creditor. IF YOU FAIL TO DO SO YOU MAY HAVE TO GO TO COURT TO ANSWER QUESTIONS OR THE COURT CAN IMPOSE PENALTIES ON YOU.

If you were sued as an individual skip this box and begin with no. 1 below. Otherwise, check the applicable box, attach the documents indicated and complete no. 12 on the reverse.

   a. ☐ (Corporation or partnership) Attached to this form is a statement describing the nature, value and exact location of all assets of the corporation or the partners, and a statement showing that the person signing this form is authorized to submit this form on behalf of the corporation or partnership.

   b. ☐ (Governmental agency) Attached to this form is the statement of an authorized representative of the agency as to when the agency will pay the judgment and any reasons for its failure to do so.

EMPLOYMENT

1. What is your occupation?

2. Name and address of your business or employer:

3. How often are you paid?

   a. ☐ daily ☐ weekly ☐ every two weeks ☐ twice a month ☐ monthly ☐ other *(explain)*

4. What is your gross pay each pay period? $ . . . .

5. What is your take home pay each pay period? $ . . . .

6. If your wife or husband earns any income give the name and address of the business or employer:

(Continued on reverse)

Form approved by the
Judicial Council of California
Effective January 1, 1981
SC-133(81)

**JUDGMENT DEBTOR'S
STATEMENT OF ASSETS
(SMALL CLAIMS)**

Code of Civil
Procedure § 117 19(b)

CASH, BANK DEPOSITS

7 How much money do you have in cash? $

8 How much other money do you have in banks, savings and loans, credit unions and other financial institutions either in your own name or jointly (list)

Name and address of financial institution	Account number	Individual or joint?	Balance
a			$
b			$
c			$

PROPERTY

9 List all automobiles, other vehicles and boats owned in your name or jointly

Make and year	Value	Legal owner if different from registered owner	Amount owed
a	$		$
b	$		$
c	$		$
d	$		$

10. List all real estate owned in your name or jointly

Address of real estate	Fair market value	Amount owed
a	$	$
b	$	$

OTHER PERSONAL PROPERTY *[Do not list household furniture and furnishings, appliances, or clothing.]*

11 List anything of value not listed above owned in your name or jointly

Description	Value	Address where property is located
a	$	
b	$	
c	$	
d	$	
e	$	
f	$	
g	$	
h	$	
i	$	
j	$	

12 I declare under penalty of perjury under the laws of the State of California that the foregoing, including any attachments, is true and correct and that this declaration is executed on (date)

at (place)

        (Type or print name)   (Signature)

Mail or deliver this completed form to the judgment creditor at the address shown on the Notice of Entry of Judgment form.

B. Finding Phantom Assets—The Judgment Debtor's Statement

As you now understand from reading the above sections, collecting on your Small Claims judgment isn't normally difficult if the judgment creditor has some money or property and you know where it is. But what do you do when you suspect that money or property exists, but have no idea how to find it? For example, you may know that a person works, but not where, or that he has money in the bank, but not which one. Wouldn't it be nice to simply ask the judgment debtor a few questions which he must answer?

Well, thanks to California CCP Sec. 117.19(b), you can do just that. Here's how it works. When a Small Claims Court judgment is entered against a person (or business) the loser (judgment debtor) must fill out a form entitled the "Judgment Debtor's Statement of Assets." This form must be sent by the judgment debtor to the person who won the case (the judgment creditor) within 35 days after Notice of Entry of Judgment is mailed out by the clerk *unless* the judgment debtor pays off the judgment, appeals or makes a motion to set aside or vacate the judgment. If a losing defendant appeals or files a motion to set aside a default judgment (or a losing plaintiff files a motion to vacate a default), and subsequently loses, he has 30 days to pay or fill out the Judgment Debtor's Statement.

If a judgment debtor does not fill out this form when required to do so, the judgment creditor can ask the court clerk to issue a

"Declaration and Order of Examination." This order, which must be properly served on the judgment debtor, requires the judgment debtor to show up in court and provide the information on the debtor's statement personally. If the debtor fails to show up, the judge can issue a bench warrant for his arrest. Oh, and one hint. At the Order of Examination hearing, the judgment creditor can ask if the debtor has any cash in her possession. If so, this can be taken to satisfy at least a portion of the debt.

C. Recovering Collection Costs And Interest

Costs (including the filing fee, costs of service, etc.) incurred prior to recovering a judgment should be included in the judgment total when it is entered by the judge. I discuss this in Chapter 15C.

Here I am concerned with costs incurred after judgment. These are the costs that result when the judgment debtor doesn't pay voluntarily and you have to levy on his or her assets. This can be expensive and you will want to make the judgment debtor pay, if possible. Most costs of collecting a judgment are recoverable, a few are not. Generally speaking, you can recover your direct costs of collecting which include such things as sheriff, marshal or constable fees, costs to get copies of required papers (i.e., "Writ of Execution," "Abstract of Judgment") issued, and recording fees. You can also recover interest on the judgment at a rate of 10% per year. Indirect costs such as babysitting costs, time off work, postage, gasoline, etc., can't be recovered.

There are two principal ways to collect your costs:

1. Writ of Execution

If you will turn back a few pages to the sample "Writ of Execution" you will see that as part of levying on wages, bank accounts, automobiles, businesses, etc., collection fees can simply be added to the total to be collected by the collecting officer, with no need for additional court action. These include the fee for issuing the Writ of Execution and the sheriff's, marshal's or constable's fee for collecting it. This can really add up as the fees for selling a motor vehicle, or placing a keeper at a place of business are considerable. In addition, you can collect any interest that has accrued on the original judgment.

2. Memorandum of Credits, Accrued Interest And Costs After Judgment

Other costs, such as money expended for an "Abstract of Judgment," County Recorder fees and costs for unsuccessful levies on wages, bank accounts, businesses or motor vehicles can be recovered only after court approval. To get these you must file a "Memorandum of Credits, Accrued Interest and Costs After Judgment." The Small Claims Court clerk will help you prepare this form. File one copy with the clerk and have a friend mail another copy to the judgment debtor. Then have your friend fill out a "Proof of Service" form (see Chapter 11F) to be filed with the clerk.

D. Collecting Small Judgments for Motor Vehicle Accidents

There is a special procedure useful for collecting unpaid Small Claims judgments in the amount of $500 or less against the driver of a motor vehicle arising from an accident on a California highway. If the judgment is not paid in 90 days, a form can be filed with the DMV. The judgment debtor then has 10 days to pay (or prove he has insurance covering the damage) or he will have his license suspended for 90 days.

CHAPTER 24

Where Do We Go
From Here?

It's easy to criticize the existing legal system—almost
everyone knows it's on the rocks. The $500 a day experts with
their degrees, titles, and well-funded consulting companies
have studied the problem to death with no positive results.
And this is hardly surprising, since most of the experts
involved in the studies and in the resulting decisions are
lawyers who, at bottom, are unable to understand a problem of
which they are so thoroughly a part.[1]

---

[1] Not everyone believes that a rotten court system is a bad thing.
David Hapgood, in his interesting book, *The Average Man Fights
Back*, reports the following statement by the Chinese Emperor K'ang
Hsi: "...lawsuits would tend to increase to a frightening extent if people
were not afraid of the tribunals and if they felt confident of always
finding in them ready and perfect justice...I desire therefore that those
who have recourse to the tribunals should be treated without pity and
in such a manner that they shall be disgusted with law and tremble to
appear before a magistrate."

But instead of my lecturing you about all the things that are wrong at the local courthouse, let's sit down at the kitchen table with a pot of tea and a bowl of raspberries and see if we can't design a better system. After all, this republic was founded by ordinary people taking the law into their own hands—they had to because most of the governor, judge and lawyer-types were quite comfortable in England, thank you. And don't forget that we have already agreed that the present legal structure doesn't work, so we obviously have nothing to lose by making our own suggestions. Hey, leave a few raspberries for me, and why don't you jot down a few of your own ideas as we go along so that this becomes a two-way communication.

Before we get to specific suggestions for change, let's take a brief look around to see where we are starting from. As a society, we obviously have a fixation with trying to solve problems by suing one another. Nowhere in the world do people come close to being as litigious as we are. The result of this love of lawsuits, or perhaps its cause—it's one of those chicken and egg problems—is the fact that, whenever we get into any sort of spat with anyone, or even think that we might get into one in the future, we run to a lawyer.[2] It's gotten so bad that people who suffer an injury have been known to call their lawyer before their doctor. But there is an odd paradox here. At the same time that we tolerate vast numbers of lawyers eating at the top end of our societal trough and are more and more likely to use them, public opinion polls tell us that our respect for lawyers has fallen so that we rate their trustworthiness below that of used car salespeople, undertakers and loan sharks. It's as if, the less we respect lawyers, the more we use them. Perhaps we're afraid that if we don't sue first, someone will get the jump on us. If you eat one more of those raspberries, I'll see you in court.

Have you ever thought about how people solved their disputes in simpler societies? Let's pretend for a moment that

---

[2] There are over 700,000 lawyers in the United States, and another 120,000 in law school. New York City alone has more than 50,000. There are more judges in Los Angeles County than there are in all of France.

we are members of a tribe of deer hunters in a pre-industrial age.[3] One fine fall morning we both set out bow in hand, you to the east and I to the west. Before long, you hit a high cliff and turn north. My way is blocked by a swift river, and I too turn north. Without our realizing it, our paths converge. Suddenly, a great stag jumps from the underbrush and we both pull back our bows and let fly. Our arrows pierce the deer's heart from opposite sides, seemingly at the same instant.

For a moment we stand frozen, each surprised by the presence of the other. Then we realize what has happened and that we have a problem. To whom does the deer belong? We carry the deer back to the village, each unwilling to surrender our claim to the other. After the deer is gutted and hung, we speak to the chief of our group about our problem. He convenes a council of elders to meet late in the afternoon to consider it. Each of us has his say as to what happened. The deer carcass is examined. Anyone else who has knowledge of our dispute is invited to speak. Tribal custom (law) is consulted, our credibility is weighed, and a decision is made—in time for dinner.

Now, let's ask ourselves what would happen today, if you and I simultaneously shot a deer (instead of each other) on the first day of hunting season and were unable to agree to whom it belonged. Assuming we didn't fight it out on the spot, but wanted the dispute resolved by "proper" legal procedures, lawyers would have to be consulted, court papers filed and responded to, a court appearance scheduled, words spoken in legalese, and a formal court decision written and issued. All of this for a deer that would have long since rotted away unless it had been put in cold storage. If the deer had been frozen, the storage costs would have to be added to court costs and attorney fees which all together would surely add up to a lot more than the value of the deer. Oh well, next time we had better go hunting at McDonald's where everything is safely delivered in plastic.

Seriously, what were the differences between the ways the two societies resolved the problem of who owned the deer? The so-called primitive one did a better job, but why? Obviously

---

[3] Anthropologists will, I hope, accept this little fable as just that.

because their solution was in proportion to the problem, while today we often make the solution process so cumbersome and expensive that it dwarfs the disputes. The hunting society handled the disagreement quickly, cheaply and, most importantly, with a process that allowed the disputing parties to participate in and understand what was going on. Simple, you say. Why then can't our dispute resolution procedure achieve even one of these goals? In large measure, because lawyers have vested financial and psychic interests in the present cumbersome way of doing things and have neither the motivation nor the perspective to make changes.

But isn't my view a bit radical? Isn't there something uniquely valuable about the great sweep of the common law as it has evolved through the ages? Doesn't the majestic black-robed judge sitting on his throne mumbling age old mantras somehow guarantee that God is in heaven, the republic safe, and that "justice will be done?" Not necessarily. History is arbitrary—our dispute resolution mechanisms could have developed in a number of alternate ways. If our present system worked well, imposing it on the future would make sense. As, in fact, it hardly works at all, continuing it is silly. Those who get quite misty-eyed recounting the history, traditions and time-tested forms behind our present ways of doing things are almost always people who benefit by their continuance. Consider, too, that in the United States, we have no pure legal tradition, having borrowed large hunks of our jurisprudence on a catch as catch basis from England, Spain, France, Holland, and Germany, as well as various Native American cultures.

Okay, granted that there have been legal systems that have worked better than ours, and granted that at least some change is overdue, what should we do? One significant reform would be to expand Small Claims Court. Like the system followed by the deer hunters, but unlike most of the rest of our legal system, Small Claims Court is simple, fast, cheap and allows for the direct participation of the disputing parties. Never mind that up to now Small Claims Court has been tolerated primarily as a way to keep lawyers' offices clear of penny ante people with penny ante disputes. It's there, it works, and we can expand it to play a meaningful role in our lives.

As you know by now, Small Claims Court as it is presently set up has several disadvantages. First, the amount that can be sued for is ridiculously low. Second, in most instances, the court only has the power to make judgments that can be satisfied by the payment of money damages. Third, many kinds of cases, such as divorces, adoptions, etc., aren't permitted in Small Claims at all. Why not start our effort to improve things by doing away with these disadvantages? Let's raise the maximum amount that can be sued for to $10,000.[4] I would like to suggest $20,000, but perhaps we should take one step at a time to limit attorney opposition. An increase to $10,000 would be a significant reform—allowing tens of thousands of disputes to be removed from our formal legal system. One logical reason to pick $10,000 is that people can't afford lawyers to handle disputes for amounts below this.[5]

---

[4] While most states limit Small Claims jurisdiction to the $1,500 - $2,500 range, there are exceptions. For example, the United States Tax Court has a very successful Small Claims procedure which allows claims up to $10,000.

[5] I believe that there are persuasive reasons for limiting the role of lawyers in addition to the fact that they cost too much. Such a limitation would require fundamental changes in our adversary system and is the subject for a broader book. For a good history of how our adversary system evolved from barbaric practices such as trial by battle, how it all too often serves to obscure rather than expose the truth, and how it protects the interests of the already strong and powerful (those who can afford a good mouthpiece) at the expense of everyone else, see Injustice For All, Strick, Putnam, $8.95.

To illustrate, let's take a situation where Randy the carpenter agrees to do $20,000 worth of rehabilitation to Al's home. When the work is completed, an argument develops about whether it was done properly according to the agreement. Al pays Randy $15,000, leaving $5,000 in dispute. Randy goes to his lawyer, and Al to his. Each has several preliminary conferences after which the lawyers exchange several letters and telephone calls. Eventually, a lawsuit is filed and answered, a court date is obtained many months in the future and then changed several times, and, finally, a two-hour trial is held. Randy's lawyer bills him $1,255 (12.5 hours x $100 per hour) and Al's charges $960 (12 hours x $80 per hour), for a total fee of $2,215. The dispute takes eleven months to be decided. In the end, Randy is awarded $3,500.[6]

This is a typical case with a typical solution. Between them, the lawyers collected almost half of the amount in dispute and took most of a year to arrive at a solution that very likely left both Randy and Al frustrated. Don't you think that Randy and Al would have preferred presenting their case in Small Claims Court where it would have been heard and decided in a month? Of course, either of them could have done worse arguing the case himself, but remember, when the legal fees are taken into consideration, the loser would have had to do a lot worse in Small Claims before he would have ended up in worse financial shape. Randy recovered $3,500 with a lawyer, but after subtracting the $1,255 lawyer fee, his net gain was only $2,245. Al ended up paying $4,460 ($3,500 for the judgment and $960 for his attorney). Thus, if a Small Claims Court judge had awarded Randy any amount from $2,246 to $4,459, both men would have done better than they did with lawyers. Of course, if this sort of case were permitted in Small Claims Court, there would be two big losers. Can it be a coincidence that lawyers (through their influence in state

---

[6] A lawyer might argue that many cases of this type are settled with a few letters and phone calls. This is true, but by the time you allow for client conferences and the fact that many lawyers charge considerably more than the fees I list here, the cost to settle would probably be comparable.

legislatures) make sure that Small Claims maximums are kept as low as possible?

The second great barrier to bringing cases in Small Claims Court is the fact that, with minor exceptions, the court is limited to making money judgments. Think back for a moment to our problems with the twice-shot deer. How does the award of money make sense in this situation? In our Small Claims Court, the tribesman who didn't end up with the carcass would have had to sue the other for the fair market value of the deer. What nonsense—if we are going to have a dispute resolution procedure, why not permit a broad range of solutions, such as the deer being cut in half, or the deer going to one hunter and six ducks going to the other in compensation, or maybe even the deer going to the person who needed it most? Or using examples more common at the end of the 20th century, why not allow a Small Claims Court judge to order an apartment be cleaned, a garage repainted, or a car properly fixed, instead of simply telling one person to pay X dollars to the other? One advantage of this sort of flexibility is that more judgments would be meaningful. Under our present system, tens of thousands of judgments can't be collected because the loser has no obvious source of income. We need to get away from the notion that people who are broke have neither rights nor responsibilities. To have a decent life, people need both.

Lawyers and judges often contend that it would be impossible to enforce non-money judgments. Perhaps some would be hard to keep track of. Certainly it might require some experimentation to find out what types of judgments are practical and which are not; however, since it is often impossible to collect a judgment under the present system, it can't hurt to try some alternatives.

The third big change that I propose, and the one that would truly make over our court system, involves expanding the types of cases that can be heard in Small Claims. Why not be brave and take the twenty most common legal problems and adopt simplified procedures enabling all of them to be handled by the people themselves without lawyers? Why not open up our courthouses to the average person who, after all, pays the bills?

To accomplish this democratization of our dispute resolution procedures, I suggest dividing Small Claims Court into several separate divisions, each one responsible for a broad area of common concern. For example, there would be a landlord-tenant and a domestic relations divisions.[7] Each division would have the authority to consider a broad range of problems and solutions falling within its area of concern. Today, if you have a claim against your landlord (or he against you) for money damages, you can use Small Claims only if the claim is for $1,500 or less. If you want a roof fixed, a tenant evicted, or to protect your privacy, etc., Small Claims Court can't help you, except possibly to award a money judgment for the intentional infliction of emotional distress.[8] The Canadian province of British Columbia has already put all landlord-tenant disputes in what amounts to a Small Claims format, easily and cheaply available to both landlord and tenant. Why can't we?

A domestic relations Small Claims Court could include simplified procedures to help people handle their own uncontested divorces, adoptions, name changes, guardianships, etc. safely and cheaply. And why not? Even with considerable hostility from lawyers and court personnel, over 20% of the divorces in California are already handled without a lawyer by people who deal with the absurd procedures inherent in going to Superior Court. When I suggest that people should be encouraged to handle their own domestic problems in a Small

---

[7] There is nothing new about the idea of dividing a court by subject matter. This is already done in our formal trial courts and works well.

[8] As I pointed out in Chapter 20, some evictions can be brought in Small Claims if a number of conditions are met, but it is commonly unwise to do so.

Claims-type forum, I'm not advocating that sensible safeguards be dropped. For example, if a divorce involves children, you would want to have someone trained in the field carefully examine the parents' plans for custody, visitation and support to see if they are reasonable.

Without going into detail, I suggest that if we took lawyers out of our domestic relations courts, we would save not only millions of dollars and many hours, but more importantly, we would lighten the heavy burden of hostility and anxiety that the divorcing spouses must now bear. Our present system, in which parents and children become clients of a "hired gun" (the lawyer) is a bad one. By definition, the client role is weak and the gun fighter role strong.[9] This imbalance commonly results in lawyers making critical decisions, affecting their clients' lives, sometimes obviously, sometimes subtlely. All too often these decisions benefit the lawyer and his bank balance to the detriment of both the client's psyche and pocketbook. The lawyer, after all, is paid more to fight, or at least to pretend to fight, than to compromise. I have seen dozens of situations where lawyers have played on people's worst instincts (paranoia, greed, ego, one-upsmanship) to fan nasty, little disagreements into flaming battles. Perhaps mercifully, the battles normally last only as long as the lawyers' bills are paid.

---

[9] In an interesting article entitled "Valuable Deficiencies, A Service Economy Needs People In Need," in the Fall 1977 Co-Evolution Quarterly, John McNight points out that "The Latin root of the word 'client' is a verb which translates 'to hear,' 'to obey.'"

I could list a number of other areas of law that could be converted to a Small Claims approach (auto accidents, simple probates, perhaps even some criminal cases), but I am sure you get the point. We must take control of the decision making processes that affect our lives. We must make ourselves welcome in our own courts and legislatures. We must stop looking at ourselves as clients who hear and obey and start taking responsibility for our own legal decisions.

Let's assume now that these obstacles can be overcome and the role of Small Claims Court will be greatly expanded. In the process of doing so, we will need to make a number of changes in the way the court now operates. It will be a good opportunity to throw out a number of existing procedures that owe more to history than to common sense. Here are a few specific ideas for changes:

1. Let's make Small Claims Court easily accessible. This means holding weekend and evening sessions. This is being done now on a limited basis in our larger counties, but should be routinely available everywhere. When court is held at 9 A.M. on weekdays, it often costs more in time lost from work for all the principals and witnesses to show up than the case is worth.

2. Let's get the judge out of his black robe and off of his throne. There is a part of all of us that loves the drama involved in seeing our magistrates sitting on high like the kings of England, but I am convinced by my own brief experience as a "pro tem" judge that this pomp and circumstance is counter productive. We would have a lot less confrontation, and a lot more willingness to compromise if we got rid of some of the drama.

3. While we're making changes, let's make a big one—let's restrict the adversary system.[10] It contributes a great deal to the posturing of the litigants and obfuscation of the dispute,

---

[10] The distinguished legal scholar Roscoe Pound made this point better than I can, "The doctrine of contentious procedure...is peculiar to Anglo-American law...(it) disfigures our judicial administration at every point...(it) gives to the whole community a false notion of the purpose and end of law....Thus, the courts...are made agents or abettors of lawlessness."

and very little to settling disputes efficiently. We must move toward systems of mediation and arbitration in which, instead of a traditional judge, we have someone whose role is to facilitate the parties arriving at their own solution—imposing a decision only if they arrive at a hopeless impasse. Big business, big labor, and increasingly even lawyers are coming to realize that arbitration and mediation are good ways to solve problems.[11] What I have in mind is something like this: All the parties to the dispute would sit down at a table with a Small Claims employee (let's drop the word "judge"). This person who would be trained for the job would not necessarily be a lawyer. The mediator would help the parties search for areas of agreement and possible compromise and, if this was impossible, at least help them define the areas in dispute.

4. Appeal rules should also be changed. The present California system which allows only the defendant to appeal to Superior Court and allows litigants to have lawyers on appeal is nuts. All too often corporate defendants who have lawyers on retainer use the present system to frustrate consumers who have won in Small Claims Court. It is my belief that no appeals should be allowed in Small Claims Court—the amounts in question just aren't worth it. If appeals are allowed, lawyers should be prohibited.[12]

I don't mean to suggest that the changes I propose in this short chapter are the only ones necessary. If we are going to put the majority of our routine legal work in Small Claims, it will require turning our dispute resolution process on its head. Legal information must be stored and decoded so that it is available to the average person. Clerk's offices, and the other support

---

[11] California has adopted an arbitration procedure which allows many types of cases that have been filed in Superior Court to be diverted to an arbitration procedure. Why not Small Claims cases?

[12] Because of the so-called constitutional right to be represented by a lawyer if you want one, there will be problems barring lawyers from Small Claims Court itself and eliminating the defendants' right to appeal (or transfer) to a court where they can have a lawyer. One way to solve this dilemma is to create a Small Claims procedure that is so desirable that very few defendants will want their cases transferred to a formal court where lawyers are allowed.

systems surrounding our courts must be expanded and geared to serve the non-lawyer. Legal forms must be translated from "legalese" into English. Computer systems must be developed to bring legal information into our offices and living rooms.

Let's illustrate how things might change by looking at a case I recently saw argued in a northern California Small Claims Court. One party to the dispute (let's call her Sally) arranged fishing charters for business and club groups. The other (let's call him Ben) owned several fishing boats. Sally often hired Ben's boats for her charters. Their relationship was of long standing and had been profitable to both. However, as the fishing charter business grew, both Sally and Ben began to enlarge their operations. Sally got a boat or two of her own and Ben began getting into the charter booking business. Eventually they stepped on one another's toes and their friendly relationship was replaced by tension and argument. One day a blow-up occurred over some inconsequential detail, phones were slammed down and Sally and Ben each swore never to do business with the other again.

Before the day of the fight, Sally had organized two charters on Ben's boat. These were to have taken place a week after the phones were slammed down. For reasons unconnected with the argument, the charters were cancelled by the clubs that had organized them. Ben had about a week's notice of cancellation. He also had $600 in deposits that Sally had paid him. He refused to refund the deposits. Sally sued him in Small Claims Court for $700 ($600 for the charter fee and $100 for general inconvenience).[13]

Testimony in court made it clear that charters were commonly cancelled and were often replaced by others booked at the last minute. Ben and Sally had signed a "Standard Marine Charter Agreement" which dealt with the issue of cancelled charters because it was required by the Coast Guard, although they had never in the past paid attention to its terms. They had always worked out sensible adjustments on a situation-by-situation basis, depending on whether substitute charters were available and whether the club or business cancelling had paid money up front, etc.

When Ben and Sally first presented their arguments about the $700, it seemed that they were not too far apart as to what would be a fair compromise. Unfortunately, the adversary nature of the court system encouraged each to overstate his (her) case and to dredge up all sorts of irrelevant side issues. "What about the times you overloaded my boat?" Ben demanded. "How about those holidays when you price gouged me?" Sally replied. As the arguments went back and forth, each person got angrier and angrier and was less and less able to listen to the other.

The result was that after an hour of testimony the judge was left with a confused mishmash of custom, habit, maritime charter contracts, promises made or not made, past performance, etc. No decision that he arrived at was likely to be accepted by both Ben and Sally as being fair. Indeed, unless he gave one or the other everything he or she requested, both of them would surely feel cheated. That is not to say that the hearing was all bad—some good things did occur. The dispute was presented quickly, cheaply and each person got to have his or her say and blow off some steam. All of these things would have been impossible in our formal court system. However, if Small

---

[13] As we learned earlier, Sally can't recover for inconvenience, so her maximum recovery would be $600.

Claims Court could be changed along the lines suggested above, a better result might have been reached.

Suppose that instead of a formal courtroom confrontation Ben and Sally are first encouraged to talk the dispute out themselves. If this fails, the next step is for the two of them to sit down in a non-courtroom setting with a court employee who is trained as a mediator and whose job is to help Ben and Sally arrive at a fair compromise—a compromise which will hopefully provide a foundation for Ben and Sally to continue to work together in the future. Only if compromise is impossible, would there be recourse to a formal court hearing. I am convinced that if this sort of three-tiered approach was available that Ben and Sally would have worked out a compromise at the first or second stage.

APPENDIX 1

Major California Consumer Laws

1. Automotive Repair Act
   (Bus. & Prof. Code §§ 9880-9889.21)

2. Collection Agency Act
   (Bus. & Prof. Code §§ 6850-6856.1 and 15 U.S.C.
   §§ 1692-1692(o)

3. Consumer Credit Laws
   (Civ. Code §§ 1799.90-1799.96)

4. Consumer Finance Lenders Law
   (Fin. Code §§ 24000-24653)

5. Consumer Legal Remedies Act
   (Civ. Code §§ 1750-1784)

6. Contractors License Law (False advertising, etc.)
   (Bus. & Prof. Code §§ 7000-7173)

7. Contracts for Discount Buying Services
   (Civ. Code §§ 1812.100-1812.128)

8. Credit Services Act of 1984
   (Civ. Code §§ 1789.10-1789.23)

9. Dance Studio Contracts
   (Civ. Code §§ 1812.50-1812.68)

10. Fair Debt Collection Act
    (Civ. Code §§ 1788-1788.32)

11. Fraud--Cancellation of Contracts Based On
    (Civ. Code §§ 1572(1)-1572(5), 1689.1

12. Health Studio Contracts
    (Civ. Code §§ 1812.80-1812.95)

13. Home Improvement Contracts
    (Bus. & Prof. Code §§ 7150-7161)

14. Home Solicitation Contracts
    (Civ. Code §§ 1689.5-1689.13)

15. Mail Order or Catalog Business
    (Bus. & Prof. Code §§ 17538-17538.5)

16. Minors Cancellation of Contract Rights
    (Civ. Code §§ 34,35)

17. Personal Loans- small loan companies
    (Fin. Code §§ 14000-16154

18. Recission of a Contract Based on Fraud, Lack of
    Consideration, Illegality, etc.
    (Civ. Code §§ 1689(b)(1)-1689(3)(b)

19. Rees-Levering Motor Vehicle Sales and Finance Act
    (Civ. Code §§ 2981-2984.4)

20. Retail Installment Accounts
    (Civ. Code § 1810.12)

21. Seller-Assisted Marketing Plans
    (Civ. Code §§ 1812.200-1812.220)

22. Song-Beverly Consumer Warranty Act
    (Civ. Code §§ 1790-1797.5)

23. Song-Beverly Credit Card Act
    (Civ. Code §§ 1747-1748.5)

24. Unconscionable Contracts
    (Civ. Code § 1670.5)

25. UCC Warranties
    (a) Express (Com Code § 2313)

    (b) Implied (Com. Code § 2315)

26. Unfair Trade Practices Act
    (Bus. & Prof. Code § 17200)

27. Unruh Act
    (Civ. Code §§ 1801-1812.20)

28. Unsolicited Goods
    (Civ. Code §§ 1584.5-1584.6)

29. Vehicle Leasing Act
    (Civ. Code §§ 2985.7-2990)

ABOUT THE AUTHOR

Ralph (Jake) Warner is a leader of the "do your own law" movement on the West Coast. As a co-founder of Nolo Press and the author of numerous books and articles aimed at giving the non-lawyer so-called "legal information" to deal with their own life decisions, he has constantly tried to expand the areas in which people can help themselves. His most recent book is the *Independent Paralegal's Handbook: How to Start Your Own Law Business Without Going to Jail.* Along with Toni Ihara, Ralph is also the author of *29 Reasons Not to Go to Law School.*

Index

K

Keeper, at place of business, 23:11

L

Landlord-tenant conflicts, 2:9, 2:15, 4:4n, 4:6-7, 4:15n, 6:6n, 20:1-15, 24:8
"Last Statement of Officers," 11:7
Law libraries. *See* Libraries and librarians
Lawyers:
  and corporations, 1:1n, 7:4
  and legal system, 13:1-3, 24:1-14
  number in U.S., 24:2n
  and own cases, 1:1n, 7:4
  and personal injury cases, 2:16, 4:11, 4:13
  and Small Claims Court, 1:1, 7:4, 13:8
  and Superior Court, 22:12, 24:11
Lease. *See* Landlord-tenant conflicts
Legal jargon, 1:2, 1:6-11
Legal research, 1:11-12, 4:2
Legal system, U.S., 24:1-14
Lemon law, 17:1-2
Levying, 1:8, 23:3-13, 23:15-16
Liability, 2:3-4, 2:10-16, 4:8-9, 17:7, 17:10
  limited, 8:5
  strict, 2:12, 2:15-16
Libraries and librarians, 1:10, 1:12, 4:2,
License number, 8:6, 19:2
Lien, 1:6, 1:8, 23:10
Limitations. *See* Statute of limitations
Limited liability. *See* Liability, limited
Loss, determining, 2:1-22, 16:3. *See also* Claim, computation of

M

Mail:
  decision sent by, 22:1-2, 22:9
  filing by, 10:5-6
  process serving by, 10:1, 10:5-6, 10:11-12, 11:3, 11:5, 11:7, 11:8
Marshall. *See* Sheriff
Mediation. *See* Arbitration/mediation
Medical costs, 4:11-14
"Memorandum of Costs" form, 15:10
"Memorandum of Credits, Accrued Interest, and Costs After Judgment," 23:16
Mental distress cases, 2:12-14, 4:14-15
Military personnel, 7:6, 8:6n
  serving papers on, 11:10
Minors:
  filing suit against, 7:1n, 8:6-7

filing suit for, 7:1n, 7:4
  and guardians, 7:4, 8:6-7
Mitigation of damages. *See* Damages, mitigation of
"Motion for Rehearing," 22:2n
Motion to vacate judgment, 1:8-9, 23:14
Motor vehicle accident cases, 4:8-9, 19:1-10, 23:16
  suit against owner, 8:6, 19:2
  suit by owner, 7:2-3
Motor vehicle finance sales, 9:3, 9:8
Motor vehicle owner, 7:2-3, 8:6, 19:2, 23:8
Motor vehicle parts, return of, 16:3
Motor vehicle purchase disputes, 17:1-14
Motor vehicle repair dealers, 7:3
Motor vehicle repair disputes, 16:1-8
Motor vehicles:
  and collection of debts, 23:4, 23:8-9
  and garnishment, 3:2n, 3:3
Motor vehicles, used. *See* Used vehicles
Multiple defendants. *See* Defendant, multiple
Multiple plaintiffs. *See* Plaintiff, multiple
Multiple suits, 4:3-5
Municipal Court:
  as alternative to Small Claims Court, 4:2, 4:3-5, 4:12n, 10:7, 12:4
  and evictions, 20:1, 20:13
  judges of, 13:8
  and right to apeal, 22:9

N

Name, of entity being sued, 8:2-3
Negligence, 1:5, 2:10-12, 2:14, 4:8, 16:3-4, 19:2, 19:4
  comparative, 2:12, 19:9
  defined, 2:10-11
  and statute of limitations, 5:2
"Notice of Entry of Judgment," 23:14
"Notice of Motion to Vacate Judgment," 10:12-13

O

Oath, in courtroom, 13:6
Obligation. *See* Contract
Order of Examination, 1:9
Owner of property, determining, 20:4-5
Owner of vehicle. *See* Motor vehicle owner

P

Pain and suffering, 4:12n, 4:13, 4:14-15
Partnerships, and filing claim, 7:2, 8:4-5

Strategy. *See* Case, preparation
Strict liability. *See* Liability, strict
Structural pest control operators, 7:3
Submission, 1:10
Subpoena, 1:10, 14:3-9. *See also* Service of
 Subpoena
"Subpoena Duces Tecum" form, 1:10, 14:6-9, 17:9
Subpoenaing:
 of documents, 14:6-9, 17:9
 of police officers, 14:6
 of witnesses, 14:3, 14:4-5
Substituted service, of papers. *See* Service of
 process
Suing:
 against more than one person, 8:2, 8:6, 9:4
 amount, 4:1-19
 for more than one person, 7:2
 location of filing suit, 9:1-8
 twice, 4:5
 who can be sued, 8:1-8, 17:3n, 19:2
 who can sue, 7:1-7, 19:2
Superior Court:
 as alternative to Small Claims Court, 4:2, 4:12n,
 10:7, 12:4
 and appeal, 1:6, 10:12, 15:1, 20:13, 22:9, 22:10-12,
 24:11
 and arbitration, 24:11n
Surety companies, 8:8

T

Talking out dispute, 6:2-4
Telephone testimony, 14:12
Television repair persons, 7:3
Tenant-landlord conflicts. *See* Landlord-tenant
 conflicts
Three-day notice, to tenant, 20:13, 20:15
Till tap, 23:11
Time limit, in filing claim. *See* Statute of
 Limitations
Time limit, in serving papers, 11:5-7
Time payments, of judgment, 12:2-3, 18:8, 20:8,
 22:3-5
Title slip, 17:10
Tolling, of statute of limitations, 5:5-6
Torts, 2:11
Transcripts, of cases, 15:5
Transportation:
 to court, 4:14
 to doctor, 4:12
 while vehicle is repaired, 19:6

Trial de novo, 1:10
Triple damages, 4:15-17, 20:8
Truck. *See* Motor vehicle
Truck drivers, 19:10
Twenty-four-hour keeper, 23:11

U

Uncontested case. *See* Case, uncontested; Default
 judgment
Unincorporated business owner. *See* Business
 owner
Uninhabitable" rental premises, 6:6, 20:7
U.S. Supreme Court, 13:7, 22:10
U.S. Tax Court, 8:8, 24:5
"Unlawful detainer" action, 1:10, 20:13-15. *See
 also* Evictions
Used vehicles, 17:5-14
 from dealer, 17:5-9
 from private party, 17:10-14

V

Vacation time, loss of, 4:12-13
Vehicle Code, 1:12, 19:4
Venue, 1:10. *See also* Suing, location of filing suit
Voluntary payment, and statute of limitations,
 5:4-5

W

Wage levies. *See* Levying
"Waiving the excess," 4:2
Warranty, 17:4-5
 breach of, 2:16-19
 disclaimer, 2:17
 express, 17:8, 17:14
 implied, 2:8, 2:17, 17:8, 17:14
 written, 16:6, 17:8, 17:14
Wife and husband, suits against, 8:2
Willful misconduct, 8:7
Witnesses, 13:5, 14:1-12, 16:7, 17:14, 18:3, 19:3,
 20:5, 21:5
 fees, 4:14, 11:5, 14:4, 14:6n, 15:9
 preparation of, 14:3-4
 subpoenaing, 14:3, 14:4-5
Work, missing, 4:12-13
Work orders, 5:3, 17:4
"Writ of Execution," 10:13, 23:4-6, 23:9, 23:11,
 23:15-16
 defined, 1:11

How To Form Your Own Corporation
All the forms, Bylaws, Articles, stock certificates and instructions necessary to file your small profit corporation.

California Edition	$29.95
Texas Edition	$21.95
New York Edition	$19.95
Florida Edition	$19.95

The Non-Profit Corporation Handbook
Includes all the forms, Bylaws, Articles and instructions you need to form a non-profit corporation in California.

California Only $24.95

Bankruptcy: Do It Yourself
Step-by-step instructions and all the forms you need.

National Edition $17.95

Legal Care For Your Software
Protect your software through the use of trade secret, trademark, copyright, patents, contracts and agreements.

International Edition $29.95

The Dictionary of Intellectual Property Law
Divided into sections on: trade secret, copyright, trademark, patent, contracts and warranties. Each term or phrase is defined and used in context, with a minimum of legal jargon.

National Edition $17.95

The Partnership Book
A basic primer for people who are starting a small business together. Sample agreements, buy-out clauses, limited partnerships.

National Edition $18.95

Plan Your Estate: Wills, Probate Avoidance, Trusts and Taxes
Making a will, alternatives to probate, living trusts, limiting inheritance and estate taxes, and more.

California Edition $15.95

WillMaker—a software/book package
Use your computer to prepare and update your own valid will. Runs on Apple II+, IIe, IIc, the Mac, the IBM PC (and most PC compatibles.

National Edition $49.95

Nolo's Simple Will Book
Shows you how to draft a will without a lawyer in any state except Louisiana.

National Edition $14.95

The Power of Attorney Book
Covers the process which allows you to arrange for someone else to protect your rights and property should you become incapable of doing so.

National Edition $17.95

Murder on the Air
An unconventional murder mystery set in Berkeley, California. $5.95

Chapter 13: The Federal Plan to Repay Your Debts
The alternative to straight bankruptcy. This book helps you develop a plan to pay your debts over a three year period. All forms and worksheets included.

National Edition $17.95

Billpayers' Rights
Bankruptcy, student loans, bill collectors and collection agencies, credit cards, car repossessions, child support, etc.

California only $14.95

The California Professional Corporation Handbook
All the forms and instructions to form a professional corporation.

California only $29.95

Small Time Operator
How to start and operate your own small business, keep books and pay taxes.

National Edition $10.95

How to Probate an Estate
Forms and instructions necessary to wind up a California resident's estate after death.

California Edition $24.95

How to Do Your Own Divorce
All the forms for an uncontested dissolution. Instructions included.

California Edition	$14.95
Texas Edition	$12.95

California Marriage and Divorce Law
Community and separate property, debts, children, buying a house, etc. Sample prenuptial contracts, simple will, probate avoidance information.

California only $15.95

How to Modify & Collect Child Support in California
How to change and enforce child support payments. Complete with forms and instructions.

California only $17.95

Collect Your Court Judgment
Winning is only half the battle. This book explains how to collect after you've won your court judgment.

California only $19.95

The Living Together Kit
Legal guide for unmarried couples. Covers wills, living together contracts, children, medical emergencies, etc.

National Edition $17.95

A Legal Guide for Lesbian/Gay Couples
Raising children, buying property, wills, job discrimination and more.

National Edition $17.95

Social Security, Medicare & Pensions: The Sourcebook for Older Americans
Most comprehensive resource tool on income, rights and benefits of Americans over 55. Social security, Medicare, pensions, etc.

National Edition $14.95

How to Adopt Your Stepchild
How to prepare all forms and appear in court.

California only $19.95

Start-Up Money: How to Finance Your New Small Business
How to write a business plan, obtain a loan package and find sources of finance.

National Edition $15.95

Patent It Yourself
Complete instructions on how to do a patent search and file a patent in the U.S.

National Edition $29.95

Inventor's Notebook
Protect your patent with the Inventor's Notebook by documenting the activities that are part of successful independent inventing.

National Edition $19.95

The People's Law Review
50-state catalog of self-help law materials, articles and interviews.

National Edition $8.95

Fight Your Ticket
Preparing for court, arguing your case, cross-examining witnesses, etc.

California only $16.95

Legal Research: How to Find and Understand the Law
Comprehensive guide to doing your own legal research.

National Edition $14.95

Tenants' Rights
Everything tenants need to know to protect themselves.

California Edition $14.95

Everybody's Guide to Small Claims Court
Step-by-step guide to going to small claims court and collecting a judgment.

California Edition	$14.95
National Edition	$14.95

Collect Your Court Judgment
Winning is only half the battle. This book explains how to collect after you've won your court judgment.

California Edition $19.95

How to Change Your Name
All the forms and instructions you need.

California only $14.95

Homestead Your House
All the forms and instructions you need.

California only $8.95

The Criminal Records Book
Takes you through all the procedures available to get your records sealed, destroyed or changed. Forms and instructions.
California only $14.95

The Landlord's Law Book: Rights and Responsibilities
Covers discrimination, insurance, tenants' privacy, leases, security deposits, rent control, liability and rent withholding.
California only $24.95

The Landlord's Law Book: Evictions
All the forms and instructions you need to evict a tenant.
California Edition $24.95

The Independent Paralegal's Handbook: How to Provide Legal Services Without Going to Jail
How to open legal typing office to provide paralegal services.
National Edition $12.95

Getting Started as an Independent Paralegal (two audio cassette tapes)
Two tapes, about three hours in all, designed to be used in conjunction with the Independent Paralegal's Handbook to get your business started.
National Edition $24.95

California Civil Code
(West Publishing) Statutes covering a wide variety of topics.
California only $17.00

California Code of Civil Procedure
(West Publishing) Statutes governing most judicial and administrative procedures.
California only $17.00

Landlording
Maintenance and repairs, getting good tenants, avoiding evictions, taxes, etc.
National Edition $17.95

Your Family Records: How to Preserve Personal, Financial and Legal History
Probate avoidance, organizing records and documents, genealogical research. For existing and future family generations.
National Edition $14.95

How to Become A United States Citizen
Explains the naturalization process from filing to the oath of allegiance. Bilingual: English/Spanish.
National Edition $12.95

Marketing Without Advertising
A creative and practical guide that outlines practical steps for building and expanding a small business without spending a lot of money.
National Edition $14.00

Make Your Own Contract
Tear-out contracts for lending money, selling personal property, leasing personal property, storing valuables, etc.
National Edition $12.95

How to Copyright Software
Covers common mistakes and how to correct them, failure to register, problems with protection and the Computer Copyright Act.
National Edition $24.95

Draft, Registration and the Law
How it works, what to do, advice and strategies.
California only $9.95

All About Escrow
Gives you a good understanding of what your escrow officer should be doing for you.
National Edition $12.95

Annulment: Your Chance to Remarry Within the Catholic Church Explains
procedures by which Roman Catholics can obtain annulments.
National Edition $5.95

Homebuyers: Lambs to the Slaughter

Describes how sellers, agents, lenders & lawyers are out to fleece the buyer & how to protect yourself.

National Edition $12.95

For Sale By Owner

Contains all the forms and instructions to sell your own home in California.

California Edition $24.95

The Deeds Book

This book shows you how to choose the right deed, fill it out and record it.

California Edition $15.95

29 Reasons Not to Go to Law School

A humorous and irreverent look at the dubious pleasures of going to law school.
$8.95

Poetic Justice

Edited by Jonathan & Edward Roth. A compendium of the funniest, meanest things e said about lawyers with quotes from Lao-Tzu Lenny Bruce. $8.95

NOLO PRESS   self-help law books

ORDER FORM

Quantity	Title	Unit Price	Total

Prices subject to change

Subtotal _____

Tax (CA only):   San Mateo, LA, & Bart Counties 6 1/2%
                 Santa Clara & Alameda 7%
                 All others 6%

Tax _____

Postage & Handling
No. of Books   Charge
   1            $1.50
  2-3 $2.00
  4-5 $2.50
Over 5 add 5% of total before tax

Postage & Handling _____

Total _____

Please allow 3-5 weeks for delivery.
For faster service, add $1 for UPS delivery (no P.O. boxes, please).

Name _____

Address _____

_____

☐ VISA   ☐ Mastercard

_____ Exp. _____

Signature _____

Phone (   ) _____

ORDERS: Credit card information or a check may be sent to:

Nolo Press
950 Parker St.
Berkeley CA 94710

Use your credit card and our **800 lines** for faster service:

ORDERS ONLY
(M-F 9-5 Pacific Time):

US: 800-992-NOLO
Outside (415) area CA: 800-445-NOLO
Inside (415) area CA: (415) 549-1976

For general information call: (415) 549-1976
☐ Please send me a catalogue